Democracy,
Race,
and Justice

Democracy, Race, and Justice

The Speeches and Writings of Sadie T. M. Alexander

SADIE T. M. ALEXANDER

Edited by

NINA BANKS

Yale UNIVERSITY PRESS/NEW HAVEN & LONDON

Yale University Press books may be purchased in quantity
for educational, business, or promotional use. For
information, please e-mail sales.press@yale.edu (U.S. office) or
sales@yaleup.co.uk (U.K. office).

Set in Minion type by Newgen North America.
Printed in the United States of America.

Library of Congress Control Number: 2020951585
ISBN 978-0-300-24670-4 (hardcover : alk. paper)

A catalogue record for this book is available
from the British Library.

This paper meets the requirements of ANSI/NISO
Z39.48-1992 (Permanence of Paper).
10 9 8 7 6 5 4 3 2 1

For Mary Elizabeth and Rae Pace Alexander

Contents

Preface

In 1991, the economist and social commentator Julianne Malveaux wrote "Missed Opportunity," an article on the first African American economist, Sadie Tanner Mossell Alexander. In it, Malveaux focused on how Alexander had been denied employment as an economist due to gender and racial discrimination. She also wondered how the profession of economics, and our understanding of the economic situation of African Americans more generally, might be different today had Alexander been free to practice her vocation. Based on the kinds of research produced by Alexander's African American contemporaries and the quality of her dissertation, Malveaux reasoned that if Alexander had been able to follow the career path she had earned, her contributions to the field would have inspired and shaped the scholarly interests of generations of students and colleagues.[1]

Sadie Alexander was denied the employment opportunities she deserved, but she still thought deeply about economic matters. Her insights, however, have been lost to the economics profession—until now. Through extensive archival research and reconstruction of Sadie Alexander's speeches and writings, I have recovered her economic thinking beyond what she wrote in her dissertation, and provide here the context for these additional works. Alexander was a highly regarded lawyer and civil rights activist who gave public addresses on the economic status of African Americans, particularly during the 1930s and 1940s. In making Alexander's speeches and writings available, I hope to include her economic analyses within the canon of significant works on economics and, more generally, within the frame of American political history.

Books that cover the intellectual history of economics contain almost no references to the scholarly productions of Black economists—and the rare work that does mention these intellectual contributions typically discusses only the work of Black men.[2] Consequently, this book is also important for being the first to examine in depth the intellectual thought of an African American woman economist, for despite her career as a practicing attorney, and although she never found employment as a professional economist, I found that Alexander continued to view herself as an economist as well as a lawyer. Racial and gender discrimination could not take away her hard-won doctoral degree in economics, and all of the knowledge that represented. In 1944, responding to the National Council of Negro Women's query about a "Negro woman Economist," Alexander stated that, as far as she was aware, she was the only Negro woman who had earned a doctorate degree in economics and was qualified as a trained economist, and further, "Although I have gone into the profession of Law I have never given up my study and interest in the Economics field. I am quite certain you have overlooked the fact that my training was in Economy and, therefore, I am calling this matter to your attention."[3]

After becoming a lawyer, Alexander continued to apply her doctoral training in economics to her assessment of problems affecting African Americans. She obtained data on workers and on economic conditions from census reports, from the National Urban League, and from economics journals such as *Monthly Labor Review, Quarterly Journal of Economics, American Economic Review,* and the *Journal of Political Economy.* In 1945, the Bipartisan Committee for a Pennsylvania FEPC [fair employment practices committee] asked Alexander to testify on fair employment issues, and in 1958 the state's Labor and Industry Department appointed her to a minimum wage board tasked with determining wages for women and minors.[4] Indeed, Alexander maintained a primary interest in the economic status of African Americans throughout her life. As her speeches will show, she argued that economic rights were a core component of safeguarding democratic rights and protections. Throughout her career, Sadie Alexander used her legal and economic skills to demand that African Americans have access to the economic and democratic rights of citizenship.

Sadie Tanner Mossell was born in 1898 in Philadelphia, Pennsylvania. Her parents belonged to highly accomplished African American families. Sadie Mossell's maternal grandfather, Benjamin Tanner, was bishop of the African Methodist Episcopal church and editor of the church's *Christian Recorder*, an influential journal of Black American intellectuals during the nineteenth century.[5] Bishop Tanner and his wife, Sarah Elizabeth Tanner, had seven children, including the renowned painter Henry Ossawa Tanner.[6] A daughter, Halle Tanner (Johnson), graduated from medical school and became the first woman of any racial group to practice medicine in Alabama.[7] The Mossell family also included notable firsts. Sadie Mossell's father, Aaron Mossell Jr., was the first Black person to graduate from the law school at the University of Pennsylvania. His brother, Nathan Francis Mossell, was the first African American to graduate from Penn's medical school. Nathan Mossell's wife, Gertrude Bustill Mossell, was a prominent journalist and author of a Black feminist manifesto, *The Work of the Afro-American Woman*.[8]

Turmoil occurred early in Sadie Mossell's life: her father left his wife and three children when she was just a year old. In response, her mother, Mary Tanner Mossell, moved the family to Washington, D.C., to live near her sister Sadie Tanner Moore and her sister's husband, Lewis Baxter Moore, a Howard University professor who was the first African American to receive a doctorate degree from the University of Pennsylvania. As Sadie Mossell grew, her family alternated between living in Washington, D.C., and living in Philadelphia. During high school, Sadie Mossell lived in Washington, D.C., at the Moores' home. In 1915, after graduating from the all-Black, well-regarded M Street High School, she moved back to Philadelphia at her mother's insistence to attend the University of Pennsylvania.[9]

Sadie Mossell went on to attend both undergraduate and graduate programs at the university and experienced racial discrimination and exclusion throughout most of her time there. The university segregated women students into the School of Education during the period when Mossell was an undergraduate. Mossell's first year was especially lonely, since she was the only Black student in all of her classes. She had no friends and study partners among her white classmates—they refused to speak to her or even acknowledge her presence in shared classes throughout her entire undergraduate education.[10]

It was also at the University of Pennsylvania that Sadie Mossell met her future husband, Raymond Pace Alexander, while he was an undergraduate student at the Wharton School of Finance and Commerce. Among the indignities to which Black students were subjected was being denied dine-in service at restaurants on campus. These early experiences with racial exclusion at the university forged a desire in the young couple to work against racial discrimination when they were older.[11]

In 1918, Mossell received a bachelor of science degree in education. Hoping to graduate early, she had taken three summer classes prior to her first semester of college and tested out of Quadratics. She graduated in just three years, with top grades.

Shortly afterward, Sadie Mossell entered the University of Pennsylvania's graduate program with a university scholarship in history, then switched to economics. She enrolled in European history and economics courses and obtained a master's degree in economics in 1919. During Mossell's master's program, she took her first class with Ernest Minor Patterson, called Economic Problems of the War. More than any other professor, Patterson influenced Mossell's economic thinking through his interest in democracy, war, world economies, and world politics. Based on Patterson's recommendation and the support of the economics department, Mossell received the highly competitive Francis Sargeant Pepper Fellowship, which funded the final year of her doctoral work.[12] Mossell had interviewed with the National Urban League in 1919 but made the difficult decision, she said, to continue with graduate studies in a doctoral program.[13] Sadie Mossell's doctoral courses covered a range of topics, including statistics, insurance, history of thought, sociology, and recent developments in economic theory. Patterson taught Mossell's economics seminar.

Although Mossell had a university scholarship in economics during the first year of her doctoral program, she took on a part-time research job in addition to devoting time to her doctoral research. Mossell and her close friend Virginia Alexander, Raymond's sister, worked for the Consumers' League of Eastern Pennsylvania as paid special investigators interviewing Black women working in Philadelphia industries. From September 1919 to June 1920, the young women canvassed the city along with several experienced white women researchers who were employed as field workers. They interviewed 190 newly employed Black women and girls about their work and training histories.[14] The women and girls had previously worked in the city as domestics or had migrated from the South.

Sadie Mossell's dissertation, "The Standard of Living Among One Hundred Negro Migrant Families in Philadelphia," examined Black migration from the South from 1916 to 1918. This was during the beginning of the Great Migration of Blacks to northward destinations in response to the World War I labor demand, and Philadelphia was an important place in this movement: of the 400,000 Blacks who left the South beginning in 1916, 10 percent relocated to Philadelphia. Mossell undertook her dissertation field research from October through December 1919. She visited the homes of one hundred migrant families and interviewed them about their household budgets. Most of the people she interviewed had migrated from agricultural areas in Mississippi, Alabama, Florida, South Carolina, and Georgia, and were living in Philadelphia's twenty-ninth ward. Prior to 1916, most residents of the neighborhood were white but by 1919, very few whites were living there.

Mossell's interviews were both broad in scope and very detailed. She asked migrants about living expenses, number of workers within the family, occupations, hours worked or not worked, wages, housing (rooms, boarders, condition), savings, debt, and various other kinds of expenses, such as medical, transportation, alcohol, and amusement. She also analyzed bills, receipts, bank accounts, insurance policies, pay envelopes, and store records of credit purchases in order to supplement and verify migrants' responses. Mossell examined household budgets on an annual basis, by family size and income, and then she calculated averages. Her goals were to compare migrants' budgets to the income that she estimated they would need in order to achieve a "fair" or reasonable standard of living in Philadelphia, and to determine the extent to which they were able to achieve that standard. Another objective was to assess the impact of migrants on race relations and living conditions in the city and to make recommendations for improving those conditions if needed.

Mossell's analysis drew on the work of recently published migrant studies, including those by Emmett Scott (1920), Carter Woodson (1918), and the U.S. Department of Labor, Division of Negro Economics (1919). Using a push-pull analysis, Alexander grouped motivations to leave the South into three categories: economic (low wages, unemployment due to boll weevil destruction, dissatisfaction with tenant farming), social (inadequate schools, segregation, lynching, monotony of farm life), and political (disenfranchisement, persecution by representatives of the law). Factors in the North that attracted migrants included increased demand for labor due to the loss of European immigrant labor, as well as migrants' desire for experiences and options unavailable to them in the South: voting rights, educational opportunities, job opportunities, higher wages, and more justice in courts of law.[15]

Sadie Mossell's dissertation asked two central questions about Black migrants. The first was whether the population of uneducated migrants could adapt to the industrial economy. The second focused on the impact of migration on the city: how did migrants' presence affect racial conditions in Philadelphia? Her study of the standard of living among Black migrants was an attempt to determine the degree of migrant adaptation to the city since she reasoned that migrants would be able to adapt if they could achieve an adequate standard of living.[16] Mossell incorporated economic theories such as Engel's Law into her study in order to determine whether or not her findings were consistent with theory, and she compared her findings on family expenditures with findings of a 1918–1919 study conducted by the War Labor Bureau. She grappled with various methodological issues, including how to determine market prices for various spending categories, how much food members of households needed, and how to weigh various expenditures for families of different sizes. Her analysis and methods stand up very well in comparison to living-wage and self-sufficiency studies generated by social scientists today.

On June 15, 1921, Sadie Mossell became the first African American to earn a doctorate degree in economics—and one of the three African American women who that year became the first in U.S. history to receive a doctorate in any field. Mossell's accomplishment received media coverage throughout the nation.[17] On the day of her commencement, she was photographed in her academic regalia wearing a hood that an economics professor, Raymond Bye, had lent to her for the occasion.[18]

Mossell's professors provided her with recommendations for employment in public and private institutions, including within her minor field of insurance, but their support was insufficient to surmount prospective employers' racial and gender biases.[19] Unlike white women economists, Sadie Mossell did not receive job offers anywhere in the North that were commensurate with her degree.[20] Although white women economists also faced employment discrimination, they were still able to secure full-time faculty positions at women's colleges (at that time, coeducational universities typically offered women faculty only adjunct positions).[21] But women's colleges in the Northeast that did not admit Black students were unwilling to hire a Black woman to serve on their faculty. Neither did Mossell receive an offer of employment at a Black university such as Lincoln or Howard, two universities that offered courses in economics. Although Howard had begun expanding its economics curriculum in 1919, it seems that gender barriers for faculty were strong: such Black universities had few women professors.[22]

Consequently, Mossell's first jobs after graduate school did not fully reflect her tremendous talent and potential. Her first was with the Whittier Center and the Henry Phipps Institute, which commissioned her for a short-term position to study the incidence of tuberculosis among African Americans in Philadelphia.[23] Later, in 1921, Mossell secured a job as an assistant actuary with the largest Black insurance company in the United States, North Carolina Mutual Life in Durham, North Carolina. Having to relocate to the South for employment was a source of disappointment for Mossell, though living in Durham afforded her the chance to witness the economic conditions and problems of southern Blacks.[24] Mossell (hereafter Alexander) left her position at North Carolina Mutual after two years when she returned to Philadelphia in 1923 to marry Raymond Pace Alexander, who had just graduated from Harvard Law School.

The career trajectories of the two other African American women who received doctorates in 1921 suggest possibilities that Alexander might have had if her geographic circumstances were different. All three doctoral recipients, Georgiana Simpson (who received her doctorate in German), Eva Dykes (English), and Sadie Alexander had been high-school students in Washington, D.C. After they received their doctoral degrees, both Simpson and Dykes returned to Washington, D.C., to teach at the Dunbar High School, the new name of the M Street School. Howard University offered Dykes and Simpson professorships in 1929 and 1931, respectively. By contrast, when Sadie Alexander returned to Philadelphia in 1923, she wanted to teach in a high school but due to racial discrimination, Black women in Philadelphia could get teaching jobs only in elementary schools, even if they had more education than the white women who taught in the high schools.[25]

By 1924, after a year spent at home without employment, Alexander decided to attend law school at the University of Pennsylvania because she did not want to be a homemaker, and more importantly, because she viewed the law as a means for advancing opportunities for African Americans.[26] She would first have to confront racial discrimination at the law school, however. The law school's dean, Edward Mikell, created a directive that excluded her from joining study clubs with her classmates. As a result, Alexander studied on her own, at home, and with the help of her husband. The dean also orchestrated a failed attempt to prevent Alexander's election to the Law Review Board.[27] Only two women out of the handful who began law school with Alexander finished in 1927. In that year, Alexander became the first Black woman to graduate from the law school and to pass the bar exam in Pennsylvania.

Alexander worked as an attorney at the law firm that her husband, Raymond, established; none of the other law firms in the city would hire a Black woman. She specialized in estate and family law and worked, at her husband's suggestion, on the orphans' court.[28] In 1927, Sadie Alexander also became the first Black woman appointed assistant city solicitor for Philadelphia and worked in this capacity for eight years. Both Alexanders were early, principal members of the National Bar Association.[29]

The Alexander law firm was one of the earliest husband-wife legal practices in the country.[30] By the 1930s, it had begun to mount an aggressive challenge to racial exclusion in Pennsylvania. The firm drafted legislation for an Equal Rights bill in 1935 and a Public Accommodations Act in 1939 that made it a misdemeanor for anyone to refuse accommodations based on race or skin color. Sadie and Raymond Alexander personally challenged establishments that refused compliance with the law, and they brought action under the law for hundreds of cases without requesting fees.[31] In an early use of auditing for discrimination, the Alexanders sent Black and white testers to theaters and hotels in order to determine if they were discriminating based on race, then filed charges against the managers or owners when the establishments denied service to Black testers. Their law firm had become the leading civil rights law firm in Philadelphia.[32]

In the mid-1930s, the Alexanders welcomed two daughters, Mary Elizabeth and Rae Pace, to their family. This period also coincided with Sadie Alexander's increased involvement in professional associations, civic associations, civil rights organizations, and increased demand as a public speaker. During the 1930s and 1940s, civic and religious organizations frequently asked Alexander to give speeches to their members. Her speeches focused on systemic barriers that prevented African Americans from having full access to democratic and economic rights of citizenship while also calling for social action and policy changes to dismantle the barriers. Among her many civic associations, Alexander held founding and or elected positions at the National Urban League, National Bar Association, Delta Sigma Theta sorority, National Council of Negro Women, Business and Professional Women's Club, Philadelphia Commission on Human Relations, American Civil Liberties Union, and Americans for Democratic Action.

In 1946, President Harry Truman appointed Sadie Alexander to a newly formed Committee on Civil Rights to investigate the provision of civil rights in the country. The committee's report, *To Secure These Rights,* was one of the most important civil rights documents issued prior to the passage of the 1964 Civil Rights Act because it enumerated the ways in which the provision of civil rights and liberties diverged from U.S. ideals.[33] In 1978, President Jimmy Carter appointed Alexander to chair the White House Conference on Aging (President Reagan subsequently replaced her).

The Alexander family donated Sadie Alexander's papers to the University of Pennsylvania Archives two years before Alexander died in 1989. The Sadie T. M. Alexander Papers provide extraordinarily detailed insights into Alexander's professional, civic, and personal life, beginning in childhood and extending through her adult life.

In addition to her dissertation, Sadie Alexander published *A Study of the Negro Tuberculosis Problem in Philadelphia* in 1923, an article on Black women workers in *Opportunity Magazine* in 1930, and a booklet, *Who's Who Among Negro Lawyers,* in 1945. The article from *Opportunity* is included in this volume along with select speeches that span a fifty-year period from Alexander's youth as an economist and newly minted lawyer to her advanced years as she reflected on the Civil Rights movement and Black protests against racial injustice that were sweeping the nation.

Alexander also gave public addresses to religious groups, benevolent societies, political party members, union workers, YMCA and YWCA affiliates, national civil rights organizations, Greek societies, university students, legal associations, and women's organizations. In so doing, she helped to shape the public mind in matters of race and economics. These speeches are Alexander's most impressive body of work and are as worthy of inclusion in the canon of economic thought as the articles and treatises published by other major economists.

They demonstrate Sadie Alexander's tremendous intellectual acumen, dogged commitment to racial justice, and foresight in recognizing the ever-emergent threat that economic insecurity poses to democratic governance. Most fundamentally, Alexander's speeches convey her deep moral convictions regarding human dignity and social welfare.

Sadie Alexander wrote many of her early speeches by hand on legal notepads, and one of the most challenging and time-consuming tasks involved in compiling this volume was deciphering her handwriting. Even her typed speeches typically had handwritten notes inserted throughout them—along margins, between sentences, and upside down on the backs of pages. She often crossed out sections or inserted arrows to show how she wanted to reorder the text. My research assistant, Lily Shorney, and I typed the speeches as Sadie Alexander wrote them, but when I found omissions within speeches, I inserted missing words within brackets; when Lily and I were unable to figure out words, I noted this within brackets. In addition, I sometimes reformatted quoted passages, added missing punctuation, corrected misspelled words that were obvious typos, and spelled out abbreviations and numbers. Footnotes within speeches are Alexander's unless otherwise noted. Any errors within the speeches are my responsibility.

Sadie Alexander spoke out against persistent racial inequities and deprivations that African Americans experienced in response to demographic, economic, and social changes that occurred throughout the twentieth century. These political and economic changes took place during major eras: World War I and the Great Migration, the Great Depression, World War II, Cold War McCarthyism, and the Civil Rights movement. Although Alexander's strategies sometimes shifted in response to these changes, the theme that permeated all of her speeches and writings is the need for social and economic justice for African Americans, a people who had survived three hundred years of racial tyranny and oppression.

Alexander articulated this theme by focusing on four major topics: racial ideology and Black achievements, Black women in the political economy, Black workers and economic justice, and democracy and citizenship rights. Alexander's speeches on racial ideology delve into the psychology of oppression and the role that dominant beliefs play in buttressing systems of oppression. Her writings on African American women address issues of Black women's agency, leadership, and status as paid and unpaid laborers. Alexander's body of work addresses topics of compensation, full employment, interracial conflict and cooperation, and redistribution of national income for Black workers. Her speeches on citizenship rights for African Americans countered the prevailing racial ideology of Black inferiority and the practice of limited democracy.

Sadie Alexander's speeches trace her personal journey to practicing economics, one guided by her strong moral compass and desire to improve the lives of others through her work. She used her economic knowledge to promote racial justice by examining the effects of macro-economic policies on African Americans. She believed in popularizing economic ideas in order to diminish economic anxiety and backlash. And she called for bold, redistributive policies to make up for the markets' failure to distribute national resources and new opportunities equitably. Alexander's approach to political economy provided an analytical framework for thinking about the connections among race, markets, law, politics, and power in a liberal democratic order.

At Sadie Alexander's memorial service in 1989, Judge A. Leon Higginbotham spoke of her notable firsts and great accomplishments, but said what was most important was that "she was excellent, wise, persistent, and fair after she got those opportunities." He included Sadie Tanner Mossell Alexander among the great voices of the past, such as "Sojourner Truth, Mary McLeod Bethune, Mahatma Gandhi, Frederick Douglass, John F. Kennedy, Earl Warren, Richardson Dilworth, Stephen Biko, Martin Luther King, Richard Allen, Charles Hamilton Houston, and Raymond Pace Alexander." Judge Higginbotham pondered "the dazzling heights Sadie would have reached if we had had a society free of race and gender bias."[34]

Remarkably, and tragically, the themes that our nation's first African American economist addressed a hundred years ago with the beginning of African American migration to northern cities remain urgent, unaddressed problems today: chronic unemployment, confinement in urban slums, police brutality, voter suppression, poverty, inferior schools, substandard housing, and unsafe neighborhoods. I hope that reading Sadie Alexander's speeches will motivate readers to think about the limitations, costs, and tremendous toll that anti-Blackness imposes on the lives of Black people as well as our larger communities, and to take action to correct the deep injustices that flow from it. For in addition to frustrating and stifling the potential of individuals, anti-Black sentiment inflicts great damage on our collective possibilities and well-being.

Part I
Racial Ideology and
Black Achievements

Introduction

Sadie Alexander was an outstanding economic historian whose speeches relied heavily on her knowledge of European and American history. Prior to taking courses in European history at the University of Pennsylvania, Alexander studied the history of African Americans while a student at the M Street High School, which was established by Congress in November 1870 as one of the first public high schools for African American students (its original name was the Preparatory High School for Negro Youth).[1] An all-Black, college preparatory high school in Washington, D.C., M Street became renowned for the many high-achieving African Americans who attended the school or worked there as faculty. The school provided young Black students with opportunities to learn from prominent Black intellectuals who either taught at the school or gave invited talks to students, including Booker T. Washington, W. E. B. Du Bois, and Mary Church Terrell.[2] The eminent historian Carter G. Woodson began teaching at M Street in 1909 and taught French, Spanish, English, and history.[3] Woodson had the greatest influence on Alexander's thinking about the important place of people of African descent in American history.[4] Her education about the critical roles that African Americans had played in the development of the nation supported her belief that public schools could decrease racial intolerance by educating their students on African American contributions.[5]

When Alexander later reflected on her own schooling, she said that her education in African American history at the M Street School gave her confidence that she could succeed at the University of Pennsylvania if she applied herself.[6]

Alexander would draw on this confidence to endure the hostile treatment of African American students and their cultural heritage she encountered as a college student. On the first day of an undergraduate sociology class, a professor asked students to list on paper the superior and inferior races and the reasons for their assessments. The majority of white students listed whites as superior and Blacks as inferior; some Black students made the same assessment.[7] White students cited wealth holding as a source of white superiority while also claiming that Blacks were "parasites." Years later, Alexander stated that the absence or belittling of Black American accomplishments in historical accounts contributed to the belief in Black inferiority.[8] It is no surprise, then, that Alexander's earliest speeches tried to dispel notions of Black inferiority and inadequacy from the minds of her Black audience members by giving a more accurate account of African Americans in U.S. history.

Alexander's proclamations about Black contributions to the nation and African American fitness as citizens came at a time when Black racial inferiority was a prevailing belief. From the Progressive era through World War II, eugenicists popularized claims that racial differences in living conditions stemmed from biology. They found fertile ground within the discipline of economics because of its embrace of scientific methods of analysis for explaining human behavior and economic outcomes. Walter Willcox and Francis Amasa Walker, both central leaders in the development of the American Economic Association, believed that statistics could provide objective facts about the "Negro problem."[9] Believing that African Americans were physically and intellectually inferior to whites, proponents of the Willcox school advanced the "Black Disappearance Hypothesis": that African Americans would eventually die out in the United States.[10] This theory helped to allay white fears that "degenerate" Black people would overwhelm whites. Other notable economists who were proponents of eugenics were Irving Fisher, Richmond Mayo-Smith, Jeremiah Jenks, John R. Commons, Carlos Closson, Thomas N. Carver, and Frank A. Fetter.[11]

Even Abram Harris Jr., who became the second African American economist in 1930 and would become the most prominent African American economist by midcentury, expressed support for biological explanations of behavior in his early research. Harris wrote his master's thesis in 1924 on Black migration to Pittsburgh, Pennsylvania. He believed that heredity and environmental factors contributed to criminal activity among migrants, and claimed that most arrests were of "feebleminded" southerners who were unprepared for the complexity of northern urban life. In discussing African Americans who were arrested, Harris wrote, "The exigencies of the economic order have thrown these feebleminded people along with their more virile kinsmen into the midst of an intricate community life where many persons who are more nearly normal find it difficult to adjust themselves."[12] Harris's views on Black southerners was in stark contrast to that of Alexander, who believed that southern Blacks' principal handicap was lack of formal education—a problem that she believed they would overcome through access to education and training available in northern cities.

Sadie Alexander challenged the prevailing anti-Black sentiment, and the intense anti-Black violence that resulted from it, by arguing that Black contributions to the nation proved they were supremely fit citizens. From World War I to the early 1970s, some eight million African Americans migrated from the South to northward destinations.[13] In the process, they transformed the African American population from primarily rural and southern into one that was increasingly urban and northern. African Americans migrated North hoping to build better lives for themselves and their children by gaining access to educational, economic, and political opportunities and rights. They also wanted to escape from the ever-present tyranny of white violence. They found, instead, that northern whites also subjected them to racial segregation, blocked job opportunities, and terrorized them just for being Black. To take just a few examples, whites confined Black workers to low-wage jobs in manufacturing or domestic service and created urban ghettos by restricting African American access to housing and mortgages. And during the World War I era, when Alexander was an undergraduate and graduate student in economics, white mobs terrorized African Americans across the country, massacring hundreds of Black people and destroying their homes, businesses, and communities. In May 1917, in East Saint Louis, Illinois, some three thousand white union members marched in protest against African American migrants, then went on a murderous rampage in July that lasted for several days. They set homes in African American neighborhoods on fire—killing African American men, women, and children as they fled and leaving approximately six thousand people homeless.[14] In the postwar economic downturn in 1919, white anger over loss of jobs and perceptions of Black social mobility led to more than thirty mob attacks that resulted in the murders of hundreds of Black people and destruction of their communities. Two weeks before Sadie Alexander received her doctoral degree in June 1921, white residents of Tulsa, Oklahoma, burned down the most prosperous Black community in the country, the Greenwood District, by destroying thirty-five city blocks, an event that resulted in the deaths of African Americans and the displacement of some ten thousand African American residents. Although whites started the violence, law enforcement arrested six thousand African Americans in the aftermath.[15]

This economic, demographic, and cultural milieu shaped Sadie Alexander's thinking about the position of African Americans. She delivered speeches to Black audiences that provided a counter history of African Americans, one that embraced the politics of racial pride, self-help, and community empowerment. Her message was a repudiation of dominant beliefs about Black capabilities. It was a recognition that African Americans needed to challenge powerful belief systems that justified, and therefore helped to sustain, material differences accorded to race.

The first speech in this section, "The Contributions of the Negro to American Life," addresses the central theme of the book—democracy—and the prominent role that African Americans have always played in keeping "the spirit of democracy alive." The history that Alexander recounted was that of African American accomplishments and cultural contributions, made under conditions of extreme oppression that stretched back to Africa. In her description of this noble heritage, African Americans are recognized as the primary bearers of democracy in the United States.

The next two documents are fragments of speeches, missing in their entirety, that illustrate contradictions in Alexander's thinking about the degree to which African Americans have availed themselves of educational opportunities and the relevance of African Americans' past accomplishments to current white perceptions of them. She wrote both speeches during the 1920s when manufacturing was the growing, dynamic sector. As a pragmatist, young Alexander believed that Black Americans could become part of the industrial sector by attending business schools and by creating businesses. Her focus on self-help and community development were in line with Booker T. Washington's views on economic development and the need for African American acquisition of business skills, but unlike her "Contributions of the Negro to American Life," these speeches did not evoke the race pride that was emerging out of the New Negro movement.[16]

The next speech, "Outstanding Achievements of Negro Women," describes African American women's gains in the fields of education, arts, politics, and business by the 1930s. Alexander's list of "ambitions and achievements" is quite impressive, particularly since some of the women she cited had parents who were enslaved; these women were part of the first generation of African Americans born in the aftermath of slavery.

In the next speech, "Address on Negro Achievement," delivered in 1936 at the Black Methodist Tindley Temple during its Negro Achievement Week, Alexander called on Black ministers to embrace a social justice vision of Christianity. She expressed racial pride in Black Americans' economic accomplishments and in their ability to survive in a hostile land, a view that countered the Black Disappearance Hypothesis. Alexander celebrated Blacks' ownership of assets, productive contributions to the nation, and educational gains. The speech cast African American accomplishments within the context of ongoing labor and housing discrimination against Black Americans. Alexander emphasized group accomplishments rather than those of individuals because she wanted to document racial progress. In this sense, her thinking was in line with that of Du Bois, who by the 1930s had become more insistent that African Americans needed to engage in cooperative consumption and production efforts to address economic problems.[17] This speech also illustrates the long tradition among African American economists in promoting the importance of wealth holding, employment training for jobs of the future, and cooperative endeavors by calling for African Americans to use their purchasing power for the benefit of Black community development.

The final work in this section is an acceptance speech that Alexander gave in 1975 upon receiving an award from the Pennsylvania Society for Promoting the Abolition of Slavery. Commenting that she was delivering her speech some sixty years after the incident in her sociology class, she noted the role the society had played in helping to remove shackles on both the bodies and the minds of Black Americans.

"The Contributions of the Negro to American Life," ca. 1920s

If you can enslave a man's mind, you do not need to put iron chains about his body. You do not have to order him to enter your house by the back door. If there is a back door, he will use no other. If there is no back door, he will either cut one or not enter. As a race our minds have been enslaved, even if the chains of bondage have been removed from our physical bodies. This has been done by a process of underestimating the deeds of black men in the histories of this country, on the lecture platform, in the press. As a result, we have come to believe ourselves that anything white is good, is bound to meet with success—while anything black is bad and bound to fail. It is expressed in the familiar reaction of nine out of ten colored persons to the thought of employing a Negro lawyer: "You had better get a white lawyer"—or the proud tone of voice in which a colored person relates that "Mr. Smith, a white man, told me so." As a result we have, with few exceptions, become so convinced of our essential inferiority in every line of human endeavor that our initiative has been trampled and that of the few who have forged ahead— destroyed by our failure to support trained leaders in the various fields of human endeavor.

I have, therefore, chosen to speak to you concerning the Contributions of the Negro to American Life, which the histories you study, prepared by white men whose purpose is to impress on your minds the superiority of their race, have either omitted or mentioned briefly and without comment regarding their true import, with the hope of leaving with you some idea of the superiority of your own race and its noble heritage.

I wonder if you realize that the acquisition of that vast territory known as the Louisiana Purchase by the U.S. was made possible by the deeds of a black man—Toussaint Louverture.

While history records the bold exploits of Toussaint Louverture, his conquest of San[to] D[omingo] has not been interpreted by historians nor appreciated by members of his own race as a cause for American acquisition of the Louisiana Territory. Triumph of Toussaint Louverture upset one of the dreams of Napoleon Bonaparte. As First Consul, he was trying to make himself the head of a French empire. In 1800 he induced Spain to retrocede the Louisiana Territory to France. Santo Domingo was to be a stepping stone in this direction. Santo Domingo, eastern end was Spanish, western, [was] French [with] fifty thousand Creoles and fifty thousand mulattoes and about a half million Negroes. The General Assembly of French Revolution extended [to] the people of color of free ancestry the rights and privileges of citizens. White people, incensed at this, precipitated revolution on the island by espousing [the] cause of [the] French King. Slaves struck in 1791. Proclamation freedom was given to slaves who upheld the cause of the French Republic. Toussaint Louverture was made general. [He] took former expelled Eng[land] and subdued the Spanish part of the island. Napoleon sent his brother-in-law General Leclerc with twenty-five thousand soldiers to enforce the claims of France in Haiti. Santo Domingo, thus upset by Toussaint Louverture, seemed to Napoleon an impediment of republicanism tainted with American ideas. Leclerc appeared upon the scene in 1802. He betrayed Toussaint Louverture into a conference on a French vessel on which he was transported to France only to die of neglect in the prison of Joux. There was immediately proclaimed the annulment of the decree of liberty to slaves. This did not, however, end the resistance of the French power. Toussaint Louverture's task of arousing his people had been too well done. The French Army was decimated not only by guerilla warfare but the yellow fever. By the end of the year 1802, six-sevenths of Leclerc's army had perished including the general himself.

In the meantime, the much-delayed retrocession of Louisiana by Spain was effected. The U.S. Government was anxious to obtain this territory as an outlet to trade in the West. In the unfortunate outcome in Haiti, the disaster in Egypt, and the inability to reach India, Napoleon could see [that] his dream for a world empire [was] a failure. He, therefore, disposed of the territory to the U.S. in 1803. Thus, the acquisition of that great rich country, 800,000 square miles in the great Mississippi valley, may be directly attributed to the revolt of Negroes in Haiti.

The Florida Purchase in 1819 for five million dollars was due largely to activities of Negroes. Florida had been an asylum for fugitive slaves who found life much more satisfactory there among the Spanish and Indians than in the sea bound slave state. In order to bring this country under the control of the U.S. and prevent Negroes from gathering in an independent country, Florida was added to the Union.

The exploration of America and its first settlement is also marked by the exploits and blood of Negro men.

The importation of Negroes was not their first contact with the Western Hemisphere. Long before the Teutonic elements established a claim to North America, the Africans had visited its shores and penetrated the interior. According to Leo Wiener of Harvard University, the Africans were the first to discover America. He has found in the American language the early African influence in words like "canoe," "buckra," and "tobacco." They could not have been brought from any other part of the world. African fetishism too, resembling a custom among the American Indians, has been considered another reason for believing that Africans saw the shores of America centuries before the Teutons had developed sufficiently to venture so far on the high seas. Inasmuch as scientists now claim that there once existed on the western coast of Africa a very advanced people who influenced even the civilization of the Mediterranean world, they have little doubt of their having extended their culture across the Middle Passage. Africa, it will be remembered, is nearer to America than Europe.

Negroes were also pioneer explorers of America. Pedro Alonso Niño, a pilot of the fleet of Columbus, has been referred to as a Negro, but this has not been proved. In the discovery of the Pacific Ocean, Balboa carried with him 30 Negroes, including Nuflo de Olano.

In the conquest of Mexico, Cortez was accompanied by a Negro, who, finding in his rations of rice some grains of wheat, planted them as an experiment and thus made himself the pioneer in wheat raising in the Western Hemisphere. Negroes accompanied Ayllon in 1526 in his expedition from the Florida Peninsula northward and figured in the establishment of the settlement of San Miguel near what is now Jamestown, VA. They accompanied Narvaez on his ill-fated expedition in 1527 and continued with Cabeza de Vaca, his successor, through what is now the southwestern part of the U.S. They went with Alarcon and Coronado in the conquest of New Mexico. They proved so valuable that De Soto, the explorer of the lower Mississippi, ordered Negroes imported. One of these Negroes wrote his name still higher in the hall of fame. This was Estevanico, the explorer of New Mexico and Arizona. Estevanico was a member of the unfortunate expedition of Narvaez who undertook to reduce the country between Florida and the Río de las Palmas in Mexico. Overcome by misfortune, only four of the expedition survived. One of these was Estevanico—who was instructed by Cabeza de Vaca to proceed in advance fifty or sixty leagues and to report the probability of success by sending back wooden crosses. If the news which the Negro gathered was of moderate importance only, he was to send back a cross the size of the palm of his hand; if the news was better, the cross was to be larger. Four days later an Indian came into camp with a cross as tall as a man. With him another Indian who told the chief of four large cities with houses of stone and lime, some of them four stories in height. The portals of the principal houses were ornamented with turquoise. Instead of awaiting the coming of his chief at the appointed distance, Estevanico pushed on to the wonderful city, where he was at once murdered. The Indians at once made up their minds that he was a liar, for it was incredible that a black man should be the agent of two white men, and killed him. The Negroes followed with the French close upon the trail of Cartier and Champlain. They appeared with the Jesuits in Canada and the Mississippi Valley during the seventeenth century. They later constituted a considerable element of the pioneers in Louisiana. In these regions as elsewhere the Negro assisted in the exploration of the country and contributed to the establishment of legal claims by actual settlement—especially emphasized in our assertion to title to Oregon.

In the wars that America has waged, Negroes have always contributed their lives—notwithstanding the command of George W., when he took command at Cambridge, to enlist no Negro soldiers. The threat of Great Britain to enroll Negro soldiers resulted in at least fourteen thousand Negroes serving in the Continental Army. Their noble deeds in battle are too well known to each of you here to be rehearsed by me. The interesting and important point for us to note regarding the Negroes' entry into this and the subsequent War of 1812, the Civil War, the Spanish-American War, and the World War, is that the Negroes actually had a purpose for which to fight: their freedom and all things that meant.

At times it might seem that this purpose had been accomplished, for long before the question of the citizenship of the Negro was established by legislation and court decisions, he was claimed as a citizen of the U.S.—when curiously enough so to do suited the purpose of the white Americans.

Thus, during Jefferson's second administration the country was beset with many troubles in its relation with England and France. These two nations, it will be remembered, had begun to fight in 1793 and the contest was still waging. In 1805 England decided, contrary to her previous policy, goods from the French colonies transported in American ships could be seized, even though they had landed in the U.S. and been reshipped. British men of war were actually stationed just outside of N.Y. harbor to intercept American merchant vessels, search them, and impress their seamen. The American frigate *Chesapeake* was overtaken not far from Hampton Roads by the British frigate *Leopard.* The British commander demanded the surrender of several (five) seamen serving on the *Chesapeake* who he claimed to be deserters from the British service, two of whom were Negroes. Ware, a mulatto from Maryland, and Martin, a Negro from Massachusetts, were declared by Commodore Barrou of *Chesapeake* to be American citizens. [This] nearly brought on war—indignation of people found expression in mass meetings, and preparation for war.

But other wars came before this citizenry was recognized and perhaps still more will come before it is fully [granted].

The presence of the Negro in America has served to keep the spirit of democracy alive which was the foundation of the country. It was

the great belief of the fathers of this country in that unalterable principle announced in the Constitution—"that all men are created free,
and equal"—which was the foundation of the nation for economic
reasons. In sections of this country we forget this and other salient
principles of a democratic government. But the presence of the Negro
brought them to our minds. And so, there was the long battle for the
freedom of the Negro which resulted in those War Amendments to
the Constitution—13th, 14th, and 15th Amendments. They were created to protect the Negro—they have been used to protect everyone
but him. Nevertheless, their application—in the fights of labor—for
freedom of contract, right to engage in any kind of trade at a wage set
by competitive bargaining—the higgling and bargaining of the market,
as Adam Smith, the great economist named it, has been an application
of rules of democracy created by the influence of the Negro citizenry of
this country.* Our fights for freedom of education have been of equal
value to other racial elements in this country and have done much to
teach democracy to the children of America, who are destined to be the
country's future leaders. Again, the presence of the Negro in America
has served to keep the true spirit of democracy alive by his valiant fight
for the franchise. The successful exclusion of any one group of persons
from the exercise of the franchise threatens the exercise of this right by
all minority groups. If the vote can be denied Negroes—it will not be
long before other groups, whose will is not that of the majority, will be
disenfranchised. The Labor Party, the Socialists, the Democrats in Republican states, and the Republicans in Democratic states would soon
find themselves disenfranchised if it were found by the majority that
any one group of the people could be denied the right of representation
through the ballot. Thus, we find in the Southern states where the Negro
has been successfully disenfranchised that other minority groups have
also lost the right of representation through the ballot. The Labor vote,
as well as the Socialist vote, are lost in the ballot boxes by some process
of assimilation, attained by means of physical destruction. The minority

---

* See Adam Smith, *Wealth of Nations* [*An Inquiry into the Nature and Causes of the Wealth of Nations*, Glasgow ed. (Oxford, UK: Clarendon Press, 1975)], bk. 1, ch. 5, p. 49.—N.B.

groups throughout this country that are represented in the government owe their representation to the Negro.

So too, the Negroes' successful fight to exercise those civil rights of jury service has assured like privileges to other minority groups. Through these various efforts the Negro has kept alive in America at least a spark of the democracy which it was the avowed purpose of the Pilgrim fathers to establish.

The Negro has contributed as is now established the only American music. The Spirituals which we once were ashamed of, thank God, we have come ourselves to appreciate and to realize are a unique contribution to American art. The jazz music of today, which has taken not only America but Europe, is the product of Negro genius. James Reese Europe and his Clef Club Orchestra created and popularized the music which Paul Whiteman and his white orchestra are now presenting to Europe and America. The only great symphony composition of this age is founded on Negro Music: Dvořák's New World Symphony. No truly great operas have been produced by Americans, but it is suggested by the musicians that any such production must be based on the music developed by the spontaneous out[put] of the Negroes of America. This music is not African, it is not Indian, it is the product of the life of the Negroes in America. Take the jazz—it represents in every detail, the blare, the rush, the discord of modern America.

The more serene music, which is known as the Spirituals, is the outpouring of the depths of distress and sorrow [in the] souls of a people in the various moods of life. It is the product of American life and the only music produced in this country—A people who are able to produce art—can never be a lost race. Greece will live on for her art and sculpture as has Rome. And now African art is reviving a lost people. Our music is destined to place us with the great gifted races of the world.

Similarly, our presence in America has contributed to the only folklore the country has produced. There are no folk stories to class with Uncle Remus—A wealth of uncollected folklore awaits those of you who are industrious enough and who have sufficient imaginations to collect and preserve it.

It seems to me that the great Renaissance among the contemporary Negro writers is but a symptom of their recognition of the facts I have been trying to place before you this afternoon. Countee Cullen, Langston Hughes, Claude McKay, Jessie Fauset, and their contemporaries, conscious of the heritage which is the Negroes'—conscious of these fundamental contributions he has made to American life which history must ultimate[ly] record as plac[ing] him among the builders of the American nation, have gained confidence in themselves and throwing aside their racial toga have felt themselves free men and women and gone to the task of contributing what is destined to be truly great American literature.

What they have done, we too can do in our individual lives. Do not make the mistake that all of us can be writers. Each has his own place, which he must fill according to his talent. If we can get in the minds of the young people, the confidence that comes from realizing the glorious position his race holds in the history of America, the confidence as knowledge of this precious heritage will develop, [and] must result in contributions from Negroes to American civilization, which are yet unthought of.

Those of you who have passed in years the age of plasticity can help by your encouragement. Those who yet have youthful minds can, freed of the stigma of inferiority which the white world has consciously developed in [us], excel the noble contributions of Toussaint Louverture—of Estevanico, of Europe, of even Dunbar.

Fragment, Speech, ca. 1920s

As I sit here and gaze upon these ladies so strikingly attired in their Revolutionary attire, my mind travels with rapidity to the days of the age they represent, when the avenue which this modern and impressive building faces was an Indian Trail, through which it is reported by history that Washington and his Revolutionary soldiers marched. I see no public schools in the entire state of Pennsylvania—the rich are educated by private tutors brought over from the old country. The poor who are fortunate enough to learn the primary rudiments are the servants in the household of the rich. But such men as Franklin [and] Rush knew the state and the nation could not progress with the masses of the people in ignorance, so after much propaganda [and] lobbying, these leaders had included in the Court of 1790 a provision for free education for paupers. Not until 1836 was $200,000 appropriated and then to Kitchen Schools—

My grandmother conducted one of these when Hallie L. Brown and other leading women of our state learned their ABC[s]. While we are a long way removed from the School in the Kitchen today, it is shockingly true that the influence of the kitchen has a marked effect on [the] educational progress of our children. If proper food doesn't come, dear souls who labor in the kitchens are making it possible for many of our boys and girls to attend these great institutions of learning which dot every section of our city.

It took more than a century to develop a really fine system of education and it has taken all of this time and will take even more for some of us to realize the necessity of our seizing these opportunities for education. We have reached the point where we appreciate the necessity of knowing the mere rudiments: reading, writing, [and] counting. But when we get beyond that—there are all kinds of objections advanced against further knowledge. 1) Can't Use It. 2) Won't Use It. 3) I made a living without it. [4)]—Even You Lose Your Mind.

As a result of the lack of appreciation on the part of the mass of our people for more than the ABC's as a race, we are rated with the disgraceful fact of having the highest mortality rate of any racial group in this city and this country, and the highest illiteracy rate and the lowest economic rating. I say this is all due to a failure on our part to seize opportunities to train our bodies and our minds. What else can it be due to? You may see economic opportunities—and those of us who know how to cook well can find jobs and keep them—those of us who know how to sew well can get all the sewing we can do—those who can serve find opportunities. The trouble is so few know how to do a specialized job well and we live in an age of specialization. I recently heard the newly elected Pres[ident] of Howard University speak; his solution was a better understanding of the true principles of Piety. I agree with this learned sense that we have not generally been taught correctly these principles but I venture my opinion against that of so learned a gentleman—that in this world of competition and survival of the fittest, we as Negroes must fight with the same instruments that our opponents use—skill, knowledge, training, wealth. Do not misunderstand me to say—leave the principles of Piety out of it—never. But the fact is—the white missionaries, while seeking to impress on the people of this and foreign countries the principles of Piety, have themselves failed to practice them. They have utilized their knowledge of science to cradle and create [an] economic world which they control while we sit, pray[ing] in poverty and ignorance.

I presume you are expecting me to offer as my panacea for our social and economic problems—a college education. Well, I am going to disappoint you, in part. Time it is that a man learned in our colleges of agriculture can raise two times as many potatoes on the same area and quality of soil as ordinary untrained uncle Joe, who has learned all he knows from his own experience. But we must face facts. Seventy-five percent of the people in the audience are adults, who left school twenty or more years ago. They have no chance of going to college—which is an opportunity for the youths. But with 75 percent of our populace [rest of speech is missing].

Fragment, "Contributions [We Can] Make," ca. 1920s

The boundaries of our country are established, and by the mandates of the Monroe Doctrine, will not be extended—so that you and I cannot hope to aid as did E[stevanico] and T[oussaint] L[ouverture] in the physical extension of the country. Having experienced in our families the horrors of war, it is to be hoped our future valor will be expended in fighting for peace and not in war, so that contributions in this field are not to be expected. But there lies before us that great field of human endeavor which has placed America, yet a frontier country, in the foreground of the great nations of the world—ahead of the ancient nations of the world. I speak of American phenomenal success in the production of goods at a market price which makes them saleable in the entire world. The man who produces goods with a world market contributes to the happiness of all mankind and to the wealth of his own nation. You do not purchase goods unless they satisfy your tastes. Think, therefore, how many millions of individuals receive satisfaction and happiness when an article which they demand is produced at a price within the reach of the masses of every nation. Such has been the result from the production of the Ford Automobile which has been introduced at a price level within the reach of the masses not only in America but in Russia, China, Africa and India. The same is true of less pretentious articles, such as Quaker Oats, a food that is sold at such a small price and that because of this reason, which is due to the physical satisfaction it gives, has a world market. The American nation produces more goods that have a world market than any other nation in the world. What does this mean?—The American label is spread on the earth's surface, and thereby American superiority is impressed on the minds of the world. Millions and billions of individuals receive human satisfaction, happiness, because their wants can be met by American products sold at a price level within their reach.

The wealth of the individual and consequently of the nation is increased. Our foreign balance sheet constantly shows a debt due [to] America and foreign money therefore exchanges at a lower rate than American money.

As a result our nation is considered powerful—we can control the great markets of the world. And when you ask the American and the European, what people in America [are] responsible for America's position in the world, he will answer every other nation but the Negro for a very obvious reason, we have no place in the economic success of America—unless it be in some such position as loading the ships with the goods produced in America for foreign shipment.

Historically we can point to contributions, but what does pointing backward mean if with this background we are not continuing to aid in the nation's development? What we did is more boys and girls going into fields of production—creating goods that satisfy human desires. The success of a nation is largely measured by its exports and imports and the success of any group of people who are a part of the nation is similarly measured by the amount of goods they contribute. We contribute practically none—our names are not written in national or international commerce. The world knows us only as gullible consumers, as it reads about us. And few books talk about us and those that do say little to our credit. All the books published could not affect our reputation for [being] gluttonous consumers, for as such we are most frequently pictured.

If the shipments of goods in America and from its shores bore goods created, made, [and] produced by black men, our products would affect the export balance of America, contribute to its wealth and influence, and our own influence and wealth would rise in proportion. Since

America is a great exporting nation, a producing nation—if we are going to be considered as a part of the life of the nation, we must contribute to the very thing that makes our nation successful. More physicians, lawyers, dentists, [and] school teachers cannot place us in a position of importance in a nation of producers. Go into the schools of business young men and women—and then do not come out and moan because some white firm will not hire you as a salesman. Do you aspire to sell the goods another man has manufactured or to manufacture goods for him to buy and sell for you? First learn the technique of business and then be willing to start at the bottom—where C. C. Spaulding, [Samuel C.] Rutherford, Madam C. J. Walker, and Mrs. Malone started—in one room. If we produce an article that is demanded by the public, and with your technical knowledge of production [and] distribution, you will outstrip our fondest expectations. Supply and demand know no racial prejudices. If your goods satisfy a human desire and can be purchased at a reasonable price they will sell [as] fast as you can produce them. Go into business young men. Go into business young women. Make yourselves a part of the economic system which has placed America as a formidable economic competitor of England, the greatest exporting nation the world has known. Write your names, the names of your race, in the annals of American industry, in the export columns, and when you have done this, no man can deny your contributions to America, for you and your race will be a part of the very life by which American greatness is measured.

"Outstanding Achievements of Negro Women," ca. 1930s

I have the privilege this afternoon to talk with you, those who have tuned in with us at the K.A.K.D. [radio station], regarding some of the outstanding achievements of Negro women. I do not hope to tell you about all the achievements of all Negro Women, first because of the impossibility of such a task in the time allotted to me and second because of human error I may inadvertently overlook some of the women who should be mentioned.

You will doubtless be surprised to learn that according to the records kept by the *Crisis*, the official organ of the NAACP, more than four thousand Negro women have graduated from the leading universities of this country. Fourteen of these women have been elected to the honorary fraternity Phi Beta Kappa, in which membership is based on scholarship. Five of these women, Georgiana Simpson, Eva Dykes, Stella [Otelia] Cromwell, Sadie Mossell Alexander, and [Anna J.] Cooper have received the degree of Doctor of Philosophy respectively from Chicago University, Radcliffe College, Yale University, University of Pennsylvania, and the Sorbonne. Of this number, twenty-five are lawyers and seventy-eight physicians. Halle Tanner Johnson, a Negro physician, graduate of the Woman's Medical College of Pennsylvania, was the first woman of any race to pass the Medical State Board examinations of the state of Alabama—where she labored with Booker T. Washington in his pioneer days.

These college women have organized themselves into three separate sororities, one of which, Delta Sigma Theta, has made possible this and similar programs brought throughout the United States. As these programs well indicate, the sorority with the Negro women has not been a social organization only but rather it has laid its greatest emphasis on movements to foster higher education among the Negro women and a greater appreciation on the part of the public of the accomplishments of Negro women of education and training. And it is with this idea in mind that I proceed to tell you something of the achievements of Negro women in art, literature, education, business, and politics.

In the field of art, Negro women have occupied a position of national and international prominence. Laura Wheeler, fellow of the Academy of Fine Arts of Philadelphia, recipient of the Harmon award of 1928, has exhibited her paintings both in Paris and America, where they have been received with much favorable comment. Meta Warrick Fuller is the most noted sculptor of the Negro race. She first attracted attention by her work in clay in the Pennsylvania School of Industrial Art. In 1899 she went to Paris to study where Rodin, the great French sculptor, saw her work and, becoming convinced of her unusual ability, took her as a pupil. Her exhibits in Paris and America have produced unusually favorable comments from the critics.

Hazel Harrison, pianist, student of Busoni and Petri, made her debut with the Berlin Philharmonic Orchestra and has since been doing concert work in America and Europe with marked success. Jessie Covington, now a scholar of the Juilliard Foundation and Helen Hagan, graduate of the Yale Conservatory of Music, are also pianists who have attained distinction on the concert stage. The position of Marian Anderson, soloist, now studying in Europe, may be judged from the fact that she was chosen as soloist for the Philharmonic Orchestra of Philadelphia for the season of 1923–24 and guest soloist at the Stadium Concert conducted in 1926 under the auspices of the N.Y. Philharmonic Orchestra after a competitive tryout by artists from all sections of the United States.

In the field of literature, Negro women have recently added two outstanding novels, *There Is Confusion* by Jessie Fauset, published by Boni and Liveright, and *Quicksand* by Nella Larsen Imes, just released by publisher Alfred Knopf. Georgia Douglas Johnson has issued two volumes of poetry of exquisite quality, which stand out as real contributions to American literature. Effie Lee Newsome is also a poet of recognized ability as are Jessie Fauset, Alice Dunbar-Nelson, and Gwendolyn Bennett. The verses of these women appear frequently in current magazines but have not yet been combined [in] single volumes. Alice Dunbar-Nelson is unusually versatile in her literary productions. She is a columnist of rare ability, a novelist and compiler, as well as a poet. Other published contributions to literature have been made in recent years by Maud Cuney Hare, Louise Alston Burleigh, Addie W. Hunton, and Kathryn M. Johnson. The latter two women relate in a single volume their experiences with the American expeditionary forces during the World War. Their contribution to the cause of the allies absorbs one's attention so greatly that the literary value of the book has often been overlooked in the comments of the critics.

In journalism we have Viola M. Falmetta of N.Y., subscription manager of *The World Tomorrow*, Geraldyn Dismond, former columnist for the *Pittsburgh Courier* and now an editor of the *Tattler*, Jessie Fauset, former literary editor of the *Crisis*, Julia Bumry, former city editor of the *Pittsburgh Courier*, and Bertha Perry Rhodes, managing editor of the *Philadelphia Tribune*.

In the field of education, Negro women have built institutions which are monuments to their industry, faith, and unselfish spirit. Mary Bethune in Florida, Charlotte Hawkins Brown in N.C., Lucy Laney in Georgia, Jane Porter Barrett in Virginia, and Nannie Burroughs in Washington, D.C., have influenced not only the lives of the students within the confines of their schools but the thoughts and lives of thousands within the communities surrounding their institutions and with whom these persons are in touch. In the midst of barren woodland, these women have gone without endowments, or even moral support, and gradually built institutions of physical respectability and of greater social importance. The story of the establishment of any one of these schools reads like a mighty novel. I have seen great audiences of stalwart men and women weep when Mary Bethune told the story of her struggles in developing an institution in the heart of Florida. Once where a simple frame dwelling stood, in which she gathered a few students, now stand modern fireproof buildings. A splendid dormitory of brick stone had just been completed when I last visited Daytona—all the result of the efforts of a single woman with a purpose. In Boston, New York City, and Chicago, Negro women have held with honor high positions in the public school systems, which are not segregated according to racial groups. Just this year Maudelle Brown Bousfield, formerly dean of girls in the Wendell Phillips High School of Chicago, was appointed principal of the Keith [Elementary] School, being the first Negro woman in Chicago to receive such an appointment.

In the field of business, the names of three Negro women stand out for accomplishments which are almost phenomenal. Annie Malone of St. Louis has built a great manufacturing company, the Poro College, for the production of cosmetics and toilet articles. She is the sole owner of this company and is rated by Bradstreet as a millionaire. Madam C. J. Walker, who died a few years ago, was the head of a similar manufacturing company with headquarters in Indianapolis. Her company, The Madam C. J. Walker Manufacturing Co., is now headed by her daughter A'Lelia Walker who is successfully conducting their company, the assets of which reach the million dollar mark. Maggie L. Walker of Richmond is the first woman in the U.S. to establish a bank and she is still among the few women bank presidents in this country. This institution, St. Luke Penny Savings Bank, has a paid-up capital of a hundred thousand [dollars]. It has never missed a year in paying, since its establishment in 1902, dividends of not less than 5 percent to its stockholders. Mrs. Walker is also the head of the Independent Order of St. Luke, a fraternal order with an insurance department operated on the legal reserve basis. Over a hundred thousand members in twenty-one states belong to the Order, which has erected an impressive office building in Richmond at the cost of a hundred thousand dollars. Here the St. Luke's Herald, another of Mrs. Walker's enterprises, is printed and distributed. These two women have done more than amass wealth; they have created standards of personal hygiene which have been adopted by the great mass of Negro women to the improvement of their health and personal appearance.

In politics Negro women have also occupied positions of trust and prominence. National Committee women have been selected in Georgia and Mississippi. And from Pittsburgh comes this year Daisy Lampkin, stated as alternate delegate at large to the National Republican Convention. Numerous positions of importance are held by Negro women in the municipal and state governments of this country.

In Philadelphia, we have Lena Trent Gordon, special investigator for the Dept. of Public Welfare; Maude Morrissette, interviewer for the Municipal Court of Philadelphia; and Daisy S. Berry, probation officer of the Juvenile Court, as well as many other clerks and assistants.

In Pittsburgh, you have Sadie Black Hamilton, a former Juvenile Court officer, now one of the chief probation officers for the Pittsburgh Schools; Mrs. William M. Randolph, her assistant; and Sarah McClaughan, a member of the police force. Similarly, in the other large eastern cities Negro women have political positions of equal importance.

And so, from this brief survey of the activities of Negro women, I hope that those of you who have listened in have had your spirits tuned in to a greater appreciation of the ambitions and achievements of Negro women.

"Address on Negro Achievement," 1936

Mr. Chairman, Honored Guests, Fellow-citizens:

In view of the fact that we are assembled here tonight to celebrate *Negro Achievement*, it seems fitting and proper that we should review some of those accomplishments which we have achieved which warrant such a celebration.

Foremost among these accomplishments, I should place the physical preservation of the Negro race. The struggle for survival of any species and its success is a standard by which we can judge the success of the species. Charles Darwin, in his essay on "The Origin of Species," first clearly pointed out that only the fittest survive and that by a process of natural selection each creature is improved in relation to its organic and inorganic conditions of life until in most cases it leads to what must be regarded as an advance in organization. For if only the fittest survive, it follows that those who survive necessarily are of the highest caliber—the fittest. Plant and animal life struggle to live, to propagate, as well as man. In order to live and create each must obtain food, shelter, and raiment. And man must, in addition, obtain sufficient wealth to secure the necessary food, shelter, and clothing. So that the mere fact that, in the highly competitive society represented by American civilization, the Negro race has been able not only to live but to increase its numbers, indicates that it has been able to meet the tests of economic competition, physical endurance, and spiritual temptations. In 140 years, from 1790 to 1930, the Negro population increased from less than one million black men and women to more than twelve millions. Approximately one third of this increase has taken place since 1900; due to the fact that our death rate declined more rapidly than our birth rate, as we learned more about caring for our bodies. The white population of America was aided in its numerical increase by emigration from every European country but the Negro population has not had any substantial increase from such a source. We have grown in numbers because of our own relegation to the lowlands, the railroad sidings, the slums, to the meanest kinds of labor and the longest hours—to jobs not protected by the N.R.A. [National Recovery Administration] or the A.A.A [Agricultural Adjustment Act]. We have won in the greatest of all known combats, the struggle to exist in a hostile country, and this is an achievement of which we should be justly proud.

As would be expected from a race of people that has grown in numbers to such proportions as the Negro race in America, we have accumulated a certain amount of wealth. If we had not obtained wealth we should have been extinguished; for the society in which we live is built on wealth. The necessities of life cannot be obtained without it. Tonight, we have a right to lay claim among our achievements to the wealth our race has accumulated. The largest asset is perhaps the homes we own. We own over 30 percent of the homes occupied by Negroes and these homes have a total value of over six hundred million dollars. Almost 30 percent or close to three quarters of a million Negroes in America own their homes. Of the fifteen cities having a Negro population of fifty thousand or more, Philadelphia leads with the greatest number of homes owned by Negroes. Over seven thousand homes are owned by Negroes in Philadelphia with an average value of $4,662.00 and a total value of over twenty million dollars. The taxable real property owned by Negroes in Philadelphia yields the city $534,000 per year. Why should we not proudly count such a substantial contribution to the maintenance of our city government [as] an achievement? Why should we not request city jobs because we help to pay for them?

In addition to our wealth represented by the value of the homes we own in America, we have accumulated church property in the value of $205,782,628 — school property owned and operated by Negroes in the value of over ten million dollars.

The Negro has also made a surprising record in his operation of retail stores. In spite of competition from the chain store, in 1930 there were 25,701 retail stores operated in the United States by Negroes with reported sales valued at $101,146,043. Our own state, Pennsylvania, reported the highest value of sales, $6,519,865. In Philadelphia alone there were sales of $3,105,007 and these 787 stores had an annual payroll of $300,747.

When it is realized that we have no inherited wealth and that a Negro must work by the sweat of his brow to accumulate wealth, such accomplishments are worthy achievements.

The Negro has undoubtedly contributed more labor in proportion to his numbers to American civilization than any other of the many racial groups that constitute this heterogeneous population. It is difficult to measure his contribution in this field because records are not made of the Negroes who build roads, subways, railroads, and factories. In the field of agriculture, however, we have a definite record of his contribution. In 1929 there was produced on farms operated by colored men and women 32.4 percent of all the cotton produced in the United States; 24.9 percent of all the sweet potatoes produced in the United States; 18.9 percent of all the tobacco produced in the United States; 16.4 percent of the total corn harvested for grain in the United States, and 10.1 percent of the Irish potatoes harvested in the United States. Yet, Negro farm operators constituted only 14 percent of all farm operators while the Negro population represented only 9.7 percent of all the total population, and this 9.7 percent of the American population produced almost one third of the staples required for American life. This is unheralded ACHIEVEMENT!

Our accomplishments in the educational field, I venture to say, have not been equaled by any race in the world. In 1870, eighty Negro persons out of a hundred could not read and write. Today, the figures are exactly reversed in that more than eighty Negro persons out of every hundred can read and write — only 16.3 percent of the Negroes ten years and over are illiterate. Sixty percent of our population between the ages of five and twenty is attending school, compared with 9.2 percent in

1870. We have seized the opportunities afforded us for education and proven our ability to make use of them.

We have in the United States today over 100,000 Negroes trained in the professions. In this number are 50,000 teachers, 6,000 nurses, close to 4,000 physicians, and 1,200 lawyers. Since 1876 we have had the degree of Doctor of Philosophy conferred by the leading American and European colleges on 107 Negro men and women and over [left blank] of our race have completed college education.

The cultural accomplishments of these trained Negro men and women in the arts and sciences will doubtless be referred to by other speakers. My failure to consider their contribution to American civilization does not indicate a lack of appreciation of their work. Rather, I am confining my survey of Negro achievements to the advancement made by the race as a mass, in the accumulation of wealth, the survival of the race itself, and the general educational advancement rather than the numerous individual accomplishments and contributions to civilization.

Having illustrated achievements as a race, I desire now to turn to the question: "What should be our program to assure further achievement of the race en masse?"

First, it seems to me that the Negro schools and colleges and churches should place greater stress upon the practical use of the power of consumption of the Negro masses. If in Philadelphia alone, without any concerted effort, 787 retail stores exist with an annual payroll of over three hundred thousand dollars, what might not be done by organized effort to increase the wage level of Negroes, and improve the economic status of the group? To illustrate what can be done I should like to tell you of a Consumers Cooperative League established in Gary, Indiana. Mr. J. S. Reddix, a high school teacher, concerned about the depths to which the twenty thousand Negroes in Gary had sunk during the depression, organized fifteen families who contributed twenty-four dollars to purchase groceries for the group as a unit. They obtained reduced prices because of the quantity of their weekly purchases. At the end of two months, thirty families had joined the group, purchasing forty-five dollars' worth of goods per week. Then Mr. Reddix proposed a cooperative store. Shares valued at ten dollars were issued with a proviso that a member could purchase any number of shares, but each person had but one vote. A store with two clerks opened Christmas 1932. In August 1935 the Consumers Cooperative Store in Gary had 371 members, [with] sales of $34,000 for the year. Now these persons have started a credit union. There are 150 members—so they no longer have to lose their furniture for a fifty-dollar loan from a loan company, the interest on which equals the principal before one can pay the loan. The progress and survival of any race of people living in the highly competitive society of today is dependent upon their economic independence. The purchasing power of the Negroes in Philadelphia is sufficient to assure our independence if it is used among ourselves. In any program for future development we must include the teaching of ways and means to harness Negro purchasing power so that it will improve the economic status of the Negro people themselves and not make rich any immigrant who establishes a corner store in a Negro neighborhood.

Second, some agency interested in Negro progress must undertake a national survey of occupational opportunities for Negroes. The jobs long considered Negro jobs are rapidly disappearing. Few of the best hotels employ Negro waiters or waitresses. Railroads are employing Filipinos in club cars and diners. The large estates are manned by an all-white corps of servants. Mexicans are seen repairing railroad tracks. Elevator operators now must have white faces. The genial smile of the agile Negro bellhop no longer greets the hotel guest and new ones are not replacing them. The old jobs are passing away. We must make a complete, exhaustive study of what can be done to keep the jobs traditionally known as Negro work and what type of training is necessary to prepare our boys and girls for new positions. Day after day, eager young boys and girls, graduates of high school, call at my office. "Mrs. Alexander, can you help me to find a job?" they ask. "What do you know how to do?" I ask, and the same answer comes back over and over again—"Well, I am a graduate of high school." Twelve years of training and still unprepared. When these children enter high school, there should be available for their parents or those entrusted with their guidance facts as to opportunities for stenographers, factory workers, dressmakers, cooks, dietitians, and facts as to the type of training required in order that one may enter a given field. If we hope even to survive we have got to find ways of making a living after November when the presidential election is over and there is no further political need for relief checks. [There must be] interest in raising standards for domestic laborers.

Third, in any program proposed for racial achievement one must consider the influence of the Negro church. Over five million Negroes belong to some church. Still more striking is the fact that we have one minister among every 475 Negroes in the United States. The full force of this statement can be realized only when it is stated that there is but one physician for every three thousand Negroes in the United States and only one lawyer for every nine thousand Negroes in the United States. To say the least our spiritual welfare is abundantly provided for. The success of any plan to improve the status of our group must be dependent upon the cooperation of the Negro clergyman and the Negro church, because they come nearer than any other group to controlling the thought of the masses. We must develop some plan by which this group of leaders will realize the social implications of Christian salvation. A real Christian cannot be satisfied with a religion that is concerned only with the technique of saving individual souls. *Jesus*, coming from a poor family, the son of a working man and himself a carpenter, had an intimate sympathy for the poor and oppressed. Combined with sympathy, He had a keen insight into their needs and problems. He knew that if the lives of the poor were to be made happier, if their souls were to be made purer, there must be an improvement in their general social conditions. His sympathy for the poor did not stop with charity but flowed out into a concept of *social justice*. The missionary who goes to a foreign country soon finds he must obtain improved social conditions in order to carry his message. First, the people must be taught to read the gospel. An illiterate people cannot obtain an understanding of the word of God. Moreover, a hungry people cannot even listen to the reading of His word. So the missionary begins to teach reading and writing. He seeks proper food and clothing for his followers. He yearns for and perhaps finally obtains a hospital where the sick can be healed and the well taught how to keep fit. So we Negro Christians and our leaders must realize that the salvation of the individual soul is but a small part of Christianity. A true conception of Christianity concerns itself with creating a fit place on earth for all of God's people, rich and poor, black and white. Our program for future achievement of the Negro race must therefore include the teaching of the social responsibility of those who preach Christian salvation.

We have come a long way from a little over a half million souls in 1870 to twelve million today; of whom eighty out of every one hundred in 1870 could neither read nor write and of whom today more than eighty out of every one hundred can read and write. We have improved not only in knowledge but in economic position. But we still have a long way to go. My plan of the way to go may not be your way. That does not matter. But it does matter that every Negro man and woman, boy and girl, catches the vision of the possibilities of his race achieving whatever has been or can be accomplished by any other people that God created and moulded in his image. What we need is a vision of Negro achievement and strength to follow that vision. When Felix Adler, the founder of the Ethical Culture movement, returned from Europe where he had been completing his rabbinistic studies, he brought news that almost broke his father's heart. Young Adler could not conscientiously enter the rabbinate. Their friends thought that old Dr. Adler, who was preparing his son to be his successor as leader of a great New York synagogue, would disown his son. Instead of his father disowning him he said in words I think should be engraved on every heart: "*Follow thy vision and God speed thee to the end.*"

Tonight, I say to you, catch a vision of the Negro race, free from illiteracy, living in homes which are owned and removed from the slums, harnessing their purchasing power by trading with one another, their ministers preaching cooperation and that cleanliness in living conditions which is next to Godliness, and follow that vision. May God speed each of you to the end.

"Acceptance Speech of the Award of the Pennsylvania Society for Promoting the Abolition of Slavery," 1975

Mr. Chairman, Officers and Members of the Pennsylvania Society for Promoting the Abolition of Slavery and Friends of this Historic Society:

I wish to express my appreciation for your affording me the opportunity to join in celebrating two hundred years of dedication to your purpose, not only to abolish slavery but to relieve Negroes unlawfully held in bondage and to improve the condition of the African race. Seldom, if ever, have I had the opportunity physically to be a part of an organization that for two hundred years has labored not only to secure the physical freedom of the American Negroes, but also assure their mental freedom. Yes, the Emancipation Proclamation decreed that the shackles be removed from the body of the Negro but left his mind enslaved . . . white was and is right!

Realizing that only education could free the human mind, this Society established, as one of its purposes, improving the condition of the African race. And, to effectuate this purpose, as early as 1790 created a Board of Education, which soon thereafter established the foundation of what is today known as Cheyney State Teachers College, which is but one of the successful products of this Committee.

The three minutes allotted me do not permit further review of the contributions of the Pennsylvania Abolition Society during its two hundred years of existence. I would like, however, the liberty to call your attention to the cooperation of the Society with William Still, a Negro, and a possible creator of the Underground Railroad. I beg your permission to tell you briefly the effect the Underground Railroad had upon my family and, hence, my life.

My maternal grandmother, Sarah Elizabeth Tanner, was born a slave in Winchester, Virginia. Her father was the master of the plantation and her mother, Elizabeth Miller, was the cook for the family. Elizabeth Miller was illiterate and had eleven children—five by the master of the plantation and six by a freeman who wanted to marry her. Each time her fiancé got enough money to pay the price the master asked for Elizabeth, his cook, the price increased. Finally, my great-grandmother made contact with the Underground Railroad; put all her eleven children in one of the master's double-team wagons, well-filled with food; and sent them away at midnight. They reached Carlisle, Pennsylvania, where members of your Society anxiously awaited their arrival. The children were divided among various families, my grandmother being sent to Pittsburgh. My great-grandmother never again saw her children and the children never again saw their mother, nor each other.

I accept your award not for any personal accomplishments but as evidence of gratitude for your unheralded efforts in freeing from bondage countless other Negroes, including my grandmother who is the mother of Henry Ossawa Tanner, one of America's greatest artists.

Part II

Black Women in the Political Economy

Introduction

By the late nineteenth century, rapid increases in levels of industrialization, immigration, and urbanization, along with imperialist expansion abroad, had led to intense nativism within the United States. Native-born whites expressed open hostility toward racial and immigrant groups that they viewed as being beneath them. Nativists claimed that white dominance was a natural outcome of evolutionary processes that had resulted in their having a superior civilization compared to so-called backward peoples.[1] Nativists also used gender differences as a signifier of racial progress and civilization. They believed that in civilized races, men and women operated in separate spheres, with men employed in the public sphere as breadwinners and women living in the private sphere as homemakers and caregivers, dependent on men.[2] Women's employment outside of their households was a mark of backwardness, according to the civilization discourse. In response to these beliefs, middle-class white and Black social reformers and clubwomen engaged in separate campaigns to "uplift" the poor segments of their communities by often focusing on morality and behavior to improve poor women's socioeconomic position.

Married women's employment was also a concern for the small group of women economists in the early twentieth century. When Alexander completed her doctoral studies in 1921, one-fifth of economists in the United States were women. By 1940, that percentage had dropped to just 7 percent, a decline that perhaps indicates the struggles women faced in becoming trained as economists as well as in working within the discipline.[3] Compared to men, women had more difficulty securing admission to graduate schools, financing their graduate education, getting hired and promoted, and publishing their work. Some universities outright excluded women from admission into their graduate programs, and even those schools that did admit women provided more fellowship opportunities to male students. After graduation, women economists' career choices were often limited to teaching at women's colleges, where women comprised 70 percent of all faculty, compared to co-ed schools where women made up just 20 percent of faculty.[4] Although women economists engaged in a range of research fields comparable to that of their male counterparts, women's ability to publish in economic journals tended to be restricted to subjects that focused on women's economic concerns.[5] It was also common for women faculty to leave their positions after marriage or when they began families in deference to expectations that married women should be homemakers.

Sadie Alexander, however, always viewed women's employment, whether her own or that of other Black women, favorably. Alexander's experience with domestic boredom during the year after her marriage, her early exposure to accomplished Black women, and the precarious economic position of her mother following Aaron Mossell's desertion must have influenced her positive assessment of Black women's employment. Women's employment, according to Alexander, gave them opportunities for gaining economic and political independence.

When women won the right to vote in 1920, it raised new political possibilities for African American women. African American women activists had expressed concern for decades that some Black men were squandering their votes and not making effective use of their positions of leadership.[6] With the right to vote, Black women activists began mobilizing Black women's voting power in order to make public officials accountable to the needs of their community.[7] Alexander encouraged Black women to use their votes against the racial violence and segregation that circumscribed their lives. As was the case with earlier generations of Black women activists, Alexander believed that African American women had a primary role to play in promoting the interests of African Americans through organizational protest and through leadership roles within Black religious and civic organizations. This was consistent with the views of other African American women activists such as Elise Johnson McDougald, who praised Black women for their organizational acumen in advancing the concerns of the Black community.[8]

In addition to African American women's leadership, Alexander focused attention in her speeches and writings on African American women's employment status. Mindful that Black wives' employment signaled the community's low status, Alexander also knew that Black women's earnings were vital for sustaining families and could possibly even contribute to their upward mobility. While most Black Americans in the early part of the twentieth century understood the need for Black wives' employment because of employment discrimination against Black men, it stood as a visible sign of Black men's inability to support their families during an era that expected men to be breadwinners. Since the late nineteenth century, however, Black women had consistently had higher labor-force participation rates than other women. By 1920, for example, the percentage of Black wives who were employed as wage laborers was five times greater than women in any other racial or ethnic group.

Social scientists who were Alexander's contemporaries were often critical of Black wives' employment since they claimed that mothers' employment caused juvenile delinquency within the Black community.[9] Although Alexander was sensitive to white perceptions that Black women's employment symbolized lack of racial progress, she nonetheless showed support for Black women's employment regardless of their marital status. The concern that she had over African American women's employment was not about whether they should work, but rather that they were experiencing discriminatory treatment that limited their opportunities for job mobility. Alexander believed that fighting this unfair treatment might enable African American women to gain a foothold within the expanding industrial sector.

Alexander framed her discussion of Black women workers within an overall analysis of racial oppression, since she believed that racism was the fundamental problem the nation faced. This was consistent with other early twentieth-century African American feminists, who similarly viewed Black women's oppression as inextricably tied to race, and who considered racial discrimination as driving the political, economic, and social problems that Black women confronted.[10] Activists such as Sadie Alexander and Mary McLeod Bethune worked cooperatively with Black men and white progressives, but by the 1930s they had also come to believe that African American women should attend to their own concerns within Black women's organizations.[11] Indeed, Alexander was a member of Bethune's National Council of Negro Women and served as the parliamentarian and chair of its legal committee. With their emphasis on race, Bethune and Alexander viewed educational and economic gains through employment for Black women as indicators of racial progress. This illustrates an important way in which African American women developed understandings of womanhood that differed from the prevailing views of the day.

The first two speeches in this section focus on Black women's leadership. Alexander delivered the first speech, "Segregation in Public Schools," at the Dunbar Theatre in Philadelphia during her second year in law school. It shows her frustration with African Americans who tried to curry favor with whites and with those Black men whom she believed were not holding elected officials accountable to the Black community. In the second speech, "A Demand for Women as Executive Officers of the Church," Alexander spoke during Women's Day at Philadelphia's Union AME Church. She envisioned women as being at least as capable as men and warned church officials to make full use of women's talents or risk losing out to competing interests.

The third entry, "Negro Women in Our Economic Life," is an economic article by Alexander that the National Urban League published in its magazine *Opportunity: Journal of Negro Life*. The article is remarkable both for its assessment of the impact of market production on women's household work and for the central role that Alexander accorded African American women's work within her analysis. Although African American women have contributed to production outside of their households to a much greater degree than other women have, most economists have had little to say about this work history. Alexander's insights that the marketization of work that was previously performed within the household contributed to a reclassification of women's household activities from production to valueless consumption is a cornerstone of the argument that a later generation of feminist economists began making during the end of the twentieth century about unpaid household work. This article also demonstrates Alexander's ongoing engagement with economic theory and practice, since she discusses the ways in which Black women's labor productivity and contribution to national output had altered economists' views.

The next speech, "The Emancipated Woman," gives a more indepth historical analysis of the impact of wage labor on women's lives and favorably assesses married women's employment during an era when domesticity was still the social expectation for married women. The speech links political with economic freedom and emphasizes the importance of African American women voting and engaging in collective action for the benefit of the community.

The fifth speech, "The Economic Status of Negro Women, an Index to the Negro's Economic Status," written in response to the failure of New Deal policies to provide equitable treatment to Black workers, is a fine example of the ways in which Alexander combined her training in economics with her knowledge of the law. The speech addresses Black women's employment in domestic service and farming rather than the manufacturing sector, and it drew attention to Black women's vulnerability to job loss as well as their abysmal working conditions and long hours of work in marginal, low-paid jobs. Recognizing the importance of Black women's earnings to family welfare, Alexander discussed the impact on families of Black women's job loss during the Great Depression. Alexander also decried the disparate treatment of Black and white women under the law, particularly with respect to domestic servants' exclusion from minimum wages and other New Deal labor protections.

The remaining two speeches in this section cover a range of issues involving African American women and girls. The Delta Sigma Theta speech in 1939 shows Alexander's favorable perceptions of changing social norms that have afforded daughters greater freedoms of self-expression, independence, and assertiveness. Alexander was one of five charter members of the Gamma chapter of Delta Sigma Theta sorority at the University of Pennsylvania in 1918. The sorority provided fellowship for members and service to the African American community. While

Alexander was at the university, the sorority sisters brought Carter Woodson, W. E. B. Du Bois, and Marian Anderson to speak on campus. Alexander was the first national president of Delta Sigma Theta from 1919 to 1923.[12] She maintained a lifelong engagement with the sorority, serving later as their legal adviser.

The final speech in this section, "Women as Practitioners of Law in the United States," is one that Alexander gave in 1941 before the National Bar Association. In this speech, she offered an overview of obstacles that women faced in admission to the bar and provided an assessment of Black women lawyers based on a survey questionnaire that she had sent to them. Alexander later revised this speech into an article for the *National Bar Journal.*

"Segregation in Public Schools," 1925

There are doubtless in this audience persons with varying opinions on the solution of the question which is before us this afternoon for discussion and possible solution. I have no doubt that in all sincerity there are those who honestly believe that the best results can be obtained by a school system the teachers in which belong entirely to the white race, while on the other extreme are those who believe Negro children should be taught by Negro teachers. Between these two extremes are persons with varying views on the subject and some, doubtless many, who believe the ideal solution is an entirely mixed faculty—colored and white teachers being assigned according to rank to the positions as they are opened. [That] there is not unanimity of opinion on the solution is not cause for alarm—it is rather a customary and a hopeful sign. The fact people have opinions is an indication they have given some thought to the subject and time will not have to be spent in creating interest in the problem. If their opinions differ from mine [and] yours neither is this cause for alarm and despondency. As long as we are individuals, we will be individualistic and see things in varying lights. Negroes are not the only people who think differently on their problem. Had Englishmen all thought alike about conditions in Britain's coalfields, the nation would not have been divided in hostile camps at a tremendous financial loss for three years. Differences of opinions on the method of solution of segregation in public schools of Philadelphia [are] not the impediment dangers we face, but rather insidious methods followed by many persons harboring these extreme views which I have mentioned. 1. The petitioner who obtains [a] list of phantom names for the opening of a new colored school—2. The regular visitors to the offices of the Board of Education to tell what we are thinking and saying—some of them will be up there tomorrow morning to explain all about this meeting—3. The interpreter for the entire race who explains to the members of [the Board of Education] that Negroes prefer to be to themselves—that is the reason they always walk through a streetcar until they see a colored person next to whom to sit— 4. Those Negro preachers who travel to Harrisburg to support segregation bills in the schools. There is a peculiar psychology to what these people do—the apparent confidence they enjoy with white men and women, who welcome them, so flatters [them] that they seize every possible occasion to call on Mr. Charlie and Miss Mary.

They can always get an audience while those of us who seek greater opportunities for our race [are] denied even a hearing. But a larger number of us suffer from utter inertia and never seek a hearing. At any rate it is a point upon which I have given thought and reached a conclusion, i.e.—Individual conferences can hurt us but cannot help us. This matter has got to be attack[ed] by an organized body—working through the Courts. Persuasion, conferences in groups, and individual [efforts] have been tried—our legal rights are the only hope. The laborer of the world faced a similar condition—individually they could command no respect—no hearing. They formed unions and carried their appeals to the Courts. You do not suppose all the members of the union agreed on the method of accomplishing their demand any more than we. They have traitors same as we have. But the influence of wide opposition is insignificant when it faces a well-organized body. So, I say, first we need a permanent organization [to show] what women can do. Whether the methods of this are the ones you would employ is not basis for failing to support it—whatever the combined thought on [the] best procedure to wipe out this growing evil is, we must follow—have faith in its success. If we support it—it will succeed.

The [additional] duties of this organization will be [to] second, gather around it every possible group. Teachers in Philadelphia schools are a potent factor whose support we have not entirely enlisted because we have failed to interpret correctly our position on the question. We are not fighting the teachers but fighting *for* the teachers. It is a disgrace that a Negro woman, ready to take her doctor's degree, should have to teach grade school children—when white women with half [the] education she has occupy executive positions in higher schools.

Women of Philadelphia must be enlisted in this fight. Women are leaders in [the] world—race rises no higher than its women. Third, vote. Women have weapons with which to fight which our men have thrown away for a few elevator operators, street cleaners, and minor clubships and women instead of leading are following men's example by giving their votes away for a few special investigators. In the spring primaries many important positions will be filled—Mayor, members [of] City Council, District Attorney. Women, *vote* but do not vote for a single man until you have written him asking where he stands on the School Lines. That's the way we can win this battle. The Board of Education is appointed by C.P. [Court of Common Pleas] Judges who depend upon constituencies and party for election. They do what their constituency favors—every city official can influence this problem. Nail them all at the next election.

Fourth, you women in Federal Clubs, Lodges, Societies and Church Organizations—you did good work when [the] Civil Rights bill was up but you have not kept up the work. Keep lobbying in Harrisburg. Demand a statement of position [from] every man [who] goes to Harrisburg and follow him up there—see [that] he keeps his word.

Fifth, support organizations financially. Expert talent must be procured [to] give full time to [the] Court issue—if [the] issue [is] improperly framed [it] can't get [to the] Supreme Court of the U.S.

It can be won, because it has been won. [unknown name], Isaac [unknown], Chris Perry [break in text] their bodies moldering in graves—along with principles for which they fought, in fact sacrificed. I have not time to tell you women who have stronger weapons than they, votes [to] control balance of power, organized clubs, and greater financial means—to use them when we have passed on as [have our] forefathers, we like they may hear those precious words, "Well done, my good and faithful servant."

"A Demand for Women as Executive Officers of the Church," 1928

In line with the recognition of women politically and economically, the AME Church at [its] 1924 General Conference decreed that women were henceforth eligible for every office held by a layman in the church, which included membership on the trustee boards, officers of individual church bodies, general officers of the connection, and delegates to the general conference. Some of the conferences, notably our own, have elected women as lay delegates to the 1928 General Conference. Few of the larger churches have filled vacancies in their trustee boards with women. As yet no woman has announced her candidacy for a General office, perhaps the campaign season has not yet opened. With, however, at least 65 percent of the membership of the connection consisting of women, who admittedly are the financial support of the church, it seems opportune upon this occasion, Women's Day, for the women to consider what steps they will take during the coming years to obtain the rights which the church has conferred upon them.

What Justification Have We for Our Demand

The mere fact that the General Conference has recognized the position of the women in the church by according them the right to representation in the controlling bodies of the church ought of itself be sufficient reason for our demanding tangible evidence of the right. But if we do not care to rely upon the mere grant of authority as a basis for asserting our demands, there are numerous reasons to support us: First, if the church is going to compete successfully with not only other denominations but more especially with other social institutions which are making such inroads on the hold of the church afar [*sic*] the people of today, it must utilize all of its forces. Women constitute one of the most potent of these forces, whose efforts throughout the history of the church in all of its fields of endeavor have been acknowledged indispensable. The church can no longer hope to compete with other institutions that are diverting the executive and intellectual ability of the women to positions of importance, if, because of convention which has no logical basis, it refuses to adopt like forces within its own borders. In every church there are some women who because of great natural gift or perseverance in the development of lesser talents are ranked among the true if not the official leaders of the church. We should derive the benefit of the services of such women, especially when their ability is greater than that of some of the men who fill positions of importance in the church, by placing them in executive control. Unless the churches in the various communities awaken to this situation and select among their leaders women, not because they are women but because they are the most capable persons to be selected, [they] shall find other institutions that have already begun to harness the talents of their capable women occupying the position of leadership, traditionally held by the church but lost because of unwise adherence to tradition.

Second, women may find ample justification for demanding representation in executive positions of the church from the effect their presence will have as an incentive to young women, whose lack of interest in the activities of the church darkens the future prospects of our great connections. Our boys have always had as a stimulus to their relations with the church the prospects of leadership. But our women have been forced to content themselves with raising the bulk of the money, the expenditure of which the men have directed. Fortunately or unfortunately, I shall not say which, our younger women are not so content to sow and not reap. Perhaps it is due to the spirit of the age. Certainly there could be no greater panacea for their state of mind than the presence of a capable woman in a general office of the church and numerous such women filling executive positions in the local churches, to whom our girls may look for inspiration and from whose position they may gather interest in applying their best labors to the work of the church.

Proposed Program of the Women Delegates to General Commerce

The extent, however, to which men and even the women of the church will recognize the necessity of placing women in positions of leadership in the church will depend largely upon the type of women selected as lay delegates and, moreover, in which women delegates to the 1928 General Conference use their power. It is to be hoped they will ally themselves with the constructive forces and not permit themselves to become a party to destructive politics. In order to safeguard themselves, the women should go to the Conference with a program, so that their combined strength may be felt, and their demands recognized. We at home have as our duty the suggesting of planks for the consideration of women lay delegates. First on their program should be the securing of a strong, capable, intelligent woman as a General Officer of the church. There should also be a demand on the Conference for a modification of the marriage ceremony. The conservative bishops of the ancient Church of England have felt the need of recommending the elimination of the word "obey" from the ceremony and of tempering the language in other respects. The women should take the lead in proposing and securing similar changes in our marriage ceremony. Moreover, the women should undertake the securing of some concrete plan for keeping the church in contact with the large group of our youth who are attending the Colleges. Every prominent denomination of the white Americans has suffered student secretaries to bring the church to the College Campus. We must work out a similar plan so that the church will not lose the youths, who are destined to be the leaders of the next generation.

There is a vast amount of work to be done for the church. If the women would be leaders in doing this work, they must lead. They can lead by thinking for themselves, developing a program, pushing its adoption, and supporting its application. The church has granted us the right to fill positions of leadership, but it rests with us to secure the privileges flowing from the right and to so use them as to warrant the confidence already placed in us and to forward the church.

"Negro Women in Our Economic Life," 1930

Not even a cursory study of Negro women in our economic life can be assumed without first considering the changing position of all women in our economic life. One hears frequently the woman of today referred to as "the new woman," much as we write and speak of "the new Negro." In my opinion there is no more a new woman among us than there is a new Negro. What has changed and what is changing is not the woman. The change is in her status in a rapidly developing social order. The advent of the mechanical age, historically referred to as the Industrial Revolution, roughly marks the passing of one social and economic order and the dawn of another that is still in the process of unfolding its undetermined course. Under the old social and economic order, the family was the economic unit of production. Under these conditions the activities of women were recognized along with those of men as productive, and the contribution of the wife was as valuable in the eyes of society as that of the husband. There was no difference in the economic function between men and women, in that they were jointly producers and consumers. But when, one after another, the traditional family activities were taken out of the home, the function of women in the home steadily lost its importance in production until it fell to a minimum and emerged associated primarily with consumption. Production in the new economic order, where standards of value are money standards, became fundamentally a matter of creating a commodity or service which demands a money price. Modern industrial processes, having robbed the home of every vestige of its former economic function, left in the home to be performed by the woman only those services which are as "valueless" and "priceless" as air and water but not recognized as *valuable* in a price economy, where standards of value are money standards. If, then, women were to answer the challenge of the new economy and place themselves again among the producers of the world, they must change their status from that of homemakers to that of industrial workers and change their activities from valueless home duties to those that resulted in the production of goods that have a price-value. The answer of women to the challenge is shown by the increase in the number of women gainfully employed from 1,321,364 in 1870, when we first had census figures in which gainfully employed persons were separated by sex, to 7,306,844 in 1920.

We are principally interested in determining the extent to which Negro women have taken their places in this price economy and the effect, if any, their presence has had on our economic life. Work for wages has always been more widespread among Negro than among white women. In 1910, 54.7 percent of the 3,680,536 Negro women in the United States, ten years of age and over, were gainfully occupied while only 19.6 percent of the 30,769,641 white women of the same age group were gainfully employed. In 1920, 38.9 percent of the 4,043,763 Negro women, ten years of age and over, were gainfully employed as compared with 16.1 percent of the 36,279,013 white women of the same age group. The Negro women in 1910 were, however, principally confined to agricultural pursuits, domestic, and personal service. Only 67,937 Negro women, or 3.4 percent of the Negro women ten years of age and over gainfully employed, were among the 1,821,570 women employed in manufacture and mechanical industries; white women workers, on the other hand, during the same decade, came into the business and industrial world at a greater proportionate rate than even men. It was not until the Great War withdrew the men from industry that Negro women were found in any considerable numbers in manufacturing and mechanical industries. The 1920 Census shows that 104,983 Negro women, or 6.7 percent of the Negro women ten years of age and over gainfully employed, were among the 1,930,241 women employed in manufacturing and mechanical industries. This is an increase of almost 100 percent for Negro women in comparison to an increase of less than 1 percent of all women so employed.

There is no question but that this unprecedented increase in the number of Negro women in industry was due to demand for labor because of the stress of war production and the reduction of available industrial labor supply resulting from the cessation of immigration and the withdrawal of three million men from normal economic functions to war activities. That these women have been retained to a large degree is established by surveys made since 1920, principally in 1921, 1922, [and] 1925, by the Women's Bureau of the United States Department of Labor. Their survey of Negro women employed in fifteen states, published in 1929, based on the study made in 1928, reports 17,134 Negro women employed in 682 establishments; an increase of nearly 1,000 over the 16,835 Negro women reported employed in the same industries in a similar survey published in 1922.

The wages of all women in industry have been found to be below that of men. It is not surprising, therefore, to find that the wages of Negro women, who are the marginal workers, should be not only lower than that of men employed in like pursuits, but also lower than that of white women. Any group that constitutes the marginal supply of labor will be paid less for their labor than those whose services are in constant and steady demand. Then, too, the labor turnover among women is greater than that among men, due largely to family duties [and] physical handicaps, but principally to the fact that women do not consider their jobs as permanent. They have not developed a philosophy of work under which they regard the production of price-demanding commodities as their life work. They are constantly expecting when the children get out of the way, or their husbands obtain better jobs, that they will then stop work. The thought of working the rest of their lives is a foreign concept and never enters their minds. Hence, women are slow to organize in unions and men are slower to accept them. The Negro woman in addition has little if any factory training and therefore no factory sense. She must accept such opening wedges [wages] at such return as may be offered her.

Not only are the wages of Negro women lower than those of white women, but Negro women as a whole are confined to the simpler types of work, and are not engaged in highly skilled labor, although many of the occupations in which Negro women are found require care and a number require some skill. This, too, might be expected; for the industrial history of any highly organized community will show, that as members of a new and inexperienced nationality, sex, or race arrive at the doors of its industries, the occupations that open to them ordinarily are those vacated by an earlier stratum of workers who have moved on to more alluring places. All industrial workers, regardless of their racial identification, have started at the bottom of the round. The important thing is *the start.*

Although Negro women are not engaged as skilled, high-priced workers, their presence in large numbers in industry during the past decade has had a marked effect on their status and on the economic life of the country.

To begin with, in the natural process of events in industry, the Negro women must eventually push on to more skilled, better paying jobs. Any other procedure would mean a waste of training, factory sense, and accumulated knowledge which the economies of big business must recognize.

Furthermore, the opportunity for participation in industrial pursuits by Negro women means a raising of the standard of living not only of Negro families but of all American families. The addition of this labor supply aids cheaper production, which in turn means more goods can be enjoyed by a large number of people. In a more direct sense, it affects the Negro family since another wage-earner is added to the family. The derogatory effects of the mother being out of the home are overbalanced by the increased family income, which makes possible the securing of at least the necessities of life and perhaps a few luxuries. If her services in the home are to be rated by the man as valueless consumption, the satisfaction which comes to the woman in realizing that she is a producer makes for peace and happiness, the chief requisites in any home.

The increased leisure that is enjoyed by women who have entered the industrial and manufacturing enterprises is giving rise to an improved educational and social standard among Negro women. Not many weeks ago, I was consulted by a colored woman sixty-two years of age, who had fallen in an unguarded, open manhole. Upon inquiry I learned that she and her witness were operators of machines in a dress factory and that they worked from 8:00 in the morning until 4:00 in the afternoon; that on the evening of the accident they were returning from night school where they had gone for a seven o'clock class to learn to be dress cutters, which would place them considerably higher up the wage scale. This is a typical example of the opportunity for economic and social advancement which the shorter hours enjoyed by industrial workers are making possible for Negro women who have industrial positions. Furthermore, the dignity of being a factory worker has resulted in Negro women thus engaged feeling a greater degree of self-respect and receiving opportunities for social intercourse and expression that as domestic servants were denied them.

The association between the various racial groups employed in a factory will prove an important factor in solving the laborer's problems. The real seat of racial friction is between the working groups, whose resistance to change in the economic status of a competing group invariably expresses itself in what we commonly define as race, or class prejudice. Could the great mass of white workers learn from industrial experience with Negro workers that they have a common purpose in life, the protection of their bargaining power, and that the sooner the untouched wealth of Negro labor is harnessed into this common purpose, the better can they bargain with capital; then and only then would industrial racial friction subside. Certainly the continued presence of Negro women in industry demonstrates that we have made progress toward reducing the resistance of white labor to Negro invasion of industry.

Surveying the field as a whole, we find over a hundred thousand Negro women employed in the manufacturing and mechanical industries of the United States in 1920, an increase of nearly 100 percent in the number so employed in 1910. This is a striking contrast to an increase of only one-tenth of 1 percent in all women so engaged during the decade. Without this additional labor supply, it is doubtful that even scientific management could have carried mass production to such a degree that we should have had a period so marked in the magnitude of its pro-

ductivity as to be called the "New Industrial Revolution." Within the
two decades during which Negro women have entered industry in large
numbers, production has increased at such a rapid rate that economists
have been forced to change their theory of a deficit economy, based on
the assumption that population would always press upon food supply,
to a theory of surplus economy. While the labor of Negro women cannot be held as the efficient cause of the mass production, it is submitted
that without this available labor supply at a low price, mass production
in many industries would not have been undertaken.

Negro families as well as all families have profited and suffered from
the effects of a surplus economy. Mass productivity has multiplied the
number and variety of stimuli which play upon the individual, resulting
in not only high-speed consumption but diversified consumption. The
result is that individual interests and standards of conduct are conceived
in terms of self-satisfaction without a stabilizing sense of group responsibility. The Negro, the furthest down in the economic scale, can least
of all afford to succumb to these varied economic stimuli. If he is going
to profit from the increased purchasing power, which the presence of
Negro women in the productive enterprises has made possible, he must
lead the way in harnessing the variety of his demands to the purchase
of commodities representing the fundamental and durable satisfaction
of life. Only in this way can we hope to promote the establishment of
factors of stability in economic demand which will materially provide
the basis of an economic balance in industry; which in turn will assure
not only the continued presence of Negro women in industry, but stability of employment and constantly improving economic position for
all workers.

"The Emancipated Woman," ca. 1930s

The story of the emancipation of women is or ought to be familiar to all of us present this afternoon. That great change in methods of manufacture and production, called the Industrial Revolution, was the fundamental cause of a new era, not only in industry, but also in domestic life. When Hargreaves (1764) invented [the] spinning jenny, operated by water power, by which six to twelve threads could be spun at one time, and James Watts discovered that steam would also operate a spinning jenny, the confinement of women to their homes, where every article of clothing had previously been produced, became a thing of the past. Then came the discovery in 1765 that coal could be used to smelt iron and liquid iron could be molded into machines that would produce many more times the amount of goods than human hands. Huge iron machines were not suitable for home use; furthermore, they required many persons to operate them. So they were congregated in what became to be called factories because it was the place that factors (commercial agents) congregated. The women and children were taken from their homes to operate the factory machines.

At the end of the week's work, instead of turning over the products to the head of the family, to trade in for staples—the women workers received a wage, which they could spend themselves—without turning it over to any man. It didn't take women long to forget that habit of turning over. Thus, we developed a large group of economically independent women.

The presence of women in [the] industrial world created a number of social problems. First, the conditions, wages, and hours of labor, which are still perplexing as illustrated by efforts [of] Congress [to] fix minimum wage for women, defeated by decision—[of the] USSC [U.S. Supreme Court]—held it was interference with the liberty to contract guaranteed by the 14th Amendment. [The] Oregon statute forbade employment of women in factories for more than ten hours in one day— [as a] valid exercise of political power for health [of] women and race. Second, social freedom: [they] feared morals of [the] nation [would] be lost when women were turned into [the] industrial world [of work]. The same argument was used against Woman Suffrage. A woman has as a bribe her self. It never seemed to occur to the men who advanced these objections that it was within their power to remove the problem. But thank God, the women have been able to handle the situation, whenever it arose, so perfectly that *Scarlet Letters* are truly figures of history and not of our modern-day acquaintance. [The] third problem was concerned with family life. Women engaged in labor, postponed marriage, or controlled births. Those who have families permitted them to rear themselves. Divorces increased—not because the contact with [the] world made women less faithful, but because she no longer had to put up with embarrassments, neglects, and cruelties in order to secure bread and butter—she could make that for herself.

Having gained a taste of freedom in the economic world, naturally women began to demand equality in the political world in order, if for no other reason that they might help legislate for their own protection. Like all other social reform movements, the grant of suffrage in the English-speaking countries had an impetus in this case, the democracy cry of the Great War. So in England in 1918 and the U.S. in 1920 the vote was granted women.

What type of woman has the economic and political freedom produced? Various types. Of course we have the Reactionists, who are always with us in every field of activity. Continually wishing, hoping, praying for the return of the good "old times" but bending every effort to live on in these times. If they are genuinely sincere in their desire,

I often wonder why these persons do not put on long skirts and bonnets and stay at home and operate a hand cotton jenny. The answer is obvious: they could not continue to exist under such conditions in this world of competition. The world is attractive enough for them to want to continue to live in it—so they take a half-handed part—in order to exist. When if they put their all in the game they might live and help others to live better. These persons to my mind are a drag on society. Their criticisms are destructive; not constructive lives are a nullity.

We have a second group, who also fail to contribute. They do not think enough about what is going on to lend even a destructive criticism—As Omar the old Tentmaker puts it:

> Into this Universe, and why not knowing
> Nor whence, like Water willy-nilly flowing,
> And out of it, as Wind along the Waste
> I know not whether, willy-nilly blowing

They drift from dinner to the movies, thence to bed, thence to breakfast and to work and so on. Or if in hard luck, they struggle and wail, cursing "our day" or society. We know the pigs' object in life. It has been beautifully and permanently outlined in Carlyle's "pig catechism." The pigs' object is to get fat and keep fat—to get his full share of swill and as much more as he can manage to secure. And his life object is worthy. By sticking at it he develops fat hams inside his bristles, and we know, although he does not, that the production of fat hams is his destiny.

But our human destiny is not to produce fat hams. Why do so many of us live earnestly on the pig basis? Why do we struggle savagely for money to buy our kind of swill—luxury, food, autos, and cease all struggle when that money is obtained?

Is fear of poverty and dependence the only emotion that should move us?

Are we merely to stay here, eat here?

A great German scientist, very learned and about as imaginative as a warthog, declares that the human face is merely an extension and elaboration of the alimentary canal—that the beauty of expression, the marvelous qualities of a noble human face, are merely indirect results of the alimentary canal trying to satisfy its wants.

That is a hideous conception, is it not? But it is justified when we consider the average human life, women whom the industrial renaissance, which we previously outlined, placed in positions of economic ease. Their existence has much to justify German's speculations.

But we have a third type of woman, who has developed out of these social forces which we have just outlined. I call her the *Emancipated Woman*. You know, when the Emancipation Proclamation was signed and the Negro slaves received [the] right to emancipation they did not automatically become emancipated. Sixty years of emancipation—hasn't emancipated some Negroes. Mr. Charlie is still God and his word is law. So the fact that social conditions decreed the emancipation of women didn't emancipate all of them. Salvation is free—but each person has to make the step to be saved for himself. So emancipation of women is possible—but like everything else in the world, it requires some effort on the part of each woman to become emancipated.

If that is all woman does, she isn't much better off than the youngsters at dinner with the Parson and his Elders, who devoured the chicken, while the kids [sop] up the gravy. When Johnny the infant could no longer restrain his comments on the unfairness of this arrangement, he was admonished by the Parson in blind faith.

Making a living—[and] casting a vote[—]are merely the substance of things hoped for, the evidence of things not seen. You haven't tasted political freedom if all you do is cast a vote and stop there—you haven't begun to enjoy economic independence if the extent of your economic activity is a struggle to get enough money to eat, sleep and drink and go to an occasional movie. *The emancipated woman* demands

1) that her vote and those she controls show tangible evidence of making this a better world to live in. Mine is a very practical kind of religion. I believe the parable of the talents is applicable to every one of us who has a vote—if we have one vote—then we must account for its use, as much as if it were one talent and if there are ten votes in our houses—I liken them to ten talents. Women, you are not emancipated if you are not using your votes—to put women and *men* (not men and women) but women first,

men second, in public offices that control our destinies. If the Italians can put a judge on the Common Pleas bench why can't the Negroes? Because neither the women nor the men are emancipated. We Negroes are truly wicked and slothful servants—to be such a religious people—we have more churches and spend more time in them yet we do not seem to have caught full import of that simple parable: Joy unto everyone that hath shall be given and he shall have abundance, but from him that hath not shall be taken away even that which he hath.

2) The emancipated woman demands (second) that her purpose in this economic struggle, of which she has become an integral part, shall be more than the securing of the necessities of life. Why do the Jews get everything they demand in this city—Municipal and C.P. [Common Pleas] judgeships, plural if you please—District Attorney, members of Council, Legislature, Congress? Because they control the money bags—and money talks. We are the poorest group of people in this city, state, or nation. If we have a candidate for a high office, we can't raise enough money to wage an effective campaign. When other races, with adverse interests, must pay our debts—we must submit to their policies. We need money, and the women who have been recently granted political emancipation, if they would be emancipated, must learn the lesson from the better experience of our men. Yes, I say strive for money—economic independence is a concomitant of political and social freedom. You cannot have one without the other. The custom of other races will teach you the same thing. The Armenians, better known [as] Queen Mary's people—are a poverty-stricken people. Persecution, plunder, war—has been their history. We do not have to go to Armenia for examples. Common, everyday examples will suffice. Who are the women in your neighborhood, who are prominent in any line of work?

I never saw a pauper [who is] president of a club—or leader of anything. Think it over for yourself and you will decide that the economically independent women and men are those who are leading in all walks of life. When all you have is a mere existence, you cannot hope to share the fruits of social or political independence. The emancipated woman is economically independent.

3) The emancipated woman uses her luxury—which affords her time and leisure—in making contacts with women of her own and other races. Wide contacts are earmarks of emancipated women. When freedom is restrained we know only those in the circles [with] which we are permitted to associate, but when we are at liberty our associations naturally increase. It is only natural that one who seeks the advantages of emancipation should form wider contacts. But if one purposefully seeks to become emancipated this is a prime necessity to accomplish her purpose. The emancipated woman is a person of wide vision, tolerant disposition and cosmopolitan nature. These qualities can only be developed by contact. Nations that are democratic in thought are those that have the greatest contact with the world. England, for example, is the pivot point for all commerce between the New and Old World. If it [is] to be wondered, with these contacts—a great democratic nation should be developed. Germany wanted to build the Baghdad Railway, so as to increase her contacts. Women who would also be democratic will build contacts—through clubs, federations—and clubhouses. There is no wonder we in Philadelphia are known to be provincial, when we haven't a single clubhouse where women of all faiths, ideals, and interests can discuss on a common informal basis their thoughts. Thoughts are things, and when a sufficient number of people think alike on a single fundamental issue—their thoughts create new mores as the sociologist term, thoughts and ideas

which are sufficiently accepted to become customs. The colored women have ideas regarding our racial advancement [that are] worthy [of] acceptance; sometimes many of us have [the] same ideas but we have no contacts by which we can bring together our ideas—thrash them out and unite in thought. We accept as a consequence the ideas, thoughts, plans made for us by the white women in their more than one hundred clubhouses in the city of Philadelphia alone. While we are meeting at this house, that church, thinking to ourselves, because when we meet it is for the formal transaction of business, they are discussing informally their ideas on our problems and formulating plans for us. The exchange of ideas brought about by wide contacts is as essential to the production of an emancipated womanhood. By these contacts a) we can unite and concentrate on our own ideas regarding racial problems. b) we can break down barriers that exist between us—the woman you do not like is the woman you do not know. You like the people you know. c) we can make impressive interracial contacts. We'll have a place to invite women of other races to confer with us. Being in our own home, we shall be more at ease and [in a] better position to put over the plan before us. d) If for no other reason because men have had clubs and we can match them.

To summarize, the Emancipated Woman will first get money—so that she can be independent in her thought and action. But if she wants to be more than a million other women, who had money but whose dead bodies are now mingled in the dust beneath, she will use the leisure, the power, that money gives her first to secure political emancipation that she will secure political recognition in a larger sense for herself and her race, [and] second, to build clubhouses that will afford such contacts that the broadening influences of club life will produce racial programs, made not by white women but by black women, for black people, who are democratic and united in thought, who are emancipated.

"The Economic Status of Negro Women, an Index to the Negro's Economic Status," ca. 1930s

I have been asked to talk to you about the Economic Status of the Negro Woman. While I shall chiefly confine my remarks to that subject, I am quite certain you will immediately realize that a picture of the economic status of our women is an index of our entire economic life. The hackneyed but nevertheless trite saying that a race can rise no higher than its women, applies to the economic status of a race as well as its moral and intellectual standing. So that a nation of women that forms, as do our women, the marginal workers in a pitifully small number of industries and the bulk of the domestic servants necessarily indicates the reduced economic status of the entire race.

The 1930 Census reports show that almost 40 percent, 38.9 [percent] to be exact, of the Negro women over ten years of age in the United States are gainfully employed. This is more than twice the number of foreign-born white women and almost twice the number of native-born white women in the same group. What does this indicate? Clearly widespread unemployment of Negro men and the fact that the wages of Negro men are so low that four out of every ten women must go out to work in order to support the home. I do not believe that the most race-loving ones of us will attribute the larger number of Negro women gainfully employed to an exceptional love for work. It is clearly [a] necessity. But what a sad commentary on the economic status of our race is the fact that 40 percent of our women over ten years of age are gainfully employed.

Further reference to the 1930 Census reports will give facts still more shocking as regards the economic status of our women. Over 60 percent (62.6 percent) of the Negro women gainfully employed are in domestic and personal service—to express it plainly, they are household servants. This may largely be accounted for by the migration during the war of southern Negroes to industrial centers, where previously there had been a shortage of servant labor. With the influx of thousands of Negro women came the opportunity for the middle-class white woman to obtain a servant. The white servant class had gone into factories and the door stood wide open to the kitchen and the laundry. The large number of Negro women in domestic service may also be accounted for by the loss of marginal jobs held by colored women in industry during the war. They were the last units of labor to be added and as it became unproductive to work the factories at full pace, they were the first fired. When we realize that the average wage paid domestic servants is four dollars per week, then we have a more exact and much more dismal picture of the economic status of our women and our race. Think of it, 62 percent of the Negro women gainfully employed (and remember that [over] a third of our women over ten years of age are at work) are servants employed at an average weekly wage of four dollars. No wonder the insurance has lapsed; the furniture has been seized by the installment house, when but [a] five-dollar balance was due on a five-hundred-dollar obligation; the children are undernourished; irritable, and unmanageable; and Johnnie has been committed to a reformatory. What other results could be expected?

But there are still other facts which we can find in our census reports, the mention of which alone will create in your minds a disheartening impression of our economic status. The second largest group of Negro women gainfully employed is to be found in agriculture, where 26.9 percent of those employed are confined. Slightly less than one-third of our women who are at work are still employed in the ancient art of crop raising. I say ancient, advisedly, because the modern farm, equipped with labor-saving devices, does not employ women workers. It is on the old farm that sows, works, and reaps with the cheapest of cheap labor that we still find barefoot Negro women hoeing, planting, and picking the crops. Theirs is not even an existence; it is a fight for the survival of the strongest against the ravages of a single diet, floods, and fever—with their only bulwark the strength which God breathed into their bodies.

I have no regrets to express over the fact that our women work. All women in all generations and races have worked. Before the Industrial Revolution, the women spun the cloth, made the clothes, cured the meat—in the home. When they entered the factories, it was merely a transplanting of the place of operation from the home to the factory, and a reduction of the number of operations as a result of division of labor. But, when I tell you that only 5.5 percent of the Negro women gainfully employed are engaged in manufacturing, mechanical, and industrial pursuits, then realizing that over two-thirds are servants and almost one-third are farm hands, you must join with me in lamenting not that our women are employed but that they are so unproductively employed.

Furthermore, not even the 5.5 percent engaged in industry are employed in any technical, well-paid activities of the factories. A report of Negro Women in Industry, published by the Women's Bureau of the United States, Department of Labor, gives us the most complete recent study made on the subject. Negro women in industry are principally found in tobacco, food, textile, and wood factories, the largest numbers being in the tobacco factories. They will not be seen running the machines that fill the cigarette paper or packing the finished product. No, they are sweeping and cleaning, and those who have any contact with the tobacco are rehandling the waste. Tobacco dust permeates the air, and many of the women have chronic coughs, notwithstanding the cloths they usually keep over their mouths. Their hair is filled with the tobacco dust, which cuts it off and makes it more unmanageable than ever.

The women in the food industries are equally engaged in the lowest divisions of labor. The Department of Labor study states that a third of the women in the meat packing industries are handling casings and chitterlings. So too we find them washing cans and dishes in bakeries;

filling and fitting fruits in canneries; pressing clothes in cleaning factories; sorting the rags in paper factories; packing nut meats in nut factories; mending and catching broken stitches by hand in hosiery and
yard-goods factories; pulling beatings or buttoning shirts for packing in
clothing plants. A negligible number are engaged in tasks requiring any
degree of skill.

Moreover, of the few Negro women engaged in industry, the vast
majority are piece workers. The earnings of the industrial workers are
higher than the domestic worker, but just as meagre in dollars and cents
when we consider the factory worker must buy every morsel she eats. In
only two of eleven states from which wage data of Negro women workers in industry was available was the median of the week's earnings, i.e.,
half of the women earning more and half less than—as high as $9.00. In
four of these states the median was below $6.00 for the week's work. The
hours of labor are as long as the wages are short for the Negro women
in industry. Only 13.6 [percent] of those included in the Department of
Labor study worked less than 8 hours—over 60 percent worked from
nine to twelve hours per day.

If then we evaluate the return from the Negro women employed
in industry in terms of their working conditions, we must conclude that
she too, receives, like her sister, the farm hand or the servant, a meagre
existence. What she enjoys over them in freedom and contact with the
world, she loses in poor health resulting from the unsanitary process in
which she works and the strain resulting from piecework and competition with machines.

The fact that Negro women are principally engaged in the two great
occupational groups which have suffered severely from the depression,
agriculture and domestic service, has led to a larger number of unemployed among colored than white workers and has therefore forced Negro workers to appear in disproportionate numbers among seekers of
relief. Negro women engaged so largely in household service have either
lost their positions or been reduced to wages ranging from promises to
$1.00, $2.00, and $3.00 per week. When the effects of depression hit the
family, the first retrenchment is made in the number of servants and the
amount paid to them—this being a kind of work in which more easily

and quickly than in almost any other an employer can retrench when income falls off.

With Negro women gainfully employed in such large numbers, their unemployment is at once reflected in the family income. Since the family income of Negro families largely determines their standard of living, the unemployment of the Negro women at once becomes an index of the economic status of the race. Consequently, with general unemployment today among Negro women, the Negro family is under a great strain and in immediate danger of its serious disorganization. The father, unemployed for two to three years, has lost hope. He finds shelter in a home for destitute men. The city places the children whom juvenile delinquency has not already sent to institutions, in homes. The mother takes a job sleeping in and doing all the housework for her board and lodging. This is not an exaggerated picture but one that is occurring daily, with the loss of the income by the large mass of Negro women who have been the background of the Negro family life.

The mercantilists of the seventeenth and eighteenth centuries craved [a] large population. This was not based upon an infatuation for mere numbers. The mercantilist considered people as factors of production, as potential sources of wealth, *when* and only when they were employed. We in America have lived to learn that our vast population is not of itself a sign of well-being but that a well-employed, large population is a source of wealth. The problem facing Negroes in America is to see that their unemployed receive a proper share of the New Deal opportunities. With 52 percent of our employed women in domestic service we must see that a code is established for their protection. With the mass of our women engaged in this kind of work, where hours are endless, the wages the lowest of any known group, it becomes of prime importance that we immediately propose and promote a code that will amply protect the domestic worker. Otherwise we cannot hope to maintain our homes, which are fast being broken up because of the low wages paid our women; nor can we hope to find ourselves in any better position at the end of the depression.

Think of the ridiculous position occupied by the Negro servant. Her employer, we will say, is a bank clerk. His salary and hours of work are protected by a code which was scientifically established by members of the Brain Trust. They determined in arriving at the proper salary to be paid the bank clerk the average cost of a proper amount of insurance protection. They made allowances for recreation and leisure, so as to induce spending. These learned gentlemen decided that a minimum of $45.00 per week is necessary for a fair standing of living for our Negro servant's bank clerk employer. Then they suddenly realize that his wife must have a maid or else she cannot leave the children at home in the evening, when the money provided for leisure and recreation is to be spent. So they add the large sum of $5.00 for a maid, and fix the minimum salary for the bank clerk at $50.00. I ask you; does not the maid have to carry insurance? Does she too not require recreation and leisure? Is she not also entitled to a place she may call home and some food when she goes there? Five dollars per week is ample to supply her needs—say the experts.

I am reminded in this regard of the needs recently stated by an applicant for divorce in Los Angeles—the cause of action being the excessive cruelty of the male of the species. The libellant requested $1,651.00 monthly alimony: $200.00 for entertainment; $160.00 for food; dresses, $500.00; rent, $400.00; automobile, $100.00; chauffeur, $100.00; miscellaneous, $100.00 and, finally, *maid* $40.00 a month. Arthur Brisbane remarked concerning this case, that "the maid must be amazed at her own moderation. She is a little lady, seen through democratic eyes, she has two arms, two legs and one body to be dressed, likes entertainment, and all this she must get for $40.00 a month, as against $1,651.00 for the other little lady. This would puzzle the angels or Stalin. In the next incarnation the maid must get herself a cruel American husband."

I fear that the real root of our trouble is that too many of us are willing to wait for the next world and are not willing to expend the energy necessary to make this world a decent place in which to live. Never did a better opportunity present itself than today, when legislation to protect the masses is being generally enacted. If we do not advocate or present legislation that particularly benefits our masses, we cannot blame others, or hope to share the results of a liberalism in government.

Not only must we place on the statute books legislation that is of special benefit to the Negro worker, but we must with equal force and zeal see that the Negro worker receives his or her full share of all relief legislation. Never since Reconstruction has there existed such a favorable chance for the federal government to influence the condition of the Negro masses. By scrupulously fair administration of all types, of direct and indirect federal aid—in farm relief, public works programs, and subsidized relief, the principle of equitable distribution can for the first time be enforced for Negro labor in America. But unless the Negro's claims are definitely, persistently, and forcibly brought before the governmental bodies there is real danger that not only will he be overlooked or neglected but that the reorganization of industry will have him in a worse position than prior to the depression. That this is the case is readily seen from the effort to force out of industry Negro workers who must be paid wages equal to that paid white workers. Unless strong and immediate steps are taken to keep Negro workers, thus forced out, in industry we are likely to find the doors permanently closed when the depression is over.

Recently in Philadelphia, the Wawa Dairies, a small and comparatively recently organized corporation, offered milk routes to Negro drivers who could obtain two hundred customers. Negroes who previously purchased from the two leading dairies gave their orders to the *Wawa Dairies' Negro drivers.* As a result, three Negro drivers are now on the streets of Philadelphia for the first time in the history of that city. A volume of Negro business has been lost by Supplee-Wills-Jones and Abbotts Dairies, the largest and oldest distributors of milk in the city of Philadelphia. The Negro employees of these companies, totaling approximately two hundred workers at an average weekly wage of $20.00, have been threatened with the loss of their positions. The three Negro drivers of Wawa Dairies probably earn collectively $150.00 per week. The discharge of all Negro employees in the two large dairies will put out of work two hundred men and will result in the loss of $400.00 weekly to the race. Neither group would lose its place, if we had proper federal protection for such emergencies, which are becoming more and more frequent. It is not too much to expect or demand, in an era of liberal legislation for the protection of labor, when freedom to contract is protected by the 14th Amendment (*Lockner v. New York,* 198 U.S. 45) and the sanctity of contracts is abrogated (Minnesota B. & L. Asso. vs.

[left blank]) we are more than stupid not to promote a statute that will protect Negro labor from discharges which are racial reprisals.

Fortunately, we have in the Urban League of America organizations equipped by training and accumulated experience to protect, advance, promote, and develop our economic position. I have often remarked that while we have many organizations working effectively to protect our rights, the Urban Leagues are the only organizations attacking cause and not seeking to remove effect, after the damage is done. The vision of Eugene Kinckle Jones, who almost twenty-five years ago began work in New York City as a pioneer social worker, has with the aid of his associates produced a force that is striking at the root of all our ills—our economic dependence. It is to the Urban Leagues that we must look, it is on their leaders that we must depend for leadership in obtaining our full share of the New Deal.

No matter how far reaching is the vision of the League nor how perfected their plan of action, the success of their action is dependent upon the financial and moral support which you who are here tonight give your League and the National Urban League. You, who have largely attained whatever degree of economic independence you enjoy because of the support of the masses, for whose economic status the League has been constantly working. When these masses of our people are unemployed as they are today, neither doctors nor lawyers can collect fees. Municipal and federal employees face payless paydays, for landlords who cannot collect rent cannot pay taxes. The entire economic life collapses when the masses are unemployed. Then it is not only the duty of those of us who have accumulated savings from the labors of the masses but it is necessary for the very existence of these persons that we should render every possible support to an organization that is working to put the Negro masses back into the line of wage-earners, that we may not be subjected to greater poverty after the depression because we have permitted ourselves to be left out of the economic reorganization plans, but that the vast numbers of Negro workers when productively employed may bring economic independence to the race and economic security to the nation.

"Address Before Delta Sigma Theta Sorority," 1939

Miss Toastmistress, my Sorors and Friends:

It is difficult for me to refrain from a few personal references or reminiscences whenever I touch a part of this great university. It was here at the University of Pennsylvania that I spent nine of the most formative years of my life. As my mind travels swiftly over those nine years of supreme happiness, of difficult struggle, of rare opportunities, I feel called upon to pay tribute to my dear mother who made them possible.

It was my mother's vision that sent me here. I had spent the better part of my life in Washington. When I graduated from M Street High School, I was awarded a scholarship to Howard University. All the following summer I spent preparing for the fall when I should enter Howard University. Within a week of the date I thought I was to leave for Howard, my mother informed me that she had decided that I should go to the University of Pennsylvania. I was stunned by such news. I did not want to go to Penn. I told her so in no uncertain words. I screamed, I cried, I pleaded. My mother was *patient, quiet but firm.* She tried to explain that there was no reason for me to go to Howard, when I was living in a city where there was one of the greatest universities. *Reasoning made no appeal, so my mother became silent but insistent.*

As I look back upon this occasion, when her will dominated mine, I cannot recall ever saying I will not go to the University of Pennsylvania, as I have heard many girls of the present generation say. But I do not claim any superiority because I did not have the nerve, nor even the idea of refusing to go to the school selected for me by my mother. I was born and grew up in a period so different from the one in which the youth of today is living that it never occurred to me to refuse to obey my mother's instruction and direction.

Reviewing this momentous decision in my life, I realize that had I been born ten years later, my reaction to my mother's command would certainly have been entirely different. I was born just after the Spanish American War, in a period of world peace. The home, the school, and the church were the orbits around which life moved. Unemployment, old age pensions, relief, were scarcely academic questions. The mills, the mines, the factories were working overtime in order to produce sufficient of the necessities of life for American citizens and a large share of the goods used by the world. The men and women of America were too busy working to think about their social problems. Life was comparatively easy and regular. The men worked five or six days. Few women were out of the home. *And the children reared in this formalized atmosphere became patterns of it.* Freedom of speech, freedom of expression, freedom from restraint for children were unthought of.

Then, there came the World War. The boys left the quiet cities where church socials were the chief diversion. They went to camp. In the evening paid entertainers came to cheer their weary souls. They wore uniforms when they came home on leave. Everybody looked at them. There was an air of excitement. The home routine was disrupted. Mother went to work. The children went to the movies after school and in the evening to celebrations where liberty loan bonds were sold, where the glowing story of making the world safe for democracy was told. Then some of the men were loaded on ships that carried them to sea—always an exciting experience. Finally, they reached the battlefields. Some visited French towns in the evening and tasted the wine [of] Montmartre and some went to the front and "over the top."

When it was all over on the battlefields the effect had just begun to be felt in American life. A woman who has tasted economic independence is slow to accept economic dependence. And so the woman remained in industry, in business, out of the home. The men who returned from the camps and especially from the front who had been over the top could no longer accept the monotony of American life as they had known it. Church socials were no substitute for the excitement of the battle field, or the allurement of French nightlife. They formed clubs. They sought entertainment outside the home. They forgot what it was to spend an evening quietly at home. Even those men who had never seen a camp, not to mention France, who were comfortably lodged in steam-heated dormitories operated by the Student Army Training Corps joined the Legion and became as active advocates of the veterans' cause as the man who saw service at Argonne.

Then followed the depression, when millions were thrown out of work. These unemployed became gradually more and more vocal. They demanded, and rightly so, protection from unemployment, protection from the vicissitudes of old age, protection from overwork for some and no work for others.

Such vital changes in American home life and attitudes could not but have their effect on the youth. I should no more have thought of refusing to obey my mother's command that I go to the University of Pennsylvania than a workman on the same day at the same hour and in the same year would have demanded that his employer provide for his old age. But the urge for freedom that followed the return of the boys from the World War, the assertion by these men of their right to demand special governmental protection, the united front of the workers of America for a larger share in the wealth of America and more time to enjoy it have created a new generation who feel that they have license to plan their own careers, to freedom of thought and action. They are but a natural product of a changed social order. These social changes had a positive effect on the youth of America and as a result we find first that generally the modern girl [is] unwilling to agree with the opinion of the older members of her family and of society. She is outspoken in her opinions. She has a sturdy readiness to differ and a positive refusal to yield her point. In this she does not differ from organized groups of her elders, such as her teachers who have formed a federation through which they express their opposition to a system that provides no tenure, or her parents who usually belong to a labor organization which is equally outspoken in its opposition to opinions contrary to its own. Similarly, there is among the boys and girls a fraternity of feeling that children should be outspoken and good fighters for their rights. There is good natured contempt for one of their number who is not a good fighter.

Second, the modern daughter refuses to be impressed. In my day, we were terrifically excited over a party, a new dress, a trip. But the girls today scorn such demonstrations. Their lips remain firmly closed, their features impassive, their gaze level and their emotions well in hand in face of all events. There is a good reason for this stoutly maintained armor of inscrutability; like the fighting spirit it is a form of self-protection. The unwary or the easily impressed girl is the object of endless jokes by boys and girls of their own age. "Poise," they say, is essential today. They call it self-possession, calmness—the same kind the boys had to have to go over the top. The same kind you and I, older ones, had to have to survive the depression.

Third, if the modern daughter is aware of her lack of charm, she remains astonishingly indifferent to it. Charm as we knew it is forbidden by the younger generation. They look with suspicion and active distrust upon the girl who has charm of manner. They feel at once the urge to unmask her. It is their instant conviction that she must be playing a part or assuming an attitude. Consciousness of self is also taboo. The girls want to be just what they are and not what someone else thinks they should be. Simplicity of manner, honesty in thought and expression are the standard. You know exactly how you are rated by such a younger generation and they know where they stand with one another. Such an attitude is only too easily understood when we consider that simplicity is the standard in every phase of life today. Even the flowery oratory of the past generation has given way to the simple, direct style exhibited so masterfully by our President. Furniture and architecture have made such a marked change in design that we refer to them as modernistic. Why should not our daughters also cast aside the foibles and consciousness of either their box-like figures or their sylph-like forms.

What is going to be the effect of this new freedom on the development of the younger generation? Perhaps this question can best be answered by a comparison with some of the results obtained from methods used in my generation. In my day, if a successful doctor had a son, from the moment of his birth it was decided the son was also to be a doctor. His personality, his ability, his own feelings on the matter were not considered in arriving at the decision. The many boys' lives that were ruined by this unscientific, illogical, unreasonable, selfish method of guiding our children are so numerous that you and I can count several in a moment without much effort. You and I know boys who failed in medical school because they did not have the ability to do the work, or because they hated the sight of blood, and whose parents have refused further financial support and thrown them out of their homes. Usually, in my day, a mother wanted to make a musician out of her daughter. Every girl had to study music. The practice hour became a period of dread for thousands of girls. If necessary, force was exercised to aid one's daughter to sit properly at the piano and correctly hold her fingers or wrist. Many girls as a result developed general sullenness of manner, the cause which their mothers could never understand. Others developed a martyr complex and many, because of their inability to execute, developed an inferiority complex. What these emotional disturbances do to our children in later life, we all know, whether or not we recognize when and by what means we are developing them. And with all the music that was taught, few girls of my generation ever became artists, and if they did, few daughters after they became grown had such a love for their music that they made use of the years of training given to them.

I am quite certain that such human waste of life will not be caused in this generation. If boys do not want to be physicians they say so in no uncertain terms. If girls do not want to be teachers they too let us know. If the piano does not interest them, no wise parent today would force it on her child and stand the risk of robbing her daughter of a love for music not to mention disrupting her emotional life. So that in the modern generation we find, first, fewer misfits. The freedom to study for the profession or vocation that most attracts and suits a child assures success for the great majority. Second, we should find fewer young people with emotional disturbances. The wise parent observes the kind of ability shown by her children. She encourages its development. She realizes that every child is different and each must with her help and assistance, not domination, carve its own place in life. Third, we are going to find the weak, as in any other struggle, eliminated before the cost to society is too great. Formerly, a child was so completely directed by its parents that not until its education was completed did the test come as to whether or not she could swim for herself. The weak failed after the resources of society had been wasted upon children who should never have been given anything but a limited type of education. Today the weak will be weeded out before they reach senior high school. If a child cannot withstand the temptation of joining too many clubs, attending too many parties, following too many cinema productions, he will soon find himself lost in the current. There are hundreds of thousands of such casualties. But, when we count those who previously failed, after completing their education, it is my opinion that the human loss a generation ago was even greater than today. Today only those who can be good physicians will find that field, and those who can be good shoemakers will work as cobblers. There will not only be greater happiness for the individual but a greater saving and safeguard to society.

While our modern daughters are exercising these rights of self-expression and freedom from restraint, what should be the attitude and conduct of the mother? It is naturally difficult for a mother to restrain herself from delivering orations on every problem that arises. But the more she orates, the less progress she makes. Restraint is much more desirable and effective. If mother could be a good listener, only dropping a word now and then to indicate her complete understanding of the problem, she would find that her daughter, surprised that mother understands, will ask guidance. When daughters do turn to us, let us not scold, lecture, but give an honest answer with tenderness and gentleness.

Many mothers concerned by the problems presented by modern daughters have attempted to put themselves on a basis of equality with their daughters. By all means let mothers be young with their daughters, but ours should be a youthful point of view rather than youthful behavior. The attempt to keep up with young people is fraught with the danger of embarrassment to our daughters, because such efforts can so easily run to absurdity. Girls have a deep respect for dignity in their mothers. They also desire us to appear dignified in the eyes of their friends. Let us therefore be young in our thoughts, understanding in our comments, but dignified in our conduct.

Finally, let not our love for our daughters be a selfish love. President William Allan Neilson of Smith College began a speech thus: "Mother love is the only element with which I have come in contact as a college president that has made me think less of human nature." Then he continued and made that now famous utterance "'nine times out of ten,' mother love is only self-love." The world of Isis worshippers flew to arms. Sob letters besieged the newspapers. One mother wrote to the *New York Times:* "Of course I want my child to make good grades in school and appear well in society. If that is selfishness—it is all right."

What clearer expression of selfish love could we find than that expressed by this mother who wants her child to make good grades because he will then appear well in society and not because good grades indicate a complete home and school adjustment. It is this kind of love that Dr. Neilson was talking about when he said: "Nine times out of ten mother love is only self-love." He referred to the kind of love that makes us want to make our sons and daughters doctors when we know they would not even make good farmers, because being doctors we think will improve our financial and social status; the kind of love that makes us deny ourselves decent food and clothing in order that our children may appear well-dressed to our neighbors; the kind of love that because we created our children out of our own flesh and blood makes us feel that we possess them. Let rather our love be genuinely creative, building a son and daughter for the child's own sake; let our love be dominated by a consciousness that the child is an independent entity belonging only to himself or herself; that our only right is to protect and nourish the child to full growth—physical, mental, and emotional. With this kind of love exhibited toward our children who have been permitted to enjoy freedom of expression and development we will find that we have built a new generation of useful, sincere, loving, constructive individuals who can be counted on the asset pages of society.

"Women as Practitioners of Law in the United States," 1941

Mr. President, Officers, Members, and Guests of the National Bar Association:

My interest in the subject "Women as Practitioners of Law in the United States" was aroused by a request from the 1939 Juridical Congress of Lawyers of the Republic of Haiti, to address that body on the status of women as practitioners of the law in the United States. While many Haitian women have been admitted to the Bar, none have been appointed to a position of public trust and not more than three have appeared as advocates in the courts. Because of the interest of our distinguished guest, the head of the Haitian Bar, M. Lelio Joseph, in the advancement of the position of Haitian women lawyers, they were for the first time in the history of the Haitian Bar included in the 1939 Juridical Congress, and I was invited to tell the Congress of the position attained by American women lawyers. In preparing my address, I was astonished to find little assembled material on the entry of American women into the learned profession of the law and shocked to ascertain that no one could tell me when or who was the first Negro woman admitted to practice before an American court. In view of the limited information on the subject of women as practitioners of the law in the United States, and in view of their distinguished success as practitioners, as indicated by the appointment of our colleague, the honorable

Jane M. Bolin, as a Justice of the Domestic Relations Court of New York City by the liberal-minded mayor of the greatest metropolis in the world, it would appear that such information as I have been able to assemble on this subject was of such a knowable but unknown nature that it should be imparted to the members of the National Bar Association, here in convention assembled.

In the United States, the entry of women into the profession of the law was not accomplished without hardship. Our courts, following as is their custom, the common law of England, repeatedly held that a woman could not be admitted to the Bar unless "the legislature shall choose to remove existing barriers and authorize us to issue license equally to men and women."* The attitude of the courts in the late nineteenth century, when American women first sought admission to the Bar, is perhaps best expressed by the words of Chief Justice Ryan of the Supreme Court of Wisconsin, when he refused the application of Miss R. Lavinia Goodell for admission to the courts of that state. For fear of being accused of possessing an uncontrolled imagination, I quote from the opinion of the learned Chief Justice:

> This is the first application for admission of a female to the Bar of this court. And it is just matter for congratulation that it is made in favor of a lady whose character raises no personal objection: Something perhaps not always to be looked for in women who forsake the ways of their sex for the ways of ours.

After discussing the question of statutory authority for admission of women to the Bar, Chief Justice Ryan continued:

> So we find no statutory authority for the admission of females to the Bar of any court of this state. We cannot but think the common law wise in excluding women from the profession of law . . . . There are many employments in life not unfit

* *In re* Myra Bradwell (1869), 55 Ill. 535.

for female character. The profession of the law is surely not
one of these. The peculiar qualities of womanhood, its gentle
graces, its quick sensibilities, its purity, its delicacy, its emotional impulses, its subordination of hard reason to sympa-
thetic feeling, are surely not qualifications for forensic strife
. . . (Our profession) has essentially and habitually to do with
all that is selfish and malicious, knavish and criminal, coarse
and brutal, repulsive and obscene, in human life . . . . Rever-
ence for all womanhood would suffer in the public spectacle
of woman so instructed and so engaged . . . . If, as counsel
threatened, these things come, we will take no voluntary part
in bringing them about.[†]

Fortunately, all of the American courts were not of the same
opinion either regarding the nature of the female who dared seek to
study and practice law, or regarding the degraded state of the profession
which they sought to enter. In the vast majority of the states, the courts
interpreting general legislation took a different view. Thus, Iowa in 1869
admitted Mrs. A. A. Mansfield, it being the first state to admit a woman
to the Bar. The Iowa statute controlling admissions to the Bar provided
that "any white male person" with the requisite qualifications should be
licensed to practice. The court held that the affirmative declaration that
male persons may be admitted is not an implied denial of the right to
females.[‡]

Similarly, the courts of other states found the statutory provisions
for admission to the Bar, broad enough to include women applicants.
Missouri was the next state to admit a woman to its Bar. In 1870 Miss
L. M. Barkalow was given the right to practice, under a statute providing
that "any person" possessing certain qualifications "may be licensed."[§]
Maine admitted Mrs. C. H. Nash in October 1872, under a statute using the words "any citizen" possessing certain qualifications "may be

† *In re* Goodell (1875), 39 Wis. 232.

‡ *Chicago Legal News* (February 5, 1870): 146.

§ *Chicago Legal News* (April 3, 1870): 212.

licensed."¶ But prior to Mrs. Nash's admittance, in May 1872, there was admitted to the Federal Court of the District of Columbia Charlotte E. Ray,** "on graduating from Howard University."††

Miss Ray, therefore, was the third woman in the United States to be admitted to the practice of law and the first in the District of Columbia. The *Women's Journal* of May 25, 1872, commenting upon the admission of Miss Ray to the Bar of the District of Columbia, stated:

> In the city of Washington, where a few years ago colored women were bought and sold under sanction of law, a woman of African descent has been admitted to practice at the Bar of the Supreme Court of the District of Columbia. Miss Charlotte E. Ray, who has the honor of being the first lady lawyer in Washington, is a graduate of the Law College of Howard University, and is said to be a dusky mulatto, possesses quite an intelligent countenance. She doubtless has also a fine mind and deserves success.‡‡

Miss Ray was graduated from Howard University Law Department in 1872.§§ She was a classmate of the Honorable J. C. Napier, who wrote me under date of May 7, 1939, "I knew and was well acquainted with Charlotte E. Ray. I sat near her in class for three years. She was a Negro girl about the complexion of Frederick Douglas[s], with long straight hair. There was never the least doubt that she was what we term a Negro. She was an apt scholar and after her admission to the Bar she went back to her home in New York." Further evidence of her ability is found in the Third General Report of General O. O. Howard, President of Howard University, Washington, D.C., wherein he quotes the following comment of a visitor to the law school regarding Miss Ray: "There was a

¶ Rev. Stat. Maine, p. 597, sec. 18; *Chicago Legal News* (October 26, 1872).

** *In re* Goodell (1875), 39 Wis. 232.

†† Phebe A. Hannaford, *Daughters of America; or, Women of the Century* (Augusta, Me., 1882), 43.

‡‡ Ibid., 649, quoting *The Woman's Journal*, May 25, 1872.

§§ Howard University Alumni Directory, 1870–1919, vol. 6.

colored woman who read us a thesis on corporations, not copied from the books but from her brain, a clear, incisive analysis of one of the most delicate legal questions."¶¶

In those states where the courts entered into the inexcusable error of presuming that women who pursue the law forsake the admirable ways of their sex, the legislators either having a better opinion of women lawyers, or of the dignity of the law than the judges, enacted laws specifically providing for the admission of women to the Bars of the various states. On March 22, 1872, the Legislature of the State of Illinois approved an Act "to secure all persons freedom in the selection of an occupation, profession or employment"; which Act by Section I provided "that no person shall be precluded or debarred from any occupation, profession or employment (except military) on account of race."*** The Supreme Court of the United States, having refused to admit Mrs. Beloa A. Lockwood to practice in that Court, Congress on February 15, 1879, passed an Act providing that:

> Any woman who shall have been a member of the Bar of the highest Court of any State or Territory or of the Supreme Court of the District of Columbia for the space of three years and shall have maintained a good standing before such Court and who shall be a person of good moral character, shall on motion and the production of such record be admitted to practice before the Supreme Court of the United States.†††

Under this statute, Mrs. Lockwood was admitted to practice in the United States Supreme Court. Similarly, the Legislatures of all other states in the union, where the Courts had failed or refused to interpret the laws as extending to women the right to practice law, enacted laws specifically conferring the right. The last state to do so was Arkansas, where until

---

¶¶ *Third Annual Report of General O. O. Howard, President of Howard University,* Washington, D.C., July 1870.

*** Hurd's Rev. Stat. [Harvey Hurd, *Revised Statutes of the State of Illinois*], 1915–1916, ch. 48, par. 2.

††† Act of Congress, February 15, 1879, ch. 81 (20 Stat. L. 292).

March 23, 1927[‡‡‡] women were denied the rights of admission to the Bar of that state, the Supreme Court of the United States having refused to grant relief.[§§§] Today, women are admitted to practice before all of the Federal Courts of the United States and all of the State Courts.

Our interest this afternoon is, however, principally in the women of the Negro race who are practitioners of the law. There are fifty-seven of these women admitted to practice before the various courts of the United States.[¶¶¶] They therefore constitute about 5 percent of the Negro Bar in America. Geographically, they are distributed as follows: One each in Indiana, Michigan, Missouri, Oklahoma, Oregon, Minnesota, Pennsylvania, Rhode Island, and Wisconsin; three each in Virginia and California; four in Massachusetts; four in the District of Columbia; six in Ohio; eleven in Illinois; and twelve in New York. This accounts for fifty-two of the fifty-seven women admitted to practice before the various state courts. Three of the remaining number are deceased, and the present location of the other two are unknown.

The education of these women equals that of the Negro men lawyers and perhaps on the whole excels the latter. Questionnaires addressed to the women lawyers whose addresses are known indicate that 80 percent of them hold undergraduate degrees from leading American universities, and 95 percent of them are graduates of approved Schools of Law. In addition, many of these women hold graduate degrees. It would further appear from replies to questionnaires submitted to the Negro women at the Bar that about 75 percent of those admitted are engaged in the practice of their profession, an unusually large percentage. And among these successful practitioners we find some of the highest public officials of the principal American cities. The list not only reads like a "Who's Who" but actually constitutes an important part of the publication *Who's Who Among Women Lawyers*:

Jane M. Bolin, Justice of the Domestic Relations Court of New York City, formerly Assistant Corporation Counsel for

‡‡‡ Acts of Arkansas, March 1927, Act. 199, p. 673.
§§§ *In re* Beloa A. Lockwood, 154 U.S. 116.
¶¶¶ See Table [2.1].

the City of New York, is a graduate of Wellesley College with honors, and a graduate of Yale Law School.

Elsie Austin, Legal Adviser to the Recorder of Deeds of the District of Columbia, former Assistant Attorney General of the State of Ohio, is a graduate of the college and law school of the University of Cincinnati.

Eunice Hunton Carter, Assistant District Attorney for the City of New York, former Assistant to the Rackets' Prosecutor of New York City, is a graduate of Smith College, from which institution she received at the same graduation the degrees of Bachelor of Arts and Master of Arts, only to be recalled in 1935, for the honorary degree of Doctor of Laws. Mrs. Carter is also a graduate of Fordham Law School.

Violette N. Anderson, deceased, of Chicago, Illinois, was the first woman assistant prosecutor in the city of Chicago, where she conducted a large and successful private practice.

Georgia Jones Ellis, *Sophia B. Boaz*, and *Edith S. Sampson*, of Chicago, have all held public positions with success. If there are others who should be added to this list, the absence of the mention of their names arises because of their failure to respond to the questionnaires mailed to every woman at the Bar.

The success that our women have had in private practice is indicated by the fact that at least 60 percent of those practicing are self-supporting. Their incomes range from $1,500.00 to $4,000.00 per year. Few men are more successful, notwithstanding their advantages of accumulated experience, of opportunities for making contacts, not to mention their appearance at the Bar centuries before a woman lawyer was admitted. Uniform success in a profession so personal as the practice of law is not to be expected. Did not Adam Smith point out ages ago before the first woman even sought admission to the Bar that "the counsellor-at-law, who, perhaps, at nearly forty years of age, begins to make something by his profession, ought to receive the retribution not only of his own so tedious and expensive education, but of that of more than twenty others who are never likely to make anything by it?"**** If Adam Smith expected only one out of every twenty lawyers to attain success, what would be his amazement to find six out of every ten Negro women lawyers supporting themselves from the fruits of their profession.

Negro women lawyers, along with all women practitioners of the law in the United States, have passed through the stage of being a source of curiosity, amusement, and doubt to one of well-founded respect. Indeed, their presence today is regarded as a normal, natural, daily occurrence. They have demonstrated their ability in public office and private practice. They have been among the leaders in promoting protective labor and social legislation. They have contributed to the legal literature and the progress of the law in America. They have sustained an excellent professional reputation. Indeed, there is nothing to distinguish them, professionally, from their male colleagues. They have proven their ability "to do as adversaries in the law, strive mightily, but eat and drink as friends."

**** Adam Smith, *Wealth of Nations* [*An Inquiry into the Nature and Causes of the Wealth of Nations*, Glasgow ed. (Oxford, UK: Clarendon Press, 1975)], bk. 1, ch. 10.

Table 2.1. Names of women lawyers and cities
in which they are admitted to practice

Name	City Admitted to Practice Law
Mrs. Thelma Davis Ackias	Oklahoma City, Oklahoma
Mrs. Myrtle B. Anderson	Address unknown
Dr. Sadie T. M. Alexander	Philadelphia, Pennsylvania
Miss Elsie Austin	Cincinnati, Ohio
Miss Tabytha Anderson, dec'd.	California
Mrs. Violette N. Anderson, deceased	Chicago, Illinois
Miss Sophia B. Boaz	Chicago, Illinois
Hon. Jane M. Bolin	New York, New York
Mrs. Blanche Braxton	Boston, Massachusetts
Mrs. Ruth Briggerman	Chicago, Illinois
Mrs. Clara Burrill Bruce	Boston, Massachusetts
Mrs. E.D. Cannady	Oregon
Mrs. Eunice Hunton Carter	New York, New York
Mrs. Lucille E. Chance	New York, New York
Mrs. Clara Christopher	Cleveland, Ohio
Mrs. Edith Clayton	Chicago, Illinois
Mrs. Ollie M. Cooper	Washington, D.C.
Miss Anna F. Crisp	Chicago, Illinois
Miss Dorothy R. Crocket	Rhode Island
Miss Ruby Diggs	New York City
Mrs. Nell Doles	New York City
Mrs. Bertha L. Douglas	Norfolk, Virginia
Mrs. Georgia Jones Ellis	Chicago, Illinois
Mrs. Beatrice Cannady Franklin	Los Angeles, California
Mrs. Sallie Gatling	New York City
Mrs. Barbary Watts Goodall	Chicago, Illinois
Miss Berniece [sic] Grandison	Address unknown
Miss Jacquelin Guild	Cambridge, Massachusetts
Miss Ramsye Hill	Address unknown
Miss Alice E.A. Huggins	Chicago, Illinois
Miss Jane Hunter	Cleveland, Ohio
Mrs. Mabel H. Johnson	Chicago, Illinois

Name	City Admitted to Practice Law
Mrs. Isadora A. Letcher	Detroit, Michigan
Miss Majorie McKenzie	Washington, D.C.
Miss Roberta McKensey	Washington, D.C.
Miss Lutie L. McNeil	New Paltz, New York
Mrs. Caroline Mason	Gary, Indiana
Miss Mildred J. Mitchell	Kansas City, Missouri
Miss Jeanne M. Mitchell	New York, New York
Mrs. Jessica Morris	Chicago, Illinois
Miss Eva Mae Parker	Oberlin, Ohio
Miss Ida Platt, dec'd.	Chicago, Illinois
Mrs. Louise Pridgeon	Cleveland, Ohio
Miss Mabel Ramey	Milwaukee, Wisconsin
Mrs. Zephyr Ramsey	Washington, D.C.
Mrs. Anna Jones Robinson	New York, New York
Mrs. Gertrude Rush	Des Moines, Iowa
Mrs. Edith S. Sampson	Chicago, Illinois
Mrs. Inez Fields Scott	Hampton, Virginia
Miss Lena O. Smith	Minneapolis, Minn.
Mrs. Dorothy Coleman Spaulding	Brooklyn, New York
Mrs. Sarah Pelham Speaks	New York, New York
Miss Virginia Stephens	San Francisco, California
Mrs. Rowena E. Taylor	Cambridge, Massachusetts
Mrs. Hazel M. Walker	Cleveland, Ohio
Mrs. Ruth W. Whaley	New York, New York
Mrs. Beulah Wheeler	Chicago, Illinois

Source: Survey Questionnaire Compiled by Dr. Sadie T. M. Alexander.

Part III
Black Workers and Economic Justice

Introduction

The speeches in this section span the period from the 1930s Great Depression era to the 1960s Civil Rights movement. New Deal policies, enacted in response to the Depression, marked a watershed for worker rights and protections in the United States. These policies provided benefits that workers had long sought, including social insurance, minimum wages, overtime pay, maximum work hours, and collective bargaining rights. In the 1930s, Sadie Alexander gave several speeches to African American audiences in which she noted that, for the first time since Reconstruction, there was a real chance that the federal government might positively influence the condition of Black Americans. But she also cautioned that the economic concerns of Black workers needed to be persistently brought to the attention of public officials. Otherwise Black workers' needs would be overlooked and they would end up *worse* off relative to their white counterparts than they had been prior to the Great Depression.

By the mid-1930s, Alexander had examined the effects of relief and other New Deal policies on African Americans and realized that her fears had been justified. New Deal policies were not set up to provide relief, reform, and recovery in an equitable manner for Black workers, and the lack of protections meant that Black workers were especially vulnerable to workplace exploitation. Southern whites in the U.S. Congress had preserved white dominance over African American labor in the South by preventing them from receiving New Deal benefits and protections. They were able to do this by writing legislation that excluded those working in jobs disproportionately held by Black workers from receiving benefits and by administering the benefits at the local level where they would have control without federal oversight.[1] The majority of African Americans in the 1930s lived in the South where whites dominated local and state politics through disenfranchisement and suppression of Black voters.

What is striking about the New Deal policies that Sadie Alexander identified as racially discriminatory toward Black workers is that they were racially neutral in language, yet they still had a detrimental impact on Black workers and their families by worsening racial disparities. Alexander was very critical of the National Industrial Recovery Act, for example, because she believed that it contributed to the loss of jobs for Black workers. In 1933, the National Recovery Administration (NRA) established minimum wage codes that enabled employers to pay Black workers lower wages than white workers by using wage codes that were based on occupational and geographical classifications. For the state of Delaware, for example, the fertilizer industry was classified as being in the South since 90 percent of workers in the industry were Black, whereas Delaware was classified as being in the North for 449 other industrial codes involving majority white workers.[2] Alexander was especially concerned with the loss of traditional Black jobs due to displacement by white workers. During the Depression, jobless whites were able to push African American workers out of traditional Black jobs such as elevator operator by intimidating employers into firing Black workers.[3]

In January 1944, after the nation had rebounded from the Great Depression and was nearing the end of World War II, President Roosevelt called for a Second Bill of Rights in his State of the Union Address, to provide a "new basis of security and prosperity." He believed that the transformation of the economy into an industrial economy since its founding required an expansion of citizens' rights to life, liberty, and the pursuit of happiness. Indeed, he stated it was "self-evident" that "true individual freedom cannot exist without economic security and independence." He also warned that "people who are hungry and out of a job are the stuff of which dictatorships are made."[4]

Sadie Alexander shared with Roosevelt this concern over economic insecurity and the danger that it posed to democratic rule in the United States. She was worried about the racial implications of economic uncertainty on workers, believing that it not only eroded peoples' quality of life, but also contributed to racial hostility. She expressed this eloquently with the hope that all people could enjoy the freedom from want and fear expressed in the Atlantic Charter.

Alexander believed that the federal government should provide jobs that paid livable wages to workers who were willing and able to work but who were unable to do so because of the failure of the private sector to create enough jobs. This was a matter of economic justice, of the federal government enacting policies that would increase workers' economic security through jobs and adequate income. During World War II, the government created jobs directly through public works programs like the Civilian Conservation Corps and Works Progress Administration. Workers' spending on goods and services then helped the economy to recover. President Roosevelt and Sadie Alexander each drew on the lessons from wartime production, which created full employment, when they called for a fully employed labor force in the postwar period.

Indeed, Alexander believed that the ability to work was a fundamental economic right that all citizens should have. Her argument for government provision of jobs during economic downturns was consistent with the ideas of John Maynard Keynes, who had published the book *General Theory* in 1936. Keynes showed that government intervention in the economy was necessary during downturns, since it would not generate full employment on its own.

Moreover, Alexander was an early economist who understood the problems of income inequality on the macroeconomy. She argued that the inequitable distribution of national income after World War I had contributed to the Great Depression. After the war ended, employers' profits increased due to lowered costs of production and increased worker productivity, yet they failed to pass on these benefits to workers through wage increases and lower consumer prices. The inequitable distribution of income eroded workers' purchasing power because "the masses had no income to purchase goods and the investors refused to place their income and capital in industry because there was no one with money to buy the products."[5] Alexander believed that peoples' decreased demand for goods contributed to widespread unemployment and economic depression. She advocated for redistributive taxation policies that would lower income inequality and benefit workers.

The first speech in this section, "Address on the Economic and Occupational Status of Negroes," examines the causes and effects of the disproportionate high rates of unemployment and relief for African American workers during the Great Depression. Alexander delivered the speech at the Elks' Educational and Economic Conference in Washington, D.C., on August 23, 1935, and before the Business and Professional Women on July 10, 1936. She believed that training Black workers for jobs with the potential for advancement would help to alleviate the problem of Black unemployment or employment in jobs that paid "starvation wages." As with other speeches during the 1930s, Alexander called for African Americans to support Black businesses and services. Her analysis of racial discrimination and the vulnerability of Black workers in regions and industries most susceptible to economic downturns is prescient: these issues have been persistent concerns of African American economists ever since.

The next speech, "The Role of the Negro Women in the Economic Life of the Post-War South," is a bold, visionary, and beautifully crafted argument for an expansion of rights. The speech, delivered on March 1, 1945, in honor of Mary McLeod Bethune, was supposed to focus on Black women. Instead, Alexander likely switched her topic to the issue of full employment because the data that she needed on Black women workers did not arrive in time for her to incorporate it within her speech.[6] As this speech demonstrates, Alexander—the first American economist to advocate for a federal jobs guarantee—prioritized the needs of African American workers in her economic arguments.[7] She understood the benefits of full employment for Black workers because of their marginal status as workers, and she wanted white workers to realize that full employment would also enhance their job security and pay.

The speech is visionary in its insistence that full employment is a citizenship right and a right that government could achieve by funding public works programs to address urgent national problems. The urgent problems that Alexander spoke of involved not just investments in physical infrastructure, such as for building and repairing roads and bridges, but also investments in social infrastructure—health, education, and nutrition—that would have long-term benefits for human welfare. Economists today note the importance of these social infrastructure investments in yielding higher and more inclusive levels of job growth than investments primarily in physical infrastructure.[8]

The next speech, "New Tempos—New Concepts," occurred a year before the passage of the Civil Rights Act of 1964 and two years before President Johnson issued an executive order for affirmative action for government contractors. Alexander delivered the speech before the Annual Conference of Commission on Human Rights in Pittsburgh, Pennsylvania, on May 22, 1963. The speech displays Alexander's abiding faith in democratic institutions and nonviolent methods for bringing about social change. As the chair of the Philadelphia Commission on Human Relations, Alexander addressed Black protests for racial justice, a movement born in slavery and nurtured by several hundred years of oppression.

Alexander skillfully blended legal and economic analysis within the speech. Believing that fair employment laws and strategies were insufficient to meet the needs of the day, Alexander said that all institutions in society—organized labor, government, schools, industry—needed to come together to develop a comprehensive plan to ensure that people who experienced neglect, deprivation, and discrimination could achieve their full potential. Alexander called for "compensatory opportunities" for African Americans in jobs, education, and housing to remedy past injustices. The commission took the position that affirmative action in hiring was the only way that excluded groups could overcome barriers to opportunities. Indeed, under Alexander's leadership, the commission maintained, "the absence of affirmative action constitutes an act of discrimination." Alexander was arguing that discrimination based on race was standard practice within labor markets and required government mandates to correct it.

In Alexander's "White House Regional Conference on Equal Employment Opportunity" statement, delivered June 10—the month before the Civil Rights Act of 1964 was signed into law—she focuses on employment discrimination against Black workers. She discusses the persistently high rates of unemployment for Black workers compared to white workers, despite recent gains from Black membership in labor unions. Alexander noted that although the educational gap between Blacks and whites had narrowed, Black workers remained concentrated in low-skilled, low-paid jobs. She called for labor unions to implement affirmative action policies and practices that would help overcome the effects of one hundred years of union exclusion of Black workers. Nearly sixty years have passed since Alexander gave her speech. Yet it bears a striking resemblance to the current research findings of African American economist Valerie Wilson on the persistence of racial pay and employment gaps despite Black educational gains.

The final speech in this section is "Response of Sadie T. M. Alexander, Esquire, at Luncheon in Her Honor" given at the Philadelphia Commission on Human Relations on January 31, 1968. In it, Alexander recounted her personal experiences with racial discrimination in Philadelphia as well as her legal work, with Raymond Pace Alexander, to challenge segregation both by drafting a stronger Public Accommodations Act in 1939 and by using testers. The speech also addressed various ways that employers practiced employment discrimination by using selection criteria that favored whites. Alexander's analysis of in-group dynamics is a precursor to the body of work in the economics of discrimination developed by economist William Darity Jr. Alexander warned that whites in the Philadelphia suburbs could not continue to ignore racial disparities in jobs, health, and life expectancy given social unrest.

"Address on the Economic and Occupational Status of Negroes," 1935 and 1936

The American Negro today faces the most critical condition that has ever confronted him. The problem of colonization that our forefathers feared, the trying days of "sixty-one" and the more confusing years following "sixty-six" by no means approach the decisively crucial problem that we face today. Over 3,300,000 Negroes of all ages are receiving relief, which means that even a larger number are unemployed. 17.8 percent of all Negroes and 18.4 percent of all cases on relief are Negroes, although Negroes are only 9.4 percent of the population.

In spite of and largely because of this volume of Negro unemployed, over one-third (36 percent) of the child labor in America is Negro. Approximately one-quarter of all women fifteen years of age and over are gainfully employed workers. About half of all Negro women are gainfully employed. Negro women form one-quarter of all married women working away from home, the ratio being about three times greater than that of all women.

I do not have to relate to you, who have personally experienced the effects of unemployment, what it means to have unemployed men in the family, with the mother working in some family of only moderate means, bringing in $5.00 or $6.00 per week, supplemented by $1.50

Mary, the oldest daughter, age fourteen, receives for washing dishes after school hours. Gone is the respect for father, as the head of the family! Gone is the influence of mother from home! Gone from parental control is the child wage-earner! Gone is the hope for the future! But this is the situation which not thousands but millions of Negro families face.

What are the causes which result in Negroes forming 18.4 percent of all persons on relief rolls, although we constitute but 9.4 percent of the population? Factors not directly related to race have been partly responsible for Negro unemployment. Negroes have concentrated in metropolitan areas. Of all urban Negroes 70.4 percent live in metropolitan areas; and 55.5 percent of all metropolitan area Negroes are in nine northern such areas—2,033,203. There are seven cities with more than a hundred thousand Negroes: New York, Chicago, Philadelphia, Baltimore, Washington, New Orleans, and Detroit, ranking in the order named. The Negro workers in cities have been concentrated in the heavy industries. Practically all of these have been in building construction and since the beginning of the depression there has been little building—outside of Washington's official center. As early as 1931 the highest recorded unemployed group of American workers was that of building laborers. For five years in Philadelphia, the Walnut-Locust Street subway projects have lain partly completed. It is nothing unusual to see partly completed constructions on city streets of metropolitan cities. So that this source of employment for the mass of male Negro labor was completely taken away.

Similarly, the curtailed incomes of persons of moderate means has curtailed the luxury of a household servant, thus reducing Negro employment in another important field. With the influx of Negro labor during the years of and following the World War, the family of most moderate means employed a domestic servant. Ninety-two percent of all Negro women gainfully employed in Pennsylvania, according to the 1930 Census, were domestic servants. But this avenue of income has either been completely taken or the result has been the same because of the low wages offered for such services.

Then came the National Recovery Act, which might well bear the nomenclature Negro Reduction Act. We all know only too well that particularly in the South, employers refused to pay Negroes the same wages as paid white labor for identical work as a consequence of which Negroes lost their jobs. Then the necessity of raising wages for jobs held by Negroes had the effect of attracting the large body of white unemployed workers to traditional Negro jobs. Next, as a measure of economy, many jobs were combined by small employers and given added dignity—too great for Negro labor to fill. Finally, and perhaps the most widespread effect, was the forced closing of the small businesses which had been able to operate only by paying unusually small wages to Negro labor.

The crippled condition of American agriculture also was a prime cause for Negro unemployment. Over one-third of all Negro workers are in agriculture. Cotton-picking and sorting has been the prime duty of these Negro workers. With the increase in cotton-growing countries throughout the world and the consequent loss of export markets, it has now become evident that the old cotton area of the southeast, where the mass of the Negroes live, will, perhaps, never regain its former position.

The recovery measures aimed at stabilizing the price of cotton suspended the collapse of the system, and assumed certain of the risks of the owners, but left virtually untouched the large tenant population, of which the Negroes constitute 55 percent. The Agricultural Adjustment Act aided the larger owner by pegging cotton prices and by providing essential credit and governmental subsidy for non-productive activity. But for the most part, the old method of handling the tenant has persisted under federal subsidy but the tenant has not always even continued to exist. The reduction program of 1933 and 1934 made possible a withdrawal of land from cultivation and resulted in a corresponding reduction in the number of tenant contracts, so that 30 percent of the Negro tenants were eliminated from agriculture. This is what the AAA did toward increasing Negro unemployment. No longer are the bulk of southern Negroes even landless tenants.

Finally, new techniques, new enterprises, mass production by machine and not manpower, cold calculating, impersonal corporation management have displaced Negro workers in tobacco manufacture, in iron and steel, in lumber and mining, and in transportation. Those Negroes who are employed are now restricted more and more to common labor and domestic service, where the wages are the lowest and the services unprotected by legislation, state or federal. The Social Security Act, which our president states is a regulation he has long cherished, specifically exempts persons employed as domestic servants or in agriculture. It is clear that in his years of planning for Social Security of the common man, Mr. Roosevelt never had in mind the security of the American Negro.

Is not our plight indeed a dismal one? Millions unemployed and the number growing. Pushed out of industry, into menial agricultural and domestic services, where there is no limit to the hours of labor, no fixed wage-level, and no provision for sickness and old age. Our labor no longer sought but spurned, we stand hungry, naked, dejected—a disorganized, dependent mass of untrained men and women.

Perhaps the solution of our problem lies in the last three words I have spoken—untrained men and women. When the rookie first comes to camp, for a short while the entire place is confusion. But every day the training continues, the smoother the organization runs and when the training is completed you no longer use individual rookies as soldiers but a unit. What we need is training that we may complete a perfect organization. By training I do not refer only to the formal education which must be the basis of every man's success in life. I refer, particularly, to training to follow trained leaders. If ever we are to establish our economic independence, upon which in modern civilization independence of every kind and nature depends, the American Negro must have trained leaders and the rest of us must learn how to follow our leaders.

The work that the educational department of the Elks is performing in training future leaders is one of the most important contributions being made today by any organization of Negroes. With millions of unemployed and the vast majority of the remaining Negroes on starvation wages, unless organized Negro effort provides the Negro youth a means of obtaining a higher education, we shall have no men and women prepared to lead the next generation. It is entirely conceivable that within a few generations, unless your organization continues and advances its educational program, that trained Negroes will be as much a part of the past as have been Negro congressmen and senators in the past two decades. The entire strength and financial power of the Elks should be thrown behind Judge Houston and his associates in this far-reaching and vital effort to afford training for Negro youth.

But as we train, we must guide those whom we train into fields where their services are most needed. Your organization should have available statistics indicating the opportunities for Negro engineers, draftsmen, mechanics, accountants, manufacturers of Elk regalia, so that the youth whom you train will be preparing themselves in fields where their services are most needed. With a consuming power of 2,800,000 Negro families, estimated at $166,000,000 per month, there should be no youth prepared for a field in which there is not opportunity for service.

As we train leaders, we must also train those who are to follow the leaders. As long as our minds remain enslaved, believing as the vast majority of us do, that a white man can build a better house than a colored man, a pound of sugar from a white grocery store weighs more and tastes sweeter than that purchased from a Negro store, there is no hope for our ultimate economic or any other kind of freedom. What is the need of raising funds to educate colored youth, if we are not going to use their services after they are available? We need trained leaders, but the need is equally acute for trained followers. If all the Elks in America made their purchases from Negro stores, operated by Elk-trained Negroes, Negro economic independence would be assured.

I say, the hope lies in trained Negro leaders, supported by Negroes trained to follow. And when this group of trained leaders and followers realizes the strength it has in its own economic power we shall not mourn as we must today our discharge from white industry, our banishment from tenancy on the land of white owners, our choice between starvation or employment as household servants and farmhands at starvation wages [with] exhausting hours of labor. But when we exert the economic strength within our own race, we shall, armed by economic independence created from our own resources, truly be free men and women.

"The Role of the Negro Women in the Economic Life of the Post-War South," 1945

Dr. Brown, our esteemed and honored guest, Dr. Bethune, the distinguished President and members of this renowned college, the faculty, students and friends of Florida Agricultural & Mechanical College:

It is with a deep sense of responsibility that I arise to address this most representative audience of the people of the state of Florida gathered to pay homage to one of America's greatest women. My sense of responsibility on this occasion is heightened by the presence of our honored guest, Mary McLeod Bethune, whom each one of us can only strive to emulate but whose accomplishments and rare ability we dare not hope to attain. How frequently have I remarked that I will never precede nor follow on the platform the matchless oratory of Mary Bethune. But here I am, in Florida, in her own happy hunting ground, attempting to bring a message which she could so much better present. Conscious of these facts, I nevertheless accepted the invitation to participate in this panel discussion because of the honor I deem it to share in a celebration of the achievements of Mary McLeod Bethune and also because the invitation was extended by my friend [and your distinguished President] whom I am proud to claim as a fellow townsman and a fellow alumnus of the University of Pennsylvania, Dr. William A. Gray, Jr., better known as "Bill Gray."

I have been asked to speak on "The Role of the Negro Women in the Economic Life of the Postwar South." To speak for or about all the Negro women of the South, among whom are many of the most capable leaders and thinkers of this nation, in itself appears to be a presumptuous task to be undertaken by any one woman and particularly when that woman lives in the North. I, therefore, must digress to remind you that I have lived and worked in the South, that as assistant actuary of the North Carolina Mutual Life Insurance Company of Durham, North Carolina, one of our greatest business organizations, I learned first-hand of the economic problems facing the Negro in the South. I learned that the economic problems that we in the South face are present in another form when we go North. I learned that the pattern out of which the problem is created may vary in its shape and form, but when the pattern is fitted together the mould that holds Negro men and women in economic subjugation in the South grips them in the North. And the pattern produces such a crazy quilt that its form in the North or South is unpredictable. This makes planning to reshape the problem vary with the many-sided patterns by which the problem of the Negroes' economic poverty is spread throughout this country.

War does not wait upon the normal processes of evolution upon which we Negroes are always cautioned to wait. The demands of our own nation and of our allies for the materials to fight this war could not be met by white hands only, nor by the hands of male workers only. Our national employment habits had to be disregarded in order to make America the Arsenal of Democracy. When our fighting men need ammunition and arms, hands must be found to produce them. As a result the employment picture of Negroes changed decidedly after Pearl Harbor. According to the data assembled by the War Manpower Commission in their E.S. 270 Report, the total number of workers in establishments covered by this report were [as shown in Table 3.1].

Therefore, the number of Negroes employed in these establishments, covered by the War Manpower Commission, increased 100 percent, from approximately a half million to slightly more than a million in the eighteen months from September 1942 to March 1944. Ammunition, guns, tanks, boats, and other weapons of war had to be produced and the progress of the War was dependent upon how quickly they were

Table 3.1. Increase in number of non-White workers, 1942–1944

	[All Workers]	Non-White Workers	
Sept. 1942	11,274,950	518,645	4.6%
Mar. 1944	14,443,079	1,054,390	7.3%

Source: U.S. War Manpower E.S. 270 Report.

Table 3.2. Expected cutback of Negro workers in war munitions

Aircraft	60,000
Shipbuilding	124,000
Ordinance & Communication Equipment	64,000
Basic Metals & Rubber	20,000
Total	268,000

Source: U.S. War Production Board.

made, not by the race nor sex of the workers who made them. That this is a fact is determined by an examination of the classification of these more than a million Negroes in industry. We find that 464,533, almost half, are employed in one of the five divisions of our war munitions industry; aircraft, shipbuilding, ordinance and communications equipment, basic metals and rubber, and "other munitions." These industries are subject to sharp drops in employment when Germany is defeated. We are told by the War Production Board that during the year after the defeat of Germany there will be a cutback of about 40 percent in these munitions industries. Under that cutback, and with Negro employment remaining at 7.3 percent, there would be 325,000 Negro workers displaced and seeking jobs during the interim period. Applying the estimated production cutback forecast to the five branches of the war munitions industry, we find these expected releases of Negro workers as [shown in Table 3.2].

or a total decline in employment of Negroes in these four branches of the munition industry of 268,000 Negroes. The cutbacks releasing these 268,000 Negroes are likely to be permanent. There remains, the fifth, "other munitions" branch, in which the proportionate Negro cutback will be 57,000 workers. This category of other munitions includes industries whose products after reconversion will be washing machines, refrigerators, sewing machines, and other consumers' durable goods industries in which Negro workers are poorly represented. The overall employment in "other munitions" is only 5.7 percent for Negroes as compared to 7.3 percent for Negroes in the five branches of war munitions as a whole.

The situation sums up this way: the mass of both white and Negro displaced by the 40 percent cutback cannot hope for reemployment in the four declining branches of our national munitions industry, and therefore must look for jobs in the fifth and only expanding branch. But in that branch Negro employment represents only 5.7 percent, so that only 68,000 out of the 268,000 displaced in the other four branches may hope for jobs in the fifth, if the 5.7 percent Negro employment is to remain during reconversion the same as it is today. But it remains clear as far as the munitions industry is concerned, and it represented in July 1944 a total of 9,500,000 workers, that displaced Negroes will be at a distinct disadvantage if they are to enter the expanding industries only in the proportion to their present employment in those industries.

There are too many variables for anyone to make accurate predictions in this field. When it is assumed that Negro workers will be discharged during the 40 percent cutbacks in the same proportion as white workers, that assumption omits certain cutback hazards which are applicable to Negroes alone. Most cutbacks will follow on-the-job seniority and so Negro workers, who by and large were the last to enter the war industries, are likely to be the first to go. There is also the very real possibility that attempts will be made to discriminate against Negroes in making layoffs.

Aside from the 9,500,000 munition workers, whom I have just mentioned, there were in July 1944, 7,000,000 workers in all other manufacturing establishments. To these establishments many displaced Negro war workers will look for employment. I will not hazard a guess as to the extent to which they will be employed by these industries but will cite the extent to which they have been employed and state that opportunities for Negroes are by and large best in those industries where

large gains have already been made. In July 1944 the percentages of Negroes in each of the industries were: (1) food and tobacco, 14.6 percent;
(2) lumber and furniture, 12 percent; (3) paper and printing, 8.1 percent;
(4) stone clay and glass, 6 percent; (5) apparel and other manufacturing,
5 percent; (6) leather, 3.9 percent. If no greater gains were made during
the urgency of war in employment in these industries than the figures
indicate, we must be realistic and face the fact that employment here
will not increase during reconversion.

What factors will determine whether Negroes will be accepted in
these industries in the post-war period? A prime factor will [be the] attitude of the trade unions representing the workers in them. There have
been men like Dr. W.E.B. Du Bois who have for years been preaching
that the best hope for the people of this country was through labor, organized on a basis of fairness to men and women of all faiths and races.
With the organization of the Congress for Industrial Organization there
was at last a strong force against racial and religious discrimination.
In the union halls and in the factories, the great question of the right
to work is being met by the CIO and by an increasing number of A.F.
of L. Unions. For those of you who are not familiar with the work of the
CIO, I need only quote a statement by its able president, Phillip Murray, who is also president of the United Steelworkers of America: "If the
steelworkers' union is going to discriminate against Negro workers or
anybody else, I do not want to be president of the union. Every member and every officer of this union must fight to drive discrimination
against Negro workers out of the steel industry." When labor, white or
black, native or foreign-born, understands that full employment means
greater purchasing power for all the people, which can be obtained only
by giving every man capable of holding a job the right to work, labor will
have solved its own problems. It is a paradoxical situation that the great
masses of labor, both white and black, fail to realize the meaning to them
of that simple axiom "In union there is strength." The right to work is
not a black nor a white problem, but a human problem upon which
depends forces of the world. The more men and women who are working, the greater is the demand for goods and the more money is invested
to build factories to produce goods to satisfy the demands of workers.

Every man should be concerned that every other man is employed, for only in full employment is the individual laborer assured a job.

Second factor that will determine whether or not Negroes will be accepted in expanding industries in post-war world—I need not state to you that full employment for all willing and able to work is also the solution of all over national difficulties. All our national and world problems stem from unemployment. But whereas this is the ultimate goal in the world's richest country, it is not to be expected that we can shift more than half of our national working force into war work and then withdraw them at the day of victory without having temporary displacements. We should face this situation with a minimum of emotion and a maximum of good, hard thinking.

In 1918, war workers poured into industrial centers as they have done before and particularly since December 7, 1941, only to discover now, as in 1918, overcrowded houses or no houses in which to live and rising living costs. The dislocation of people and the war nerves of [the] 1918 period brought a sorry aftermath; not the least of which were the race riots stimulated between Negro and white workers by their fear of insecurity during the 1919 reshuffling of employment. Unemployment did not cause the riots but rather fear that production cutbacks would leave workers stranded. The men at the top knew that reconversion to peacetime production would supply jobs. But the workers only knew that the war jobs with high wages were gone and high prices remained. The fear of what might happen put men in a mood to fight for jobs and wherever that struggle took a racial turn there was trouble.

To mention the twenty-six race riots which happened in 1919 is not to be pessimistic about the coming post-war period. We have profited by our experience in the last war and learned how to manage things better on the present home production front. Today, the orderly supply of war workers by the War Manpower Commission, the brakes placed by the War Labor Board on wildcat bidding for workers, the curb on rising living costs imposed by OPA [Office of Price Administration] rationing and price controls, the restraint on luxury production by the War Production Board, implementation of improvements in savings through investments of salary and wages in government securities, and last but by no means least, the making of employment non-discrimination in war work a national policy by President Roosevelt's now famous executive order 8802 [which] is thereby making available a much needed supply of labor, all these precautions have kept American war workers better satisfied, their dispositions more even, and their relations toward each other healthier. Will these safeguards to economic opportunity for the Negro be continued in the post-war world? Will they carry us through the reconversion period when as we have seen great shifts in war employment are inevitable and 325,000 Negro workers now in industry will be displaced and seeking jobs during the interim period?

This is a question of foremost concern not only to the Negro but also to the American nation. Therefore, in posing this question, I do so not as one pleading for special post-war privileges for Negro employment, but rather as one concerned about my country's attaining for all of its citizens those freedoms guaranteed most recently in the Atlantic Charter. Freedom from want and freedom from fear cannot be attained at home, when hordes of unemployed men and women are pounding the city streets, and bargaining on street corners against each other for a chance to do a day's work. I hold it the obligation of every American to remove those iniquities which have crept into our national life and caused men to fear want and to fear each other. Just as Congress and the courts have recognized the need to protect child labor, the ... [right of] workers to organize for the purposes of collective bargaining and to picket to enforce their contracts with management, as well as the unfair economic treatment of women workers, so too by act of the courts or by congressional act must the right to work in the post-war world be guaranteed every able-bodied man and woman in America, regardless of his race or religious beliefs. Discrimination in employment because of race, color, or religion is an abuse of a right as fundamental as denial [of] freedom of religion or freedom of speech.

Whether or not the controls that produce freedom to work and result in freedom from fear are invoked by the courts and the Congress, as well as the state law-making bodies, will depend much upon the attitudes of the communities to which Negroes have migrated, i.e. the attitude of the people of Los Angeles and Portland on the West Coast; Chicago and Detroit in the Middle West; Philadelphia and Baltimore on the East Coast; and Tampa, Mobile, and Birmingham in the South. What will be the attitude of the people of these cities or others to which Negroes have gone in great numbers at the request of industry to help turn out the weapons of war? The destructive community attitude will forget that the Negroes were invited to come to their community to help build desperately needed ships and planes and tanks, just as some of the descendants of those men who brought our fore parents from Africa have forgotten that we Negroes are the descendants of these guests of their forefathers, brought to America on ships with passage prepaid to give our services to till the soil, level fields, conquer mountains, and stem the tides and not immigrants seeking a return back to a native land. The destructive attitude will demand that when the need for the Negro's services has ceased, that he return home, go somewhere, but not stay and compete with the home folks for the declining numbers of jobs. The constructive community attitude will say, "we can use all the good workers who want to stay here. We are going to clear slums, build decent houses, fine schools, supply labor for busy factories, workers remain with us! Reconversion will be a short period!" The good worker who is invited to remain will be the man and woman who have worked regularly and punctually in their war jobs, who have been courteous on the job and to those people they met in the street or on the buses going to work, who bought bonds and saved them to convert into cash during the reconversion period. This community, with the constructive attitude, will educate the workers as to the causes of unemployment during reconversion and thereby remove from their minds fear of permanent insecurity. The newspapers, radio, and public halls will carry announcements that the temporary unemployment during reconversion results principally from time lags caused by the geographical difficulties of having available workmen in the same places as expanding plants. Workers will be urged to remain until the plants are reconverted, when all good available labor will be in demand.

The Negro industrial war worker may be assured that his war record will have listed him among the good workers needed in every postwar plant; he should tone his jubilation over high wages for an eight hour day, with time and a half for overtime, his pride at the possession of a union card and his satisfaction at being accepted as a fellow

American industrial worker, with a deep sense of responsibility. Upon the character of his performance largely depends the opportunity or lack of opportunity for Negro workers in the post-war world.

The day [that] fourteen Negro men and women walked on the platforms of the street cars of Los Angeles a local Negro paper wrote these patriotic, prophetic words:

> The eyes of all Los Angeles are on these fourteen Negro conductors and conductorettes. Our enemies, as well as our friends, are watching every move that will be made. Every word that will be spoken . . .
>
> Hold your head high, little Negro girl! Collect your fares, direct your passengers to their destinations with the courtesy only you know how to show. Help that old lady, brother, that cripple, with the kindliness and gentleness that seems to have been born within you. You may have nasty things said to you, mean things, things that will make your cheeks burn and your fingers itch to strike down the person who said them. But don't do it, brother, don't do it. You are fighting as great a battle on your streetcar platform as those in Europe and the South Seas. You are fighting for the dignity and honor of your race. You have won a bridgehead. You have taken a hilltop held by the enemy. Keep them, hold them, and go on winning others by your high moral courage, your friendliness, your sense of humor, your native tact and courtesy.

Upon the performance of the million and a quarter Negro workers in Los Angeles and other American cities who have been keyed into the working gangs of the vital American industries depends to a large extent the degree to which they will be admitted into post-war industry. These are facts we cannot over stress. Absenteeism, lateness, loafing on the job, imperfections in vital work, will be used as justifiable excuses for firing when the first cutbacks are ordered and for refusing to hire when the post-war plants are opened. Knowing that we are the marginal workers, the last to be hired and the first to be fired, the workers whose services are only needed in periods of full production, not a single Negro man or woman who has gained a bridgehead in American industry can abandon it, for by so doing he loses for himself and his race the first foothold toward permanent integration in post-war industry.

We Negroes must, therefore, be concerned about any plan for full employment for only by attaining this goal can we be assured of employment. In 1939 there were less than 45 million workers in America with jobs. Now there are 55 million workers with jobs and 11 million men under arms. Experts state that 60 million jobs, or 15 million more than we had before the war, will be necessary if we are to achieve post-war full employment. How are 60 million jobs to be provided? Perhaps we can find the answer by studying the factors that produced 10 million additional jobs for war time full employment. There were as follows:

1. A pressing need for goods

2. Availability of materials, resources, and skills to produce

3. A people and a government determining to use every resource to win the war

4. The establishment of planning and controls to keep the productive machine rolling and to protect worker purchasing power, by controls such as rationing and rent regulations; allocation of materials and control of prices; and supplying the needed labor to operate the plants by inserting non-discriminatory clauses in war contracts.

The first two of these factors will be present after the war ends. First, there will be pressing needs. Two out of three farms are without electricity. Large portions of the population are undernourished and improperly clothed. We have 10 million illiterates and literally millions live in slums. Dr. Warren Banner in a recent study of Economic and Cultural Problems in Dade County, Florida, points out that 15 percent of the houses occupied by non-white dwellers in Dade County need major repairs. Less than 2 percent had private baths and flush toilets. Ten percent were without running water in the dwelling units and over four in every ten units were overcrowded. These are facts that can be duplicated in many other counties and cities of this and other states, north and south. These are needs which demand the production of goods.

As regards our ability to produce goods, we will come out of this war with the greatest industrial plants the world has known. We will have improved techniques and superior materials. We will have more skilled workers than ever in our history. What this could mean in living standards can best be realized by noting that even back in pre-war days if our plants and labor had been fully utilized, the incomes of all the lower income group would have been above $2,000 per family.

Before discussing the two remaining factors, the determination of the people and government and the establishment of proper planning and controls, let us examine our economic machinery as it existed in pre-war days, to determine if possible, what caused the unemployment and depressions so well remembered by all of us. During the prosperity of the Coolidge era, there was a great increase in productive efficiency which we referred to as technology, but there was no corresponding reduction in selling prices. Instead of passing on the benefits of reduced costs of production in higher wages and lower prices, which create a demand for goods, industry either held or raised prices. These profits were not spent and thereby returned to circulation but were held for future investment which, because of fear of depressed market conditions, never materialized. As a result, the demand for goods no longer existed, producers' warehouses became overstocked, dividends ceased, employees were discharged, and on came the depression. Our economy went into a downward spiral, not because of deficiencies in ability to produce or desire to consume, but because our distribution of income was such that the masses had no income to purchase goods and the investors refused to place their income and capital in industry because there was no one with money to buy the products. America had the skill, the techniques and the materials, the labor supply, but lacked a mass purchasing power because of inequitable distribution of the lowered cost of production.

How can we create this mass purchasing power, which is dependent upon raising money [and] wages and lowering commodity prices, without creating bankruptcy? Only by adopting a national post-war placing policy based upon (1) an equitable tax program that will keep in circulation excess profits which previously have been stored away but should be used for a public works program to clear slums, provide electricity for every farm, and reduce illiteracy; (2) higher and broader social security benefits embracing migrant labor [on] farms and domestic labor; (3) unemployment insurance that will provide migrant war workers with transportation costs back home or to new areas of labor shortage; (4) higher and broader workmen's compensation benefits; (5) a guaranteed minimum annual wage that is based upon the relation of a fair standard of living to the cost of living; [and] (6) non-discrimination in employment of guaranteeing to work. This is a national not a local problem. It can only be met as we have met our war needs, through a people and a government determined to use every resource to keep the peace, by planning to provide full employment.

We Negro women of the North and South must make ourselves first informed and then vocal concerning the methods of obtaining economic freedom for the masses of our people in the post-war world. I hope that my discussion has made it clear that two factors will determine the Negro workers' post-war status: first, the degree of his integration in the present war economy. We have seen that between September 1942 and March 1944 there was a 100 percent increase of Negro war workers. The presence of a million and a quarter Negro workers keyed into working gangs of vital American industries is proof that Negro and white workers can work together. In war plants this is a certain, if unheralded fact. Every opportunity for training and employment in war production plants must be sought by Negroes. Only those who have had experience and hold seniority can hope to be retained when reconversion comes. Equally important is their record for faithful, conscientious capable work which will influence work. The second factor that will determine the Negro workers' post-war status is the kind of post-war economy we have. Whether we retain our gains and whether we are certain to lose them depends upon whether this nation attains full employment—60 million workers. Anything short of full employment, the marginal worker is pressing the brick on the streets [looking for work] which creates fear in fellow workers and racial friction and the Negro will continue to be the marginal worker so long as he has less seniority than other workers. Full employment would mean for the Negro worker continuing occupational advancement, increased seniority, and the removal of fears of economic rivalry on the part of his fellow white workers. Full employment is the only solution to the economic subjugation of the Negro, and of the great masses of white labor. If full employment by determination of the people and the government could be obtained for the destructive purposes of war, why can we not unite to achieve it for the constructive purposes of maintaining the peace? A vocal, informed, concerned home guard of Negro women must combine with every agency and force working for full employment, if the Negro and the great mass of white labor are to be permanently relieved of the fear of those destructive forces which play one against the other and result in economic poverty and want of the masses of the white as well as the black workers of America.*

* Alexander inserted a handwritten extension at the end of this sentence but did not complete it. It read "resulting unemployment, which [causes]." Handwritten notes appearing further down on the page included "unemployment in racial friction, closed factories, depressions, nation unrest, world wide depressions, fascisms, nat.l socialism, recessions," and still further down: "followed by the 'cures' of nat.l socialism, communism, fascism, nazism not to mention Hooverism, ending in total war." We can infer from these notes that Alexander likely extended her speech to include the tendency for severe unemployment to heighten racial animosities and intolerance, leading eventually to the infringement of civil liberties under the guise of curing the nation of communist influences.—N.B.

"New Tempos—New Concepts," 1963

Mr. Boyer, Members of the Conference of Commission for Human Rights:

We are in the midst of a crusade. Eric Sevareid has called this crusade the "Negro Passion" and has said it is the nearest thing to a people's revolution we have ever seen in America.

We are all caught up and affected by the movement—we in the cities of the North as well as the people of the South. The protest of the Negro in America is not new. Martin Luther King, whose leadership has inspired all of us, did not give birth to it. It was born with slavery and has been nurtured by degradation, discrimination, and segregation until it has become the greatest single moral issue of the twentieth century.

What is new, or at least what now characterizes the protest, is its vigor, its growing unity, its articulateness, its variety, and its youthful leadership. The basic dynamic in the movement, however, is that Negroes sense their power—economic power, political power, and moral power. The power is beginning to be used effectively. We see this not only in Birmingham, Alabama, but in Philadelphia, in Englewood, N.J., in New Rochelle, N.Y., and in hundreds of other cities and towns across the country. We see it in a variety of ways—from the awkward, zealous efforts of a few students in a picket line to the highly organized and disciplined program of Negro ministers in their selective patronage programs.

The significance of these developments for commissions like ours is that under the pressures generated by the Negro protest movement, the tempo of social change with all its implications for the restructuring of traditional forms of relationships is accelerating. The changes that are occurring are being compressed—timewise—in the pressure cooker of the people's revolution. (I shall have something to say a little later about our own pressure cooker in Philadelphia.)

I am saying not that we must slow down the tempo of the change (which is hardly possible). On the contrary, we must maintain the tempo and in some instances speed it up. Unless we do, we risk the danger of seeing the leadership of the struggle for equal rights in America pass in the hands of the more extreme groups. Let no one doubt that a new day is at hand. The only true issue is whether it will be peaceful or bloodstained.

What is the significance of all of this for our agencies? My thesis is this: we must become much more influential as the designers and the engineers of social change in our state and local communities. We must do this, not because we will be left in the backwash if we don't (or as some people say: we'd better hurry up or they'll integrate without us). We must do this first because I believe that by virtue of the frustration of our agencies we have a greater responsibility, greater experience, yes, and greater skill than anyone in the community. We must do it, above all, because the accelerated tempo of change—this revolution we are in—must take place with the framework of our democratic structure in as orderly a way as possible, without violence and within the law. The alternative could be disorder, chaos, violence, and a very real threat to our form of government.

The laws we administer then must be regarded as only one of a number of tools that we must use as we attempt to help design and engineer social change.

Let us examine briefly the limitations of the narrow approach which we call compliance with our fair practice laws. The first fair employment practices committee came into being just twenty-two years ago, created by President Roosevelt under his wartime powers. By 1950 eight states had enacted FEP [fair employment practices] legislation, and since then ten more have been added. We who work under these laws have pointed to the progress we have made and have noted with satisfaction that the laws have stood up in the courts. No longer do we hear much opposition to such laws; they have been established in the public mind as fair and just. They do, in fact, represent the conscience of the community.

In attempting to determine the degree of progress actually attributable to the laws, however, we run into difficulties. Few figures are available. That progress has *not* been spectacular is at least suggested by figures from the 1940, 1950, and 1960 censuses. Concentrating on the four states where FEP laws were passed or became effective late in the decade of the forties (New York, New Jersey, Massachusetts, Connecticut), one can compare occupational distributions of non-white males from one decade to another. The gains in numbers represented in the clerical and sales occupations, in skilled and semi-skilled labor, were relatively greater during the forties than during the fifties. It seems likely that the greatest gains occurred during the war years.

I am sure your experience with the disposition of individual cases of discrimination is similar to ours in Philadelphia. Since the enactment of our fair employment practice ordinance in 1948, we have received, investigated, and closed 2,088 cases. Of that number only 26 percent have been settled on the basis of an unlawful practice found and adjusted. In how many of these successfully adjusted cases did the complainant, whether a Negro or other minority group person, finally get the job for which he was qualified and which had been closed to him because of discrimination? (Pause) Probably less than a hundred—and this over a period of fifteen years.

I think we will agree that our original expectations of the results of fair practice laws have *not* been realized. For one thing, we expected too much of legal procedures; we assumed that all discrimination is deliberate and therefore accessible to prohibitions. A strictly legal approach works itself out to the point where we are dealing with narrower and narrower questions while larger problems continue to grow. We can never expect the courts to deal adequately with what are essentially moral attitudes and social processes. A court order is in many instances like a "bull in a china shop" of human sensitivities and traditional patterns of behavior.

Even with their limitations, the laws can be used in a positive, creative way to achieve results that the case-by-case compliance—proof of discrimination—method did not achieve. Many of us have demonstrated this.

One device has been the industry-wide investigation. Our Philadelphia Commission has been investigating the hotel restaurant industry, commercial and savings bank, the insurance, and the entertainment industry.

Let me tell you briefly about our banking study.

After an initial site survey to determine [the] amount of employment of non-whites in public banking areas, 202 visits were made to 92 offices of the 16 major banking institutions; the visits were intensive investigations using an interview schedule. The 16 banks included comprised the bulk of banking employment in Philadelphia. An average non-white distribution of slightly less than 3 percent overall was found. During the survey and immediately thereafter the Commission was instrumental in the banks' increasing their total of non-white employees in public banking areas by more than 30 percent. Furthermore, and most important, as a result of conferences with top officials of the banks all meeting together, the banks are now on the verge of making public an affirmative statement of policy and program of fair employment. Among the factors that contributed to this favorable outcome was the dynamic ingredient of the Negro ministers' selective patronage program, and also the previous publicity given to the Commission's investigation of the hotel and restaurant industry.

I know that other commissions have also been successful in conducting similar industry-wide studies and negotiations. I am familiar with some of the work that the New York State Commission has done in such fields as employment of stewardesses by the airlines and east-side apartment house employment.

Another approach which is aimed at reaching a broader segment of private industry than can be reached through complaint investigation is what we call our plant inspection program. It seeks to ascertain whether a given firm adheres to a policy of merit employment. If not, efforts are made to bring about the adoption of such a policy. We utilize a set of six specific criteria to determine whether an employer has taken affirmative measures to assure non-discrimination. These criteria have been published and widely circulated in the business community. They are, briefly:

1. The issuance in written form of a fair employment policy statement, brought to the attention of all employees.

2. The issuance of written instructions to personnel departments to remedy existing patterns of exclusion, and a periodic request for progress reports.

3. A policy of recruitment through sufficient channels to acquaint minority persons of job openings.

4. Written notice to all sources of recruitment of the employer's merit policy.

5. The avoidance of geographical (distance from work) criteria resulting in exclusion of particular ethnic groups.

6. A program of policy discussions and supervisory staff training sessions on techniques for implementing merit employment.

In one such inspection program covering 71 firms, which employed over 21,000 persons, of whom 10 percent were Negroes (in Philadelphia 26 percent of the labor force is non-white), recruitment practices were revealed that tended to limit employment opportunity for minority groups. These practices included referrals by employees, private employment agencies, labor unions, and specific high schools having only majority-group graduates. However, sixteen of the firms were found to have affirmative programs of merit employment and six others were complying with the criteria quoted above but were not actively implementing a policy to lead to full compliance. Fourteen companies agreed to revise and/or formalize their policy statements regarding merit employment, and to expand their recruitment programs to encourage additional non-white applicants. We are reviewing the practices of the remaining firms.

There are other creative uses of the law which we could cite. At the federal level, the President's Committee reporting system and the Plans for Progress agreements are noteworthy. There are other non-legal examples such as the efforts to motivate minority youth to prepare and train for broadening job opportunities. The California plan for a clearing house for apprenticeship information which was established with the help of the State Commission demands our attention.

As creative and useful as these programs are, they have been inadequate to meet today's needs. What is required is a comprehensive plan and a total process in which government, industry, labor, the public schools, and the representatives of the organized community join together to provide those who have not participated and shared fully in our society the assurance in concrete ways that they truly have an equal chance. We must provide the hope and the certainty of productive employment to everyone, and especially to Negro young people.

The basic purpose of this comprehensive design, this total process, is the development of the deprived, the neglected—the discriminated against—the minority—to its full potential. This is necessary not only to meet the ends of social justice and morality, to fulfill the guarantees of our constitution and laws, but because in this era of automation, when tens of thousands of unskilled and semi-skilled jobs are being eliminated, it becomes an economic imperative which is basic to our very existence as a free society.

What I am saying is that Negro children have to *feel* that they have as much of a chance as any white child to get that job, live in that suburban house, go to that particular school. To do this we are going to have to do a lot more than change the self-image of Negroes. We're going to have to restructure our society.

There is another basic concept I want to put forward.

The principle of compensatory educational opportunities for [the] so called "culturally deprived" (really Negro pupils) I believe must be extended to other areas of our life—in employment, in housing as well as in education. I submit that our agencies, because they have the responsibility, the knowledge, the experience, the skill, and the understanding, should take leadership in helping to design, promote and "sell" such comprehensive plans and programs—including programs of compensatory opportunity.

In Philadelphia—and if I seem to overemphasize Philadelphia it is only because I can speak from first-hand knowledge—I believe we are only now beginning to recognize and act on these concepts.

We have stated forthrightly and publicly on the front pages of the newspaper that public schools must become *color-conscious* instead of color-blind in order to compensate for past deprivations. We have said that no other issue confronting our city is more important than the need to train tens of thousands of disadvantaged children for useful, productive lives in our democratic society. We are working with community groups and with the Board of Education to achieve this goal.

We are experimenting to find new ways to encourage Negro families to take advantage of the Fair Housing law and to move away from the traditional segregated areas of the city to the new, outlying residential areas.

We have sponsored a citizens committee which has recruited, selected, trained, and is trying to place a group of highly qualified young Negro citizens on governing boards and committees of public and private social agencies.

We have worked with the press, radio, and television executives of the city to enlist their aid in bringing these issues to the public and in changing the image of the Negro. Next fall, in cooperation with the local NBC-TV affiliate and the American Jewish Committee, we will broadcast a series of documentary films on human relation problems in Philadelphia. As government agencies, we do not have to try to "manage" the press. We have to learn to be unafraid of it and regard it as an ally.

At this moment we are on the verge of a significant breakthrough in the employment of Negroes in the traditional, construction crafts. Two days ago, on May 20, we issued a public report of our findings and recommendations based on public investigative hearings we have been conducting since May 3rd on the question of compliance with the non-discrimination provisions of city work contracts.

In that report we have made a finding that certain local unions covering skilled trades (plumbing, steamfitting, electrical, sheet metal, roofing) have followed customs and practices in the selection of apprentices and in admissions to unions which have inevitably resulted in the exclusion of non-whites from particular trades. We have declared that contractors working on city contracts have an obligation to prevent discrimination, by refraining from hiring through discriminatory unions. We have stated that the barriers to opportunity are overcome only through affirmative action which enables and causes qualified members of the excluded groups to pass through the traditional barriers and become established in those jobs from which they were so long excluded. Our recommendations include an interim requirement of hiring a reasonable number of qualified journeymen who have hitherto been excluded from certain trades and the adoption of guarantees that a reasonable number of qualified non-whites shall be included in apprenticeship programs until past inequities have been remedied. The Commission will help in the implementation of these recommendations by establishing an information and referral office which all contractors must notify of their hiring requirements and schedules, and a similar service for apprenticeships. These offices would then refer any minority group persons, hitherto excluded, for jobs and apprenticeship training. The Commission will assign inspectors to review all hiring and union referral procedures, to assure compliance with its requirements. The most significant aspect of our report is our finding that certain contractors performing work for the city have violated non-discriminatory provisions of their contract by default in the sense that they have not taken corrective steps. In other words, we have said that the absence of affirmative action constitutes an act of discrimination, I am delighted to report to you.

I believe we are breaking ground and using the law creatively when we put forth, concretely and specifically, proposals which are designed to remedy past injustices. This is the concept of compensatory opportunity to which I have referred. To those of you who would like to study our report further, I have brought a number of copies with me.

Please note the time from the start of our hearings to our preliminary report—May 3rd to May 20th. We did in 17 days what we have not done—or been able to do—in all the years of our existence. We did it because we were in a "pressure cooker" of our own peoples' revolution in Philadelphia, where social changes—and the need for social changes— are being compressed into days instead of years. This current crisis has been building up for sometime but was triggered by sit-in demonstrations in the Mayor's office on April 26th by CORE. You probably know that NAACP threatened mass picketing at the construction site of the new municipal services building in order to close down operations, that CORE charged the Mayor with reneging on his original assurances to it and staged another twenty-one-hour sit-down in the Mayor's reception room; that the Mayor gave additional assurances to CORE and in addition closed down construction operations at the building site and ordered the Commission to negotiate with the leadership of the building trades unions. He publicly accused the unions of racial discrimination—this before our investigative hearings had been concluded.

This is only an incomplete and inadequate description of events which have occurred in the last few days which has seen unpaid commissioners spending days and nights in marathon negotiations, caucuses, and meetings. If you do not think that we have been in a pressure cooker, I invite you to come to Philadelphia.

What I am trying to say, finally, is that this protest movement— this revolution—which is accelerating and compressing changes at an almost incredible rate, is forcing us all to reshape our thinking and our strategy. Some of us in some of our commissions used to like to think that *we* generated the pressures for social change. The thrust, the pressures today are being generated by the Negro community which— deficient as it may be in organization, communication, and representation—senses its growing power and is asserting it.

We could not stop this thrust and these pressures if we wanted to. And I hope none of us thinks we ought to contain it. They can be the greatest opportunity we have ever had for achieving our goals. But we do have to get in there and help guide the direction and process of these pressures. We have to relate them to a total plan and design and we have to see that they take place with a minimum amount of disorder, without violence, in a lawful way. And we have to make sure that the community participates in these plans and processes. This means we have to become knowledgeable and skillful—if we aren't already—in a whole kit full of disciplines—not just the law. Community organization, skill, and techniques are probably just as important to us now as expertise in the law.

As this process takes place a lot of people are going to be bruised—including some of us. To put it in the words of the President's Commission on National Goals speaking on the "sordid or timid techniques of unequal treatment that still leave millions outside the circle of first-class citizenship": "If this means that some men must renounce old privileges in order that other men may enjoy new liberties, then that is the way the knife of democratic aspiration will have to cut."

Let us help hold that knife and help guide it.

"Statement of Mrs. Sadie T. M. Alexander at the White House Regional Conference on Equal Employment Opportunity," 1964

Mr. Secretary, I will confine my remarks to labor's obligation to assist in efforts to overcome the disadvantage and lack of qualification of many of those who have been discriminated against in the past. My comments will be made with a full recognition of the significant role unions have played in the area of social and economic reform. I fully appreciate the tremendous strides made by organized labor as regards non-white workers and recognize, as well, the contribution of labor in the civil rights struggle.

In spite of the past and present efforts of unions, however, we have today an unemployment rate for non-white males that is more than double that of white males. Reports published by your department, Mr. Wirtz, show that non-whites, while representing 11 percent of the civilian labor force, account for 21 percent of those who have been out of work for fifteen weeks or longer and 28 percent of those unemployed for twenty-seven weeks or longer.

In the area of occupational distribution, non-whites continue to show improvement in their proportions employed in professional and clerical occupations. However, they have not made significant gains in managerial, sales, or skilled blue-collar jobs recently. Negroes, who make up more than 90 percent of the country's non-white population, are generally found in low-skilled, poorly paid, and frequently declining occupations. Relatively few of the occupations enjoyed by Negroes can be characterized by growing labor demand. The Negro male is largely employed as a laborer or an operative.

At the same time this trend is continuing, Negroes are narrowing the educational gap between themselves and whites. The educational level of non-whites rose two years during the past decade as compared with a one-year rise for whites. In spite of this educational improvement, the economic gap between Negroes and whites is becoming wider.

An appreciable amount of the economic gap between whites and Negroes results from underutilization of Negro workers. While 80 percent of white males with four years or more of college are in professional, technical, or managerial jobs, only 70 percent of the similarly educated non-whites are so employed. Among men with one to three years of college, the proportion of non-whites in these occupations in 1962 was less than half that for whites. Whereas white male high school graduates are largely white-collar or craft workers, non-whites of similar education are unskilled, semi-skilled, or service workers.

The Manpower Evaluation report issued by the U.S. Department of Labor in November 1963 revealed that 23 percent of all Manpower Development and Training Act enrollees are non-white. The report also disclosed that non-white MDTA trainees are younger and have had more schooling.

I do not suggest by the foregoing that it is not difficult, if not in some instances impossible, to find qualified non-white applicants when opportunities in training or employment are made. The Philadelphia Commission, for which I do not speak on this occasion, has often been unable to locate qualified non-white persons to take advantage of such opportunities. However, I am sure we will all agree that a very major cause of the dearth of qualified non-whites for some opportunities and the underutilization of many other non-whites, is the long existence of discriminatory barriers that have traditionally barred such persons from the mainstream of employment. Government, industry and labor as well, must all reinforce their efforts to correct this situation.

A recent report prepared by the Bureau of Employment Security of the Commonwealth of Pennsylvania dealt with the manpower skill requirements and training needs of the Pennsylvania portion of the Philadelphia labor market area. This report indicated the five-county area (Bucks, Chester, Delaware, Montgomery and Philadelphia) will need 56,000 new workers for skilled and semi-skilled occupations by November 1967. Existing sources are expected to produce a supply of about 29,000, leaving a deficit of some 27,000 workers by 1967.

It is important to note that the labor supply for many of the jobs in question does not originate with any identifiable training source, formal or informal. Traditionally, this supply has come from partially qualified, experienced workers. Registered apprenticeship programs do not provide a very large portion of skilled labor requirements outside the construction industry. Most of this supply comes from vocational training which is supplemented by long periods of on-the-job training conducted by private companies. In most cases these private companies are unionized.

In my opinion, labor's obligation to its past as a strong supporter of social and economic reform demands that it play a more active and effective role to help overcome the disadvantages of those who have been discriminated against for so long.

1. I urge the labor representatives present today to force-fully inject themselves and their organizations into the fight for equality of opportunity, in a manner that goes beyond support for legislation and the adoption of non-discrimination policy statements.

2. I ask that they take the affirmative and go on record with the firms with which they have bargaining agreements as supporting immediate and effective steps to see that non-whites have an opportunity to be employed and enrolled in on-the-job training programs and upgraded to appropriate positions.

3. I further suggest that union representatives in private companies establish committees and ask management to do likewise for the purpose of developing plans for the recruitment and encouragement of non-whites.

4. I propose that central labor bodies, state and local, meet with Chambers of Commerce and other business groups to develop machinery for working with school administrators to reassure, encourage, and recruit non-whites for vocational training and subsequent employment in on-the-job training programs.

5. I propose and urge with all the force at my command that labor take positive steps toward the upgrading of non-white employees, who frequently have demonstrated their qualifications for advancement by performing work of a higher grade than that for which they are paid.

6. I recommend that, to provide equality of opportunity for men and women denied for one hundred years the right to work at jobs for which they are qualified, preferential action be taken to implement labor force integration in those union shops where restrictive practices have precluded their employment.

I am confident that labor can make another historic contribution if it accepts this challenge with its traditional fervor and vigor.

"Response of Sadie T. M. Alexander, Esquire, at Luncheon in Her Honor," 1968

Madame Toast Mistress, Mr. Mayor, President D'Ortona, Bishop Bright, Father Washington, and distinguished dais guests and my friends, to all of whom I am most grateful for having made this most significant occasion in my life: To be so honored while one is yet alive is a frightening experience. I feel certain that my humble efforts do not warrant such acclaim and that in the years left to me I have the responsibility of proving myself worthy of your confidence. This I assure you I shall attempt to do. I thank each one of you and hope I will be forgiven for expressing special appreciation to my husband and children, who have too often been left alone while I attended meetings, conferences, and conventions at home and abroad.

I wish also to express gratitude to all the people of Philadelphia who by adopting in 1951 the Home Rule Charter created a Commission on Human Relations on which I have had the privilege to serve from its organization on January 12, 1952 by Mayor Clark, following the reappointment of Mayor Dilworth and under the administration of Mayor Tate, as Chairman. Long before any of us conceived a Commission on Human Relations, my husband and I dedicated ourselves to helping make equality of opportunity a reality in Philadelphia. Comfortably seated in this beautiful ballroom of The Warwick, one of American's best hotels and courteously received by management and its employees, it is difficult to realize what was the plight of our Negro citizens forty years ago when, in our youth, my husband and I first felt the sting of prejudice. When students at the University of Pennsylvania, we had daily to carry our lunches, which I ate at a table under the steps in the lobby of the library. We could not buy a cup of coffee or any food at a restaurant nor a lunch counter in the University area, unless we carried it out to drink or eat which we refused to do. I personally presented this grievous situation, a hazard to the health and an insult to the dignity of the colored students, to the Provost. He listened sympathetically but stated there was nothing the University could do. After spending nine years at the University, where I was privileged to be appointed a graduate scholar and fellow but during which time I could not buy a hot meal, my husband and I determined that some day, some way we would open places of public accommodation to all the people of Philadelphia.

We found, upon our respective admissions to the Bar, that the only law controlling discrimination in places of public accommodation was the *Act of May 19, 1887*, P.L. 130 Sec. I, 18 P.S. 4554, which prohibited discrimination in places of public accommodation, such as restaurants, hotels, theatres, concert halls, and places of amusement. However, the Superior Court, in an opinion by Kiphart, J. concurred in by the entire bench, held that a theatre proprietor who sets aside a portion of his theatre for accommodation of colored people cannot be convicted of violating the Act of May 19, 1887 (supra) unless it is shown to the satisfaction of the jury that the accommodation afforded by the portion set aside is not equal to that afforded by other parts of the theatre. Citing *Plessy v. Ferguson*, 163 U.S. 539, which as you know held that separate railroad accommodations—the Jim Crow Railroad Car—did not violate the 13th and 14th Amendments to the Constitution, the Court held "civil and equal rights do not mean the same or identical rights," *Commonwealth v. George*, 61 Pa. S 412 (1915). Our colored citizens were therefore legally confined to the "peanut gallery" and either denied seats in a theatre without a gallery or sold tickets only in the last row. My husband and I have suffered this indignation, when long before either of us was going what is today "called steady." I asked him to my home to meet a girl friend of mine who was attending Cornell. My boyfriend for the time suggested we make a foursome and go to the Shubert Theatre. My friend, who was of my complexion but with Caucasian features, bought the tickets. We were refused admission until we began to speak French and Spanish interchanged according to our respective abilities. Whereupon the manager offered us a box, which we refused—claiming not to comprehend what box was. Then the manager said: "They're not niggers, so give them their seats." The only restaurants open to colored people were self-service automats. Not a hotel afforded a separate but equal bed or meal for a tired traveler.

The only solution, we decided, was a stronger Public Accommodations Act, which was drafted after many hours of discussion and work in our office and introduced by Hobson R. Reynolds, then a member of the Legislature. It became the *Act of June 24, 1939*, P.L. 827, sec. 654 and provided not only "whoever refused to accommodate" but that "whoever . . . withholds from or denies to any person, any accommodations, advantages, faculties, privileges thereof . . . to any person on account of his race, and/or color or that the patronage or custom thereof of any person belonging to or purporting to be of any particular race, creed is unwelcome, objectionable or not acceptable, desired or solicited, is guilty of a misdemeanor and shall be sentenced to a fine of not more than $100 and shall undergo imprisonment for not more than 90 days or both."

We were now able to prosecute cases of discrimination in public accommodation. Time does not permit me to detail the full facts. Let me give you a few examples. When the theatre at 19th and Chestnut then named The Aldine was built it opened with a showing of the Ten Commandments. It had no balcony. Can you believe that people were denied admission to even the last row of the presentation of the Commandments? Mrs. DeHaven Hinlsson, a lady of my complexion, was pulled out of line but her sister, Mrs. William Upshur of a very fair complexion was admitted and entered not knowing what happened to her sister. The Earl Theatre at 11th and Market, a popular vaudeville house particularly among Negro actors and actresses, refused admission to Dr. and Mrs. Wilbur H. Strickland and Dr. and Mrs. Frederick Douglass Stubs. Numerous colored athletes, who came with their teammates to the Relays, were refused accommodation at Philadelphia hotels. Ethel Waters, Katherine Dunham, Etta Moten, all holding confirmed hotel reservations, each rang our telephone at various hours of the night seeking a bed in which to sleep.

In all of these cases and literally hundreds more my husband with my assistance brought action under the Public Accommodations Act of 1939. We served without receiving or requesting costs or counsel fees. Our compensation was securing the accommodation sought and the promise, too often broken, that it will not again happen. When it happened again, another and another warrant was issued and served. I recall so well the manager of the Aldine coming to our office, opposite the theatre, waving a white handkerchief and saying: "I surrender. My wife cannot stand of my telephoning 'I'm arrested again.'" Other defendants did not comply with the law so readily. Salt was put in the food of colored patrons in some restaurants; some theatres claimed they were sold out and some hotels said they were filled. So we started testing by sending white and colored persons to seek accommodations. Marjorie Penny was one of our most loyal testers.

We still have no legal means of combatting discrimination in employment. What benefit was it to have the legal right to eat in a restaurant or attend the theatre if the vast majority of our people had not the money to pay the cost? Numerous organizations and literally thousands of people of all races began a concerted effort for a Fair Practice Law prohibiting discrimination in employment because of race, color, religion, or ancestry. On March 12, 1948 the City Council passed such an ordinance and established a Fair Employment Practice Commission (Sec. 9-104 — The Philadelphia Code) and granted the F.E.P. Commission a budget of $49,817, increased to $82,379 in 1951. The staff consisted of fourteen paid employees. Gimbels was the first major department store to employ Negro salesgirls and men, clerks, stenographers and bookkeepers. Previously Negroes had been employed in the department stores only as elevator operators, stock men and women, restroom attendants, and laborers. Gradually and often only after much persuasion the other major stores and shops also employed Negroes. The Fair Employment Practice Ordinance had set a standard of democratic conduct. Laws may not change men's hearts but they do change their conduct.

When the Charter Commission was appointed, organizations and individuals concerned about equality of opportunity for all our citizens determined that our Home Rule Charter must create an agency of government dedicated to removing every vestige of discrimination based upon race, color, religion, or national origin. Great credit must be given to The Philadelphia Fellowship Commission which spearheaded the drive to write into the Charter a provision for a Commission on Human Relations. Murray Shusterman, Esquire and I served as members of the Philadelphia Fellowship Commission Committee on the Charter. We drafted the proposal for a Commission on Human Relations, which I was privileged to present to the Charter Commission and which proposal, as I recall, was accepted with only minor changes. Under the provisions of The Home Rule Charter adopted in 1951, a Commission on Human Relations was established with power to administer and enforce all statutes and ordinances concerning prohibiting discrimination against persons because of race, color, religion, or national origin and also with the power and duties heretofore exercised and performed by the Fair Employment Practice Commission (Chapter 7 Sec. 4-700). Thus, under this Ordinance the Commission has power to deal with problems such as discrimination arising in the hiring of city employees. It was also granted subpoena power; [as well as the] right to hold public hearings and make public findings as a part of its duty to promote education and yield factual data for any necessary executive or legal action.

On January 7, 1952, the Commission was established with Robert J. Callaghan as Chairman; Nathan L. Edelstein, Vice-Chairman; Sadie T. M. Alexander, Secretary; Albert J. Nesbitt, Francis J. Coyle, Lawrence M.C. Smith, Leon C. Sunstein, Elizabeth M. Fetter and James Jones. Do you now understand why I said upon the opening of these remarks that I was grateful to the people of Philadelphia for adopting the Home Rule Charter which created a governmental agency through which the power of the city administration could work to create equality of opportunity in employment, public accommodation, housing, and the control of tensions? From the year of my admission to the Bar, September 1927 to January 1952 almost twenty-five years, my husband and I had waged a lonely, legal struggle against discrimination for which we were frequently criticized. Some people said my husband's Harvard education had gone to his head and that any woman with my education is a fool! Can you not also comprehend my appreciation of having had through the appointment of three mayors the privilege of serving on the Commission and under the administration of Mayor Tate, serving as Chairman. Let me remind you that historically it has been thought that a white person should be President or Chairman of an organization working in the field of race relations. I can name organizations, local and national, working only in the field of intergroup, race, or human relations that have distinguished Negro board members but no one of them is ever elected President or Chairman of the Board. Today, I salute Mayor Tate for having expressed his approval of placing the reins of the Philadelphia Commission on Human Relations in the hands of a Negro woman.

Let me now direct your attention briefly, and therefore incompletely, to some of the problems of the Commission, their possible solution, and what, in my opinion, is the direction it must take in the future.

Very soon after my appointment to the Commission, I learned that the wheels of administrative justice grind exceedingly slow. Each member of the Commission with whom I have had the privilege to serve believed unquestionably in equality. But we all came from different backgrounds. Those who had lived in affluence all of their lives, as well as those who had not, seldom had felt the strangle of the chain of denial to secure any kind of job, or to buy and eat in a restaurant a hot meal or to sit in a movie house, not to mention buy a decent home— not a mansion. Only our colored Commissioner had ever lived in the ghetto. I know Commissioners who had never seen the ghetto until after they were appointed. They all had read and discussed at meetings or in the quiet of their well-appointed homes the problems of the minorities and were eager to learn first-hand. This takes time. It may take several years of hearing testimony, witnessing brutality, visiting the ghetto before all the members of the Commission comprehend fully that action is required now. Too often they leave the Commission before becoming thoroughly aware of the necessity to make an immediate change in the lives of our minority citizens if we are to save our city. Others, who remain on the Commission, do "protest too much" their concern while at the same time urging educational programs as the solution when the ghetto threatens to burn. I would strongly recommend that each year the Mayor request from both the Chairman and Executive Director a confidential, independent evaluation of the work and contributions of members of the Commission.

The Commissioners are the policy makers. The staff executes the policy they set. Too often staff is far in advance on programs for the consensus attained by the Commission. This is caused largely by resignations of Commissioners resulting in a continuous process of educating new members not only about the responsibilities of the Commission but convincing them, based upon past experience, how these responsibilities can best be met. There are presently two vacancies on the Commission and one Commissioner only recently appointed. Based upon my experience it is my personal opinion that it will take a strong Chairman, respected for his or her wide experience in inter-group relations, with strong community acceptance by the white and Negro community, at least a year to produce any kind of consensus of the Commission that will fully comprehend the goals of the professional staff so as not to crush their initiative but wisely guide it; meet the demands of the community so as to maintain, if not secure, their faith in and support of the Commission as an effective agency in solving problems of discrimination.

The character of the work of the Commission and its image are dependent upon the professional competence and dedication of the staff and equally upon the character [of], dedication of, and public respect for the members of the Commission. All appointments to staff, except that of the Executive Director, are subject to Civil Service regulations. I wish to take this opportunity to congratulate the members of the staff, all of whom are hard-working, skillful, and dedicated to the work of the Commission. My constant concern is that the higher salaries paid men and women of their training and experience by the numerous federal agencies, which our budget cannot match, will cause the Commission to lose their inestimable contributions to the development of work of the Commission.

The members of the Commission are appointed by the Mayor (Home Rule Charter 1951—Sec. 3-208). Mayors Clark, Dilworth, and

Tate each have made the very best appointments each could find. Our present Commission are men and women of training, dedication, and liberal views, respected in the community. However the present seven members are either Catholic, Jewish, or Negro. Three of them are lawyers, two are clergymen, one a pharmacist, and another a community worker. With the death of Herbert J. Graham, a retired industrialist, who served faithfully for almost ten years, we lost our only Commissioner who was representative of the business community and was a white protestant. The few white protestant businessmen who have accepted appointments to the Commission, with the exception of Mr. Graham, have all resigned after fairly short periods of service. Why, you may ask, do you want them on the Commission? We need a cross-section of the community to help interpret the problems the Commission has been charged to resolve. On the other hand, the members of the Commission need the support and the thinking of the white business community if we are to save our city. I do not wish to appear to be condemning all white Anglo-Saxon Protestants. I know what the banks have done in providing mortgage money in the ghetto. I know their affirmative response to the Commission's appeal for employment of Negroes. I ask that the community commonly referred to as WASP provide Mayor Tate with the names of members of their group so influential in shaping policy, to help the Commission interpret its work and secure the full cooperation of the white Anglo-Saxon community to the only municipal agency charged with eliminating discrimination based upon race. In Philadelphia where the unemployment rate for non-whites is more than twice that of whites, the infant death rate during the first year also twice that of whites, and the life expectancy of non-whites seven years less than that for whites, those who control access to jobs can no longer retire, be safe in their suburban homes, shut their eyes to the rising discontent, and fiddle while Rome burns. As Oliver Wendell Holmes told us: "Life is action and passion; it is required of a man that he should share in passion and action of his time, at the peril of being judged not to have lived."

The success of the Commission cannot be judged by the number of complaints filed by individuals or on the initiative of the Commission, the investigations conducted, hearings held, or the amount of publicity given to our activities. We are charged by City Ordinance 9-1101 Sec. 4(a) to endeavor to eliminate the unlawful practice complained of by persuasion. Some respondents will not sign a Conciliation Agreement if publicity is given to the facts. We secured for a complainant, who was unlawfully refused employment, a settlement of two thousand dollars, representing loss in wages. In this case, as in others, where the majority of the Commissioners or the respondent insisted upon no publicity, we have obtained more than money. The mere investigation of respondent's practices and a finding of discrimination have in most cases caused him to change his unlawful practice.

Furthermore, discrimination in employment is no longer blatant and overt. No small or big businessman is going to say as they did prior to the passage of the Fair Employment Practice on March 11, 1948, "We do not employ Negroes." Discrimination as pointed out by Samuel C. Jackson E.E.O.C. Commissioner has become institutionalized. The personnel system for hiring, assignment, promotion, lay off, transfer, or discharge was developed long before the employer was required by law not to discriminate. His method of selection of employees was focused only at the average white employee and not to the employment equally of Negroes, Spanish-speaking Americans, or native-born Asiatics. The intelligence or ability tests measure cultural, educational, and work experience; the personal interview is heavily weighted on appearance and the quality of voice and English spoken; promotion systems requiring work histories that only the "in" group possess; seniority systems that result in first "ins" being retained regardless of the ability of the last hired under compulsion of the law. If the Philadelphia Commission on Human Relations is going to make in the foreseeable future any inroads on discrimination in employment, it must conclude that the system of hiring, promotion, and discharging developed when white-only employees were accepted has proven to be discriminatory and its present use is unlawful under the intent of Fair Employment Practice Ordinance in order to eliminate arbitrary personnel practices which perpetuate discrimination in employment.

We are grateful to Mayor Tate for submitting to [the] City Council a Fair Housing Ordinance, Title of The Philadelphia Code Chapter 9-1103–1104 and to President D'Ortona and the members of the City

Council for adopting the same on October 11, 1967. This Ordinance makes available to minority home seekers 65 percent more housing than was available under the Fair Housing Ordinance adopted June 10, 1963. Adequately to enforce this much-needed law requires a larger staff than eight persons allowed by the present budget to cover discrimination in housing in the entire city of Philadelphia. We have one supervisor, four field representatives, one field inspector, and one stenographer and one clerk typist, eight employees in all. We do not help solve but only increase the unrest among our minority citizens when we create hope without providing the means of securing that for which all men yearn: a decent home. The budget of the Commission is presently $437,581, admittedly a vast increase from its budget of $82,379 in 1951. With a non-white population of 535,033 according to the 1960 Census, we are spending less than $1.00 per person to secure to our non-white population equality of opportunity so long promised and long denied.

Finally, by no means last, the citizens of Philadelphia and its elected officials cannot expect non-salaried Commissioners, all of whom presently, except one, are engaged in their professions, to give not only endless hours but sometimes days of their time in hearings and writing opinions for which task some members feel they are not qualified, placing a greater burden on those who accept these assignments. Members of the Commission are not ordinary board members, who attend monthly meetings of the Board and committee meetings. In addition they preside frequently as often [as] weekly at long hearings; in times of threatened crisis meet daily and are available round the clock; attend innumerable meetings as representatives of the city and the Commission. The Commissioners should be either compensated for their labor or provision made in the budget for paid hearing Commissioners. We owe a great debt to every man and woman who has unselfishly served without even the payment of transportation, not to mention loss of income, in order to promote the work of the Commission. In addition, the Commission has only one attorney, assigned by the City Solicitor to represent it at all hearings. There is a limit to the number of cases one lawyer can prepare and handle in one day or one week. We are also dependent upon Yale Bernstein, Esquire, a most capable and dedicated lawyer, for all legal opinions, which he must first have approved by the

City Solicitor. Both because of the load of work on one attorney and the difficulty of finding convenient hours for Commissioners to set at hearings and leisure time in which to write opinions, our work cannot progress at the speed it should.

The responsibility that confronts government, Municipal, State and Federal, private industries, and every citizen is not transporting our form of democracies abroad but making it work at home. We cannot overlook Watts, Newark, Detroit, Milwaukee, Plainfield, Tampa, Buffalo. No army or civilian police force has even been able to quell man's demand for freedom. I am pleased to note that Mayor Tate, recognizing this fact, has developed a plan to secure financial support from business and the Federal government to create jobs for the coming summer in Philadelphia. The search for the dignity of holding a job cannot be satisfied by a few weeks' work in the heat of the summer to cool things. Young and old men have lost their own respect and that of their wives because they have not been able to assume responsibilities of the bread-winner and the head of the family. They are despondent, discouraged, hopeless—yes, extremely restless, and defiant. We have a chance to quell their dissatisfactions now a threat of violence if private industry will voluntarily change its personnel practices; if private citizens will comprehend that either we destroy the ghetto or it will destroy us and comply with the Fair Housing Ordinances; and [if the] government supplies the budget necessary for the agency specifically created to "establish a form of improved municipal self-government in which all citizens may participate equally without any distinction based on race, religion or national origin."

Part IV
Democracy and Citizenship Rights

Introduction

During the 1930s, Sadie Alexander spoke presciently about political developments that have since occurred in Europe and the United States, as economic and cultural anxieties fueled the ascent of right-wing populism and authoritarian practices. She saw parallels between the rise of racial hostility and fascism in Germany and increased racial animosity in the United States caused by economic uncertainty and racial demagoguery. As the prospect for job losses increased toward the end of World War II, Alexander worried that unemployed white workers would scapegoat and attack vulnerable racial groups as they had in the economic downturn following World War I. Alexander also feared the possibility that white Americans—who, like so many of us, lack an understanding of how economies recover—would embrace fascism, that is, they would sacrifice freedoms and civil liberties in order to elect a "self-proclaimed Messiah" who claimed to be able to fix all of their economic problems. Alexander made eloquent and compelling arguments for the need to ensure democratic rights and protections for marginalized communities, and explained why these protections were also in the interest of majority groups.

Indeed, Sadie Alexander believed that most national and global problems were tied to some form of economic deprivation. She maintained that economic security was vital not only to enhance well-being, but also as a foundation for the maintenance of democratic institutions. As stated earlier, Alexander favored full employment as the solution to the general problem of economic insecurity and as a means for countering job discrimination, income inequality, marginal work, inadequate wages, and the racial disparities that all of these injustices exacerbate. Economic policies that more fairly redistributed national income and resources, Alexander believed, would expand citizens' rights to life, liberty, and the pursuit of happiness. Access to jobs and livable wages, therefore, provided the basis for democratic rights and safeguarding of the rule of law. Democracy, she argued, was contingent on the provision of these economic rights.

In December 1946, President Truman convened a commission to investigate civil rights in the United States. The NAACP was putting pressure on Truman because of a surge in white mob violence against African Americans.[1] Truman appointed Sadie Alexander to his fifteen-member Committee on Civil Rights, making Alexander the first African American woman appointed to a presidential committee. Tasked with investigating civil rights enforcement and violations, the committee was the most important civil rights commission that had ever been organized. In December 1947, the committee announced that it had documented severe civil rights violations throughout the nation—particularly against African Americans—and provided recommendations to strengthen civil rights protections in a powerful report, *To Secure These Rights*. The committee called for an end to racial discrimination in all aspects of life, including desegregation of the military. Its report laid the foundation for civil rights policy until enactment of the 1964 Civil Rights Act.

After the publication of *To Secure These Rights*, Alexander sought to disseminate and promote the committee's recommendations by asking members to give public talks on the committee's findings. In her own public addresses, Alexander usually discussed the findings by focusing on four rights: (1) the right to security of the person, (2) the right to citizenship and its privileges, (3) the right of conscience and expression, and (4) the right to equality of opportunity. Citing the "central theme of our American heritage" as the importance of each individual to dignity and integrity, Alexander stated that in order for individuals to secure their own individual rights as members of groups, they must be "willing to respect the rights" of other people. The failure of Americans to meet this requirement, however, meant that democracy had been undermined, and that government would have to step in to enforce these rights.[2]

Less than a decade after the release of *To Secure These Rights*, African Americans began waging a nonviolent, grassroots campaign against racial injustices. Protests included marches, sit-ins, demonstrations, and boycotts that often resulted in mass arrests. Having spent more than three decades engaged in civil rights activism, Sadie Alexander called on the human rights and civil rights communities to radically reassess their methods for diminishing racial disparities.

The speeches in this section are, in many ways, an indictment of our national failure to provide a guarantee of citizenship rights based on the principles of economic and racial justice. In the first speech in this section, "Constitutional Guarantees of Civil Rights to American Negroes," presented at the National YWCA Conference on May 9, 1934, Alexander skillfully laid out the logic of the Bill of Rights within a democratic form of governance, then demonstrated the many ways in which actions of the state and private parties had denied African Americans their fundamental rights. Although the speech is missing part of a sentence, Alexander told white Americans in her conclusion that their violation of African American rights was morally corrosive and had served to undermine the rule of law.

The next speech, delivered on September 6, 1935, to the Eastern Federation of Negro Republicans at Wesley AME Zion Church in Philadelphia, showed Alexander's frustration with the Republican and Democratic parties' lack of responsiveness to the needs of African Americans, though she remained unwilling to switch her party affiliation at the time from Republican because of the power of southern white Democrats. Alexander rightly condemned Roosevelt's willingness to enact, with southern Democrats' support, legislation that excluded Black workers from labor protections. Alexander also raised concerns over the politicization of the judiciary. In her frustration with the lack of party responsiveness to African Americans, Alexander advocated that Black voters elect Black legislators who would protect Black Americans' interests, even if the party did not endorse those candidates.

The next speech is an anti-war talk by Alexander on the theme "War Must Cease," to Black churchwomen at Bethel AME Church in Baltimore Maryland, on October 13, 1935. The speech drew on her moral convictions about the value of life as well as about war's economic cost. A substantial portion of the talk was devoted to the macroeconomic implications of the war and its disproportionate effect on Black Americans.

The speech "For the Republican Party in the Lackawanna County Elections," given November 1, 1935, in Scranton, Pennsylvania, on the eve of local elections, is unusual compared to Alexander's other speeches in that it makes claims for limited government. Alexander warned of overreach by both the Democratic Party and the executive branch of government. In the latter part of the speech, Alexander presented an economic analysis that was critical of government deficit spending because it contributed to inflationary pressures without increasing production. By the time Alexander delivered her Bethune speech at Florida A&M in 1945, however, she had changed her views in favor of government spending programs given their success in generating full employment.

The next speech, "Coming Events Cast Their Shadow/Address in Detroit," is one of Alexander's most eloquent and prescient speeches in which she sounds the alarm on the risk of an economically insecure citizenry embracing autocracy and racial scapegoating. She outlined a program to preserve democratic institutions during periods of great economic uncertainty. Alexander gave this speech in response to open expressions of racist hostility toward African Americans by mainstream institutions, as well as anti-Semitic and anti-immigrant pronouncements by public figures such as Father Coughlin and Major George Van Horn Moseley. The speech drew on Alexander's extensive knowledge of world history and affairs: she discussed the significance of these events in the United States by comparing them to racism directed against Jews in Europe and Latin America.

Although the next speech, "The Place of a College Fraternity in the Life of a Student, in the Life of a University, in the Life of the Negro Race," includes portions of "Coming Events Cast Their Shadow/

Address in Detroit," the first part of the speech discussed the role of sorority graduates in curbing the spread of racism by cooperating with national agencies in educational campaigns. Alexander recognized the need for popular education that would increase racial knowledge and understanding of the dynamics of economic downturns in order to diminish the likelihood for racial scapegoating.

In "On the Status of the Philadelphia Negro," a powerful speech condemning suppression of minority rights, Sadie Alexander chronicles the ways in which the legal system and customary practices have failed to provide equal rights and protections for African Americans through everyday occurrences. Alexander delivered the speech before the Whittier Committee on Race Relations of the Society of Friends on February 12, 1942. Although Alexander discussed cases of infringement on Black freedoms in 1942, the speech provides powerful documentation of the continuity of criminal justice abuses against African Americans through over-policing, unlawful entry, and coerced confessions. Linking policing to politics, Alexander stated that the indiscriminate rounding up and harassment of Black people under the pretext of a crime having been committed often occurs in concert with attempts to suppress Black political agency.

The next selection, a fragment of "Concerning the Loyalty Pledge," is part of a larger address that is missing. The small portion of the speech contained in this volume boldly challenged the House Un-American Activities Committee's violation of freedom of expression while also describing the role of African Americans as drivers of social justice. Alexander called American global leadership into question for its denial of equal rights and protections to African Americans.

In the next two speeches, made after the release of *To Secure These Rights*, Alexander drew on some of her earlier speeches to provide a fuller discussion of the committee's report. She delivered the *To Secure These Rights* speech at a luncheon meeting before the Americans for Democratic Action on January 10, 1948. At the invitation of Rabbi Roland B. Gittelsohn, another member of Truman's Civil Rights committee, Alexander gave "The Responsibility of Minorities" address at Central Synagogue, Rockville, Long Island, on April 9, 1948. Both speeches examined government abuse and suppression of personal liberties by enumerating the consequences of violating constitutional rights. Alexander presented the prospect of an erosion in democratic governance and creation of a police state with ongoing denials of civil liberties and protections. She drew a connection between mental health and civil rights by incorporating the concerns made by 150 leading psychiatrists of the Group for the Advancement of Psychiatry (GAP), who stated after the release of the *To Secure These Rights* report that civil rights infringement impairs mental health and can contribute to the rise of fascist leadership. In earlier periods, Alexander had called for white and Black workers to unify around their common interests as workers; here she called on all disaffected groups to unite against denials of their rights of citizenship.

The next speech, "Progress Made in Civil Rights in the United States Since the Publication of *To Secure These Rights*," reviewed some of the changes in the protection of civil rights since publication of *To Secure These Rights* ten years earlier. Alexander believed that the report's release had played a role in shifting public opinion in favor of civil rights protections. During that decade, major changes had occurred in civil rights provision and enforcement—for example, the Supreme Court had outlawed segregation in transportation and education and the federal government had sent troops to enforce this right for Black children in Little Rock, Arkansas.

The next entry, "Founders Day Address," is a speech that Alexander gave to Spelman College students on April 11, 1963, about the role of Black colleges and universities in producing leaders of civil rights initiatives and strategies. She discussed the continuous efforts of African Americans to secure rights denied to them, efforts that had moved the nation closer to fulfilling its democratic ideals. Alexander passed on "guiding principles" for racial justice to her young audience, noting that African American college students in the United States were the first young people to engage in sustained, direct protests against social injustice. In an unusual departure from earlier speeches, Alexander made disparaging comments about the aspirations of the Black working class, suggesting that a lack of opportunities had diminished their drive for mobility. Alexander also challenged the students to work on behalf of marginalized people at home and abroad.

The next speech, delivered possibly in 1966, was in response to Black protests for racial justice. The Civil Rights Act of 1964 and Voting Rights Act of 1965 had done little to address the reality of life for African Americans who lived in urban slums. Racial disparities in cities had been caused by a complex set of problems involving public disinvestment, police brutality, substandard schools, inadequate housing, poverty, environmental squalor, and joblessness. From the mid- to late 1960s, African Americans who lived in urban areas rebelled against these unjust living conditions. In "Education and Social Change," Alexander argued that the dual, racially segregated school system was not a Black problem but rather an "American problem" that hinders the development of both Black and white children and undermines democracy.

Alexander's final speech in this volume, "The Catalytic Role of Commissions in Helping Alienated Communities," was delivered on July 5, 1967, at the nineteenth Annual Conference of Commissions for Human Rights held in Toronto. It is a powerful criticism of human rights and public service agencies for their failure to reach their professed goal of ameliorating racial disparities. In it, Alexander addressed the all-too-familiar litany of conditions in housing, education, policing, jobs, and health that have created—and continued to burden— disaffected and alienated Black communities. Noting the limitations in budgets, staffing, and enforcement of antidiscrimination legislation, Alexander proclaimed the need to move beyond merely enacting such legislation. Instead she called for a "radical and agonizing reappraisal of our old methods" of assisting alienated communities, in order to address systemic barriers both to shared prosperity and to the full, equal participation of Black Americans in all areas of civic life.

"Constitutional Guarantees of Civil Rights to American Negroes," 1934

The necessity to insert restrictions in the Constitution of the United States, which should guarantee to a class of its population the fundamental civil rights already possessed and enjoyed by the general population, was never contemplated by the framers of the Constitution. As the government of the United States was to be one of enumerated powers, it was not deemed important by the framers of the Constitution that a bill of rights should be incorporated among its provisions. If, among the powers conferred, there was none which would authorize or empower the government to deprive the citizen of any of those fundamental rights which it is the object and duty of the government to protect and defend and to insure which is the sole purpose of bills of rights, it was thought to be at least unimportant to insert negative clauses in that instrument, inhibiting the government from assuming any such powers, since the mere failure to confer them would leave all such powers beyond the sphere of its constitutional authority. And, as Mr. Hamilton argued, it might seem dangerous to do so. "For why declare that things shall not be done which there is no power to do?" Why, for instance, should it be said that the state shall not deprive any person of liberty without due process of law? It might be argued with a semblance of reason, that the Constitution ought not to be charged with the absurdity of providing against the abuse of authority which was not given.

It was also thought that bills of rights, however important under a monarchical government, were of no moment in a constitution of government framed by the people for themselves and under which public affairs were managed by means of agencies selected by popular choice and subject to frequent change by popular action. "We, the people of the United States, to secure the blessings of liberty to ourselves and our posterity, do ordain and establish this Constitution for the United States of America." Here, in strictness, the people surrender nothing; and, as they retain everything, they have no need of particular reservations.

The failure of many of the states of the United States to afford to colored citizens after the Civil War those fundamental rights of citizenship that were retained and enjoyed by the people of the United States, necessitated certain constitutional amendments which would authoritatively settle the question as to the status of the Negro population. The first of these with which we are concerned today, as effectively establishing the civil rights of the Negro, is the 14th Amendment, which became effective July 1868.

"All persons born or naturalized in the United States and subject to the jurisdiction thereof are citizens of the United States and of the states wherein they reside. No state shall make or enforce any law which abridges the privileges or immunities of citizens of the United States; nor shall any state deprive any person of life, liberty, or property, without due process of law; nor deny to any person within its jurisdiction the equal protection of the law."

Clause one of this first section established affirmatively the *citizenship* of free Negroes which had been denied in the opinion delivered by Chief Justice Taney in the now famous *Dred Scott* decision (*Dred Scott v. Sandford*, 19 How. 393). The opening sentence of this amendment put beyond all doubt that all persons, white or black, and whether formerly slaves or not, born or naturalized in the United States, and owing no allegiance to any alien power, are citizens of the United States and of the state in which they reside: *Elk v. Wilkins*, 112 U.S. 101.

The subsequent clauses of this amendment have been interrupted by numerous court decisions and have resulted in securing the vast majority of those civil rights which are today assured [to] the colored population of America. An examination of these decisions will give a comprehensive picture of the civil status of our colored population.

A fundamental right of citizenship is the right to serve on juries and to have one's own peers on a jury that is to judge the guilt or innocence of the accused. This right by statute was denied Negroes by many statutes. But such a law, after the passage of the 14th Amendment, was declared invalid as a denial of the equal protection of laws, which is enjoyed by other persons and classes, *Strauder v. W. Va.,* 100 U.S. 303. While these laws have generally been declared invalid, the officers performing the ministerial duties of selection of the jury have in many cases refused to select Negroes for jury service. As recently as 1932, the Supreme Court of Maryland granted a new trial in a case involving a Negro defendant where there was evidence that no Negro had been drawn on jury for many years (*Lee v. State* [Md. 1932] 161 A. 284). So that while we have the right to serve on juries guaranteed by this provision of the 14th Amendment, yet the fact that in state after state evidence is being presented in various cases, notably the *Crawford* case in Massachusetts, the *Scottsboro* case in Alabama, and the *Lee* case in Maryland, that no Negroes have been called to serve on the jury for many years, clearly indicates how general is the circumvention of the law and how dependent is the enforcement of any law upon honest officers.

Similar to the statutes denying Negroes the right to serve on juries were the many statutes or ordinances of the southern states and cities in general and of a few other states that prohibited property in certain localities from being sold to Negroes. In *Buchanan v. Warley,* 245 U.S. 60, the famous Louisville segregation case, the United States Supreme Court held such a provision unconstitutional, as a violation of the due process clause of the 14th Amendment, in that the right to alienate is an incident of property and the ordinance destroyed this right. Although a state or local government cannot create such a plan of segregation, the individual property owner has been able to effect the same result by the insertion of a covenant in his deed, which prohibits the sale or rental of property to a person of Negro descent. A recent case arose in Washington, D.C. Dr. Arthur Curtis, a prominent and well-respected Negro physician, contracted to purchase a house, only to find such a restriction in the deed. The restriction in the deed was upheld by the court. Since the prohibitions of the 14th Amendment apply only to state action, there was no discrimination within the civil rights clauses of the Constitution (*Corrigan et al v. Buckley*, 299 Fed. 899). So that we are again forced to rely upon the fair-mindedness of our citizenry in whom reposes in the final analysis the power to secure the enjoyment of the life, liberty, and happiness which it was the intention of the founders of our government to assure all of its citizens. While the states cannot legislate so as to confine us to the lowlands, the swamps, the slums, the individual property owner can be inserting restrictive covenants in his deed. The consequence is that in the segregated Negro community, municipal improvements such as paving, drainage, and sanitation are denied the inhabitants and as a further consequence the welfare of the entire population is threatened. If you would remove such centers of possible infection from your cities and towns, you will blaze the trail of public opinion, opposing the restrictions on ownership and tenancy and allow economic power to control land development and not some stifled idea of race superiority, which future generations must condemn not only because thereby the value of their inheritance is destroyed, but more especially because of the danger to public health and morals.

The education of colored youth has also been largely dependent upon judicial interpretation of the 14th Amendment. It has been declared constitutional by our United States Supreme Court for a state statute to provide for the education of white and colored children in separate schools—*Hall v. DeCuir*, 95 U.S. 504 (1877)—provided each race is given equal accommodation. As a consequence, in those communities which I regret to state are numerous, where the law is administered by public servants who permit their own opinions to control rather than the law, the accommodations afforded colored school children are inferior as to length of school term, salaries paid teachers, physical equipment, and in every other conceivable manner. So that again I call to your attention the power and duty that lies in the hands of the American people, if they would enforce the law and the principles of American government.

Similar to the status of our educational rights is the situation regarding transportation. The United States Supreme Court has held that a state statute which provides for separate railway coaches for white and colored persons does not deny equal protection of the law, provided equal accommodation is secured each race (*Plessy v. Ferguson*, 163 U.S. [537], 539). Those who have seen, or better still, ridden in the railroad car that is provided for Negroes, after the train starts South from Washington D.C., know that there is no more equal accommodation in railroad trains for white and colored persons, than there is in the white and colored schools. Frequently on short runs, part of a baggage car, or of the smoker, is designated for colored people, while the white people have a clean, single car, with comfortable seats. Furthermore, the colored car is usually next to the engine or closest to it, while the coaches for white people are on the rear, as far away from the heat and dust of the engines as possible. This is equal accommodation in the dwarfed opinion of those entrusted with the enforcement of the law.

It is not surprising after reviewing the above rights of colored people, to find that city ordinances assigning portions of parks for the exclusive use of Negroes have been declared constitutional, *Warley v. Board of Park Commissioners*, 26 S.W. (2d) 554 (1930). So that even in recreation and play the races are lawfully segregated provided equal accommodations are secured each race. That the white children get accommodations equal to the colored can never be doubted, but do the colored get facilities equal to the white is the important question, to those interested not only in race relations and racial development but more especially in law enforcement.

Another amendment, the 15th, had to be added to the Constitution to assure to colored citizens that fundamental right of citizenship—the right of suffrage—which was freely enjoyed by all other American citizens.

"The right of citizens of the United States to vote shall not be denied or abridged by the United States or by any state on account of race, color, or previous condition of servitude."

The southern states had all passed laws limiting suffrage to the white, male population. After the ratification of this amendment in March 1870, these laws became invalid. Then we were confronted by a series of laws establishing requisites for voting, such as the ability to read and write any section of the state constitution. Very recently a colored man, a Doctor of Philosophy from Cornell University and a professor at Hampton Institute, was subject to such a test in Virginia. Thousands of white farmers and laborers qualified to the entire satisfaction of the election officials. No reasonable, fair-minded person can believe that the colored professor failed to interpret the Constitution of Virginia as intelligently as these voters. We must be forced to the conclusion that the election officials did not fairly administer the law. Such maladministration of the law results in the almost general disenfranchisement of Negro citizens in many of the southern states.

What then is the civil status of the colored population, as far as constitutional guarantees of the U.S. Constitution affect it?

They are citizens of the United States.

As such citizens what fundamental rights do they enjoy?

1. The right to vote, provided the applicant can pass the qualifications established by the states as administered by its citizens.

2. The right to serve on jury, provided the selection of jury members is administered in accordance with the law.

3. Equal accommodations in public schools, public conveyances, and public parks with the white race. The equality of accommodation is, as we have seen, practically unknown in a completely segregated society.

Each of these rights, however firmly established by law, is dependent for its full enjoyment upon impartial administration of the law. The right to vote in many southern states is either flatly denied by maladministration of the qualification or is refused the vast majority of the colored citizens. By similar means, the right to jury service is denied colored men and women. Equal accommodations in public schools, public conveyances, and public places of recreation are unheard of in any segregated society. The result has been that in those communities that realize the economic loss of segregation as well as the moral degradation to the entire community, Civil Rights Bills have been enacted by the state legislatures to assure to the entire population the enjoyment of those fundamental rights which it is the object and duty of government to protect and defend. The states of New York, Massachusetts, Ohio, Pennsylvania, Illinois, California, Colorado, Iowa, and Michigan have enacted such statutes. These states have gone beyond assuring the colored citizens the right to suffrage and the right to serve on jury. They have declared illegal separation in public schools, theatres, hotels, and other institutions operated for the benefit of the public.

The further recognition of the civil rights of the Negro is dependent upon the enlightened public opinion of the people in the various states. That the Y.W.C.A. has devoted a place on its program to this and similar topics affecting the status of the Negro population is a hopeful sign of the support that may be expected from its members.

. . . . greater disrespect for law than America. That this is true should not be marveled at by those of us who know for how many years we have shut our eyes to the fact that in our own communities colored citizens are denied the right to suffrage, the right to serve on jury, the right to an education similar to that afforded the white population. Disabuse your minds from the thought that only Negroes are affected by such discrimination. The continuous disregard for law, yes even those laws that apply only to Negroes, destroys the moral fiber of a community because it establishes a basis for the general disregard of law. You cannot build up a substantial regard for law by permitting any laws, whether they apply to Negroes or Prohibition, to be disregarded.

Until the American people realize how substantially their peace and security as well as the moral fiber of the race [are] being destroyed by the almost general disregard of law which has been enacted to assure to its colored citizens those fundamental rights which already rested in all of the people, and demand that these and all other laws be enforced, we shall continue to face lawlessness and all the accompanying dangers to our homes and to our national security that follow in the wake of disrespect of law.

"Speech Before the Eastern Federation of Negro Republicans," 1935

It would scarcely have been conceivable even a few years ago that Negro Americans who today register Republican and vote for Republican candidates would be criticized by members of their own race. But that is the present situation. Not many weeks ago, I was attending a dinner given in honor of a former Republican friend, now a Democratic office holder. I noticed a quiet discussion at my table of which I was not a part. Finally, in order to settle the argument, a woman of my own race spoke out and asked me, "Mrs. Alexander, are you still a Republican?" In other words, can it be possible that after all the appointments by the Democrats of Negroes to offices for which the Republicans never considered Negroes, are you still sticking to the Republican Party?

We are reminded by Negro converts to the Democratic Party that the Republican Party has ignored us in its distribution of patronage. In Pennsylvania, they point with pride to the appointment of two assistant Deputy Attorney Generals, a position the Republican Party steadfastly refused to give a Negro; to the appointment of a Referee for the State Workmen's Compensation Board, another new birth for Negroes; and to the endorsement by the Democratic Party in the impending election of a Negro candidate for City Council, while the Republican Party in the same district endorses a white leader. They proudly boast that Democratic national campaigns have no Negro committee; that there is but one Democratic Campaign Committee; that members of the Speakers Bureau are indiscriminately assigned regardless of the color of the audience—that Negroes and all other minority groups are represented in Democratic Party conferences, whether the subject of discussion be slate-making or job-seeking; while Negro Republicans enjoy none of these privileges and opportunities. We must confess that the group popularly referred to as "silk stocking" or "blue blood" has long been the lone dictator of the policy of the Republican Party and the recipient of its choicest patronage. In 1860 the Republican Campaign song portrayed and emphasized the lowliness of the Presidential candidate.

> Old Abe Lincoln came out of the wilderness
> Out of the Wilderness, out of the wilderness
> Old Abe Lincoln came out of the wilderness
> Down in Illinois.

Today Old Abe, an unknown country lawyer, would find his low birth a disqualification for an officer holder of the Republican Party.* On the other hand, the rejuvenated Democratic Party places in prominent positions representatives of every minority group—Jewish, Italian, Negro, Catholic—whether or not they have risen from lowly ranks. Furthermore, notwithstanding the fact that the Republican Party throughout the nation in the present election, faces a crucial test, it is continuing its previous policy of ignoring the Negro voter. We form no part of the round table conferences of leaders in states where our votes far exceed those of other minority groups, who are there represented. We are given no important place on the ticket. We are frequently held in such low esteem that even promises are seldom made to us.

Why are blocks of Negro votes held in such apparent disdain by Republican leaders in the face of an election which threatens defeat? Why are we given no consideration in face of the fact that in recent elections the Republican Party carried only those Negro districts where

---

* Alexander crossed out several words in her typed speech and added other words by hand that changed the meaning in a manner that contradicted the point that she intended to make—that in 1935, Lincoln's low status would have made him unacceptable for a high-ranking office within the Republican Party.—N.B.

Negro candidates were slated for office and lost in Negro districts where the Democratic party slated Negro candidates? Being more familiar with the political situation in my own city and state, I shall take my illustrations from what took place in Philadelphia at the last election. In North Philadelphia, Hobson Reynolds was slated by the Republican organization for the Legislature. The Negro wards, 47th and 29th, gave an overwhelming majority vote for the Republican Party. In West Philadelphia, Marshall L. Shepard was slated by the Democratic Party for the same position. The 24th, 34th and 44th wards, where Negro votes predominate, gave a similar majority for the Democratic Party.

In spite of these facts which are fresh in the minds of all, no Negro has been slated in either of these important districts for a position by the Republican Party in the coming election. The reason is that the political leaders do not believe it is necessary to give Negroes places on the slate in order to obtain their votes. They have frankly told us that we must not ask for too much. When we asked them to endorse Linton Fisher, from North Philadelphia, for Councilman, we were told that we had just got Dr. John P. Turner appointed to the Board of Education and we should be satisfied. Satisfied, because after years of struggle for representation on the School Board to which we were entitled twenty years ago, we should not seek representation in the body that governs all the people of Philadelphia.

If the previous psychology of the Negro Republicans was to be satisfied with small favors thankfully received, I can assure the Republican leaders that it is not the reaction of old or young Negro Republicans today. We will not be satisfied; we will not cease our demands until Negroes are given representation in all branches of government in accordance with their voting strength. In order that our demand may effectively be made known, we must vote solidly for Negro candidates. Only by showing that these candidates have the backing of their voters can we overcome the belief of the political leaders that Negroes will not support each other and therefore Negroes do not have to be given a place on the ticket. To accomplish this purpose effectively, we must organize, locally and nationally, so that we can demonstrate the power of Negro candidates in every state where there is a substantial voting strength. If in the coming elections Negro candidates—whether endorsed by the dominant party or not—could carry the Negro vote, the facts will talk for themselves and we shall not have to beg for representation which is justly due us.

I know that such advice does not conform with the orthodox rules of politics; that political works are supposed to vote for the party slate. But I also know that the party slate is supposed to represent the people and when it fails so to do, then the people not represented have a right to rise up and take such steps as may best afford them protection. What then are the steps best calculated to protect the Negro voter?

Some Negroes answer, join the Democratic Party. I have not been able to see the efficacy of this suggestion, notwithstanding the positions which I acknowledge the Republican Party has denied us. If Negroes obtained in eastern and middle-western states the number of political positions from either party to which they are entitled in accordance with their political strength, the welfare of the Negro in America would not be fundamentally improved. Our concern should be and must be to improve the general status of the Negro race. This cannot be done through even a few thousand appointments to office in northern states. Alliance with the Democratic Party which is controlled by southern Democrats can never yield a return to the mass of American Negroes.

What hope can there be for legislation that is beneficial to Negroes when southerners are the chairmen of the most important and the majority of the United States Senate and House Committees? Let me read to you the names of the chairmen of these important committees in the House and Senate [see Table 4.1].

Twenty-two of the thirty-three Senate Committees and Twenty-eight of the forty-six House Committees are in the control of chairmen from southern Democratic states.

The number of jobs that we in the eastern and middle-western states can expect from any party by no means balance the effect upon the Negro legislation which a southern-controlled Democratic House and Senate pass.

What benefits have we derived from the so-called relief legislation of the Roosevelt Administration? Let us examine our present economic status. The number of Negroes on relief has steadily increased. Today over three million Negroes of all ages are receiving relief, which means

Table 4.1. Chairmen of important House and Senate congressional committees

[Committee]	House	Senate
Agriculture	Jones, Texas	Smith, S.C.
Appropriations	Buchanan, Texas	Glass, Va.
Banking and Commerce	Steagall, Alabama	Fletcher, Fla.
Civil Service	Ramspich, Ga.	Bulow, S.D.
Finance		Harrison, Miss.
Education	Palmisano, Md.	Walsh, Mass.
Foreign Affairs	McReynolds, Tenn.	Pittman, Nevada
Interstate and Foreign Commerce	Rayborn, Texas	Wheeler, Montana
Judiciary	Sumner, Texas	Ashurst, Calif.

Source: Compiled by Sadie Alexander from U.S. Congressional Data.

that even a larger number are unemployed. 18.4 percent of all cases on relief are Negroes, although Negroes are only 9.4 percent of the population. In spite of and largely because of this volume of Negroes unemployed, over one-third (36 percent) of the child labor in America is Negro. Approximately one-quarter of all women fifteen years of age and over are workers, but Negro women form one-quarter of all married women working away from home. The ratio is about three times greater than that of all women. The cause for this appalling economic condition can largely be traced to the effect of relief legislation of the Roosevelt Administration.

We all well know the effect of the National Recovery Act, which specifically exempted from its provisions outside and casual labor—into which groups the Negro either actually fell or was actually pushed. By its terms Negroes were practically excluded from the provisions for a reduction of hours and an increase in pay. So that even during its short life, Negro labor was only further suppressed. Then came the Agricultural Adjustment Act, which was principally aimed at stabilizing the price of cotton but which left virtually untouched the large tenant population of which the Negro constituted 55 percent. The reduction of acreage in 1933 and 1934 made possible a withdrawal of land from cultivation and resulted in a corresponding reduction in the number of tenant contracts, so that 30 percent of the Negro tenants were eliminated from agriculture. This is what the AAA did toward increasing Negro unemployment. No longer are the bulk of southern Negroes even landless tenants. The Social Security Act which President Roosevelt states is a realization he has long cherished, specifically exempts from its provisions for old age pensions, employment insurance, pensions for the blind and all of its magnanimous provisions to alleviate suffering among the masses, all persons employed as domestic servants or in agriculture. No, it does not say Negroes shall not share these advantages, but it boldly provides that in these jobs where the bulk of Negro labor is found—the provisions of the Act shall not apply. Is it not clear that in his years of yearning and planning for the social security of the common man, neither Mr. Roosevelt nor his Democratic colleagues had in mind the security of the American Negro? Nor did the Democratic controlled Legislature of Pennsylvania have him in mind. Recently I appeared before the House Committee of our Legislature to oppose House Bill No. 371 that proposed to decrease from fifty-four hours to forty hours labor by women in Pennsylvania except domestic servants and those employed in agriculture. Ninety-two percent of all Negro women in Pennsylvania gainfully employed are domestic servants. I ask you, what advantage to the Negro laborer are a dozen Assistant Attorney Generals in Pennsylvania, New York, Ohio, and Illinois when legislation specifically dooms the masses to starvation wages, unemployment and poverty?

The ultimate solution of our problem lies in obtaining the favorable laws to protect and advance the Negro masses. These we shall never obtain from a Congress, nor a Legislature controlled by Democrats who must curry the favor of the bourbon South to assure the continuance of their own party in power. Nor shall we obtain the needed legislation from a Republican Congress and Legislature until we are represented therein and an integral part thereof. Representation in the lawmaking bodies of our country is vital to the life of the Negro race. We cannot hope for favorable legislation until we oust southern democratic control, which every Negro who votes the Democratic ticket in New York or Pennsylvania helps to forward and continue; nor can we hope for favorable legislation until Negro representatives are a part of the lawmaking bodies of the United States. If Negroes return to the Republican Party and if the Republican Party assures their return by endorsing and slat-ing in Illinois, Ohio, Pennsylvania, and New York, where there are large blocks of Negro votes, Negroes not only for the state Legislatures but Negroes for Congress, then not only is the Republican Party assured of winning back these states in the Presidential Election of 1936 [but also] Negroes will be guaranteed the representation they have so long been unjustly denied as well as the protection of their rights which have been so long sorely neglected and will again rally to the Republican standard. Nothing short of such representation can overcome the deflection of Negro votes in the east and west to the Democratic Party. We cannot overcome the unwillingness of Republican leaders to slate Negros for such positions unless we unite our strength behind Negro candidates. Then and then only will Republican leaders realize our strength. Negro leaders here assembled, the solution lies in your hands. If you would lift the Negro masses from the depths into which they have been thrown by Democratic legislation designed to keep us forever down, support, encourage, vote for Negro candidates. When we thus demonstrate our strength, we guarantee the future welfare of the Negro race.

"Address on the Theme 'War Must Cease,'" 1935

If I should ask the persons here assembled whether they approved of war, and if they wanted another war, there would be a storm of "Noes!" Each day, however, draws us closer to another war. England, the mistress of the sea, whose island is supported by her colonies, is not going to allow Italy to take any land without her permission. When France and England apply pressure to Italy, Mussolini, in a vain effort to save himself, can only reply with war. Again the question will arise—can America remain neutral? Whether or not she can depends upon public opinion, and opinion depends upon the information given to the public, upon which the great populace bases its opinion. In the Great War, propaganda against Germany was rampant. A democracy can be brought into a war only by whipping it up to a fury against the enemy. [In] an autocracy, we were told in a thousand insidious ways imaginary tales about the atrocities the enemy commits against women, children, and civilians. We were urged to join in making the world safe for democracy. Finally, to bring the war fright closer to the American citizen, a letter disclosing that Herr Zimmerman planned to get Mexico on the German side, with a promise to restore it the lost territory of Texas, was given out through British agencies at just the right time to be, as Senator Lodge said, "of almost unlimited use in forcing the situation." We shall, in the course of the next few years, meet similar propaganda. Whether we shall be overcome by it and submit to another devastating war will depend upon the force of the propaganda by such an organization as is here assembled against war. If you do not want another war, the fury of which is at the moment threatening, you must with all your power oppose it *now*.

It seems to me that the initial step should be the dissemination of salient facts regarding the effect of war. Do you know that in the World War there were fifty-three million men engaged on the sides of the allies and of the central powers? Had all the men in the entire world, three hundred and sixty million, been gathering in one spot, one in every seven men would have marched away to produce that fifty-three million. An army so gigantic, equipped with weapons more destructive than any previous army had had, poisonous gas, tanks, submarines, automatic guns that could be carried by one man, with a capacity of a hundred shots per minute, left behind it an astonishing number of dead. The number of those killed is stated by Field Marshall, Sir William Robertson, Chief of the British General Staff during the World War to be 10,873,000. General Tasker Howard Bliss gives the total death list as 12,991,000. Field Marshal Robertson adds that if the victims of army and navy blockades, of revolutions, of sunken and shipwrecked boats, of bombardments be added to this list, the number of dead would amount to 37,000,000 "otherwise wounded." Even more serious than the numerical loss, in its effect upon the future, is the loss through race deterioration. Considered first from the point of view of the physical, it is inevitable that war should take its heaviest toll from the physically fit. The physically fit die for their country; the physically unfit live and propagate for it; that is an inevitable outcome of war.

When ten million of the ablest men of the world are killed and millions more left physically unfit, such human waste threatens the destruction of mankind. Hundreds [of] years and numerous generations will be required before this sacrifice of life can be made good.

The cost of the World War in dollars is as appalling as its cost in lives. Immediately following the war it was computed at the International Financial Conference at Brussels, 1920, that the total national indebtedness incurred by the warring nations during the period from August 1, 1914 to November 11, 1918 had been *two hundred and twenty-five billions of dollars.* The estimated wealth of the United States is three hundred billion. Yet this sum covers only the cost as represented by the national indebtedness of the warring countries. The real cost of the war is so vast that it could not possibly be indicated on any ledger, but I shall enumerate a few facts which will indicate the vastness of the total cost. The Army has admitted that it costs $25,000 "for every man who was put in action." Then the total cost for the American Expeditionary Forces was $102,427,525,000. For temporary crosses and stars (for Jewish dead) to mark the graves of slain soldiers the allies, it is estimated, paid $5,000,000. There is another phase of the cost which defies accurate computation. That is the cost of human lives that were lost. Who can compute the value to the world of the ten million young men who were killed; the six million permanently disabled; the thirteen million partially disabled. Nor does this figure include the cost of maintaining the armies of occupation which continued until ten years following the Armistice. Nor has the cost of restoring the devastated territory, the pensions, compensation and other provisions for veterans and their dependents been added. In June 1930, the estimated cost of soldiers' pensions of various kinds was $40,583,000,000. Nor does this estimated cost include the war-time distortion of economic activity which was diverted to production of war materials. The mere enumeration of the costs directly and indirectly attributable to the war justify [*sic*] the claim that it is impossible to write down in monetary figures the war cost.

While we may not be able to define or visualize in dollars the cost, there is not one of us who has not felt the cost. The economic depression following the World War has been for Americans a more vivid experience than the war itself. When the World War broke out, the world was practically an economic unit. Rapid transportation, communication, and international division of production had created a world market upon which all nations were dependent for their prosperity. In 1914, the principal industries of many countries, and therefore the jobs and livelihood of their citizens, depended upon raw material controlled by other governments. Those countries, like the British Isles, that had specialized in industrial production were dependent on others for food. Furthermore, machine production had so far increased output beyond home consumption that foreign markets were necessary for profitable operations. Trade being conducted at such long distances, it required a considerable outlay of capital and extension of credit for their production and distribution.

In order to carry on such a system of international trade, it was necessary to have first: a constant relationship between the currencies of different countries and a common standard of value into which the money of various countries can be translated. Gold had generally been agreed upon as this standard. Second, it was necessary that the relationship of the price of goods in different countries remain practically the same, in order that trade transactions covering any period of time may be carried on with some degree of certainty. In the years before the war, this could be counted upon because of the following set of facts: If the exports of one country were greater than its imports, the balance due was paid in gold. As gold increased in any given country, the quantity of available credit, if not of actual currency, was increased. This tended, in part by increasing purchasing power, to increase prices. When the price[s] of goods in one country were higher than the prices in another, its exports decreased and its imports increased. It, in turn, was forced to pay for the excess of imports over exports with gold. Its quantity of gold decreased, and the balance tended to be restored.

The World War immediately threw this balance of trade out of gear. Trade with foreign countries was cut off by blockades, seizure of shipments, curtailing of shipping facilities. The production of peace time goods was stopped, while labor was transferred to the production of war materials. A sharp rise in prices followed the demand for peace time goods. Such a rise in prices is bound to be followed by a severe drop in prices when the extraordinary conditions created by war no longer exist.

Another result of the war on our economic structure was the large sums of money borrowed by the belligerent governments. Faced with the necessity of expending in excess of their revenues and fearing the effect upon the morale of their people of increasing taxation, war governments borrowed enormous sums first from England and then from the United States. Now this borrowed money could only be repaid by the debtors' governments giving us goods, services or gold. But a spirit of intensive nationalization and desire for self-sufficiency, natural products of war, led to quota systems for the limitation of imports and to new and increased tariffs which protected uneconomic industries developed during war years from the production of goods that it was cheaper to import. So that the debtor nations could not pay us in goods, as we refused to take it. Similar quotas prevented the importation of labor, so we could not be paid by service. The debtor nations had spent their gold on war materials and had none with which to pay us. So that unless we allowed them to come into our country there was no way in which they could pay us.

With European countries unable to produce because they were without markets in which to sell, due to the vicious circle of depreciated currencies and high tariffs, capital began to flow to America. For a time our industries flourished, prices rose, stocks soared. But we had no foreign markets in which to sell our high surpluses. The European countries had no gold with which to pay us and we refused to accept their goods in exchange. The financial crash of 1929 came just ten years after the "peace settlement" in which governments laid down their guns only to continue warring with tariffs and quotas.

The economic chaos produced by the last war has endangered civilization as much as the war itself. More than thirteen million workers were unemployed in the United States at the beginning of 1933. It is estimated in the world more than thirty million had no employment. More than nine hundred thousand American farm families were turned out of their homes through foreclosure of mortgages. Up to June 1934, the fifth year of the depression, the total emergency expenditures of the Federal government amounted to $6,452,846,304. This does not take into account over three million dollars spent in direct unemployment and farm relief. These figures cannot possibly portray the human suffering, which even such immense expenditures have been unable to alleviate . . . . Surely, no person who thinks at all can fail to realize the unfathomable depths of misery into which the human race has been plunged by the World War and his or her duty to avoid another such futile but devastating conflict.

As Christian women, we should particularly be concerned about the demoralizing effects of war. In war, acts which constitute the major crimes in peace times are the everyday work of the soldier. Killing men, which under every civilized code constitutes a major felony, is rewarded by promotions and gold medals in time of war. Raiding the enemies' country, taking her cattle, food, clothing, and destroying her property were daily occurrences. Dr. Lorenz in an article appearing in *Mental Hygiene,* written in 1923, tells us that for a soldier to help himself to necessary equipment by taking it from someone else in his unit was common practice. He says a shortage was often made up by stealing from nearby organizations and not unfrequently with the knowledge of the commanding officers. The influence of such an experience commonly practiced and occasionally sanctioned by those in authority was not conducive to respecting property rights at home.

Thus we see following the war a general increase in crime. The statistics in the United States Department of Commerce figures from the Bureau of Census (Prisoners for 1923) show that for the years 1910 to 1923 there was the following increase in crime percentages:

Table 4.2. Percentage increase in crimes, 1910–1923

Forgery	68.2
Homicide	16.1
Rape	33.3
Violating drug acts	2,006.7
Robbery	83.3

Source: United States Department of Commerce figures from the Bureau of Census (Prisoners for 1923).

The mere increase in these figures does not begin to tell the story. As marked features of the period [were] the youth of the criminal and the extreme cruelty of the crime. More than half of the criminals today are twenty-four or younger. The abnormality of the crime is characterized by the Leopold and Loeb case. While these young people were not in the war, the acts are indicative of the fact that the war neurosis was not limited to soldiers in the field. Society, like the soldiers, had thrown off restrictions and the children felt the relaxation of ethical and moral restraint.

Broken families and divorces also increased in the period immediately following the war. The figures for divorce per one hundred marriages, as given in the *World Almanac,* show an increase from 10.6 percent in 1917 to 16.3 percent in 1932. While other causes were at work, such a[s] great economic freedom for women, [and] emotional instability fostered by the "free love" doctrine—the irresponsibility engendered by the war had a direct bearing upon divorce and the breaking up of the family. A man who had gone over the top, who had enjoyed the company of various types and races of women, who had felt no restraint when he was on furlough, settling down to the ordinary details of a plain life, in a plain house, with a plain woman, was just too boring.

It was during this same period that organized crime received its start. Gault, in his book on criminology and penology, states that in the autumn of 1927 some fifty rackets were uncovered, while by April 1928, 117 separate rackets had been identified. Crime during the last decade has been organized on a scale and with reserves unprecedented by the world's history. The brutality and the lawlessness released by war after the war ended not only disrupted homes and established mores, but stimulated organized crime. The technical skill developed in the army and displayed to the populace at home resulted in the machine gun and the bomb being turned to criminal purposes at home. The racket is a natural sequence of the war.

To no group of people should the plea "War Must Cease" appeal more than to ours. We who in years of plenty are compelled to accept reduced wages, low standards of living; whose family life is disrupted because mother and father must work away from home and children rear themselves, with the consequent result of high juvenile delinquency; whose death rate is high because of economic and social handicaps— such a race of underprivileged people face annihilation from the effects of war. What other group of people in America has suffered as we have from the depression. Already at the bottom of the world, the chaos that followed the war and which I have just described to you is about to push us off the face of the world. Negro Christian women, you are recreant to your trust if you fail to heed this call and to carry to your people the facts [of] that unanswerable decree, "*War Must Cease.*"

"For the Republican Party in the Lackawanna County Elections," 1935

Mr. Chairman, Ladies and Gentlemen:

We are facing the most important election that has ever confronted the American voter. The decision of our forefathers to make Lincoln the standard-bearer of the nation in the crises that [were] about to divide the nation in 1860, the decision of many of us who are present here tonight to elect Woodrow Wilson President of the United States, which decision resulted in our being engaged in the World War, do not equal the importance of the questions which are dependent upon the decision you will make when you cast your ballot on November 5th: the liberty of the citizens of America, the security of the nation. The Democratic Party in the Gubernatorial election of 1934 blatantly declared that a vote against George H. Earle was a vote against Roosevelt. We were told that the election of every candidate on the Democratic ticket was vital to the success of the New Deal; which was to bring us the return of the prosperity which we enjoyed under the administration of Calvin Coolidge. Today, however, when men and women are aware that the New Deal has been a raw deal for the average citizen, this same Democratic Party that preached a year ago, a vote for Michael Mahoney for constable is a vote for Roosevelt, says the present election is a local matter; that your election of local officers in Lackawanna County in November 1935 bears no relation to the issues of the Presidential Campaign of 1936.

When Justice and Mrs. George W. Maxey invited me to come address you tonight, it immediately occurred to me how broad were the issues in this political campaign; that although we have but two candidates-at-large, Judge Horace Stern, that learned, liberal-minded jurist who will soon take his seat beside Justice Maxey on the Supreme Court bench and lend his support to the liberal minority of which Justice Maxey has for so long been the leading standard-bearer. Equally important to our judiciary is the return of Judge Jesse E. B. Cunningham of the Superior Court, whose fair, liberal, learned opinions have brought honor to the bench. Yet the Democratic Party, breaking all previous precedents, is seeking to unseat the learned jurist. The courts of the Commonwealth are the safety valves of liberty. You cannot permit political parties to tamper with the judiciary. If you wish to be assured of fair, honest, liberal, learned decisions, you must repudiate the threat against judicial freedom of thought and action by returning Justice Cunningham, the Republican nominee, to the Superior Court bench and electing to the Supreme Court of America's most respected jurists, a liberal, kind-hearted, honest and learned gentleman—Judge Horace Stern.

Equally vital as the protection of the courts of our own state is the protection to the American people of the safeguards which have been guaranteed us by our Constitution—a problem which confronts the voter in the present election. You doubtless are wondering what relations has the present election with assuring to the American people their constitutional rights and privileges. Do you realize that for the past two years you and I have been ruled under an Act of Congress which had seventeen thousand rules and regulations promulgated by the Executive Department of the government and five thousand laws [which] had been promulgated by the same department of the government, the violation of any one of which constituted a crime punishable by fine or imprisonment or both? Over five hundred persons were awaiting trial for violating these executive orders when they were declared to be unconstitutional. So rapidly were new rules and regulations promulgated by the Executive Department that you and I, the common man and woman, did not know what was the law. Case after case arose and came to trial before it was discovered a new regulation made necessary the

noll [null] processing of the old case and the drawing of a new indictment against Mr. Citizen. To enforce these 22,000 laws, rules and regulations 146,490 additional employees were put on the federal payroll at a
cost of a million dollars a day.

The man or woman who voted last fall for George H. Earle, in
order to support the Roosevelt policy, was voting to subject himself to
this insufferable regulation which the United States Supreme Court declared to be repugnant not only to the letter of the law as stated in the
Constitution, but repugnant to the spirit of freedom guaranteed by the
Constitution.

Since the United States Supreme Court denied the right of the Executive branch of our government to govern 130,000,000 people from
Washington under the rules established through the N.R.A., the administration has not changed its policy. It has continued to press its efforts
to prescribe every detail of our daily lives. Congress recently passed a
law containing 15,400 words and providing that if a farmer raises more
potatoes than he is told in this law, he is penalized by a tax of 45 cents a
bushel on the extra bushels. If he sells any of his potatoes in a package
different from that which the law prescribes or without a stamp; or if a
person buys potatoes not packaged and stamped as the law prescribes,
both buyer and seller can be fined and sent to jail. This law is more severe
than the repudiated prohibition law. The seller was subject under that
law to fine or punishment but the buyer was not. Now the purchaser of
potatoes, a basic American food, must beware. "Buyer Beware" Market
Overt Warranties Sales Act.

The framers of our Constitution took the utmost precautions
against such attempted establishment of bureaucracy. Henry VIII,
Charles I, James II, George III. He declared himself invested with the
power to legislate for us. They not only limited the powers of the federal
government to matters of general concern but they expressly declared
that "the powers not delegated to the United States by the Constitution,
nor prohibited by it to the states, are preserved to the states respectively
or to the people." To permit the present administration to transfer to
itself the power to regulate matters which are essentially for state and
individual decision is to create a dictatorship, such as we are now witnessing under Hitler, Mussolini, and Stalin.

The time to strike is now. The date is November 5th. The way is, vote Republican. If Grant had not captured Fort Henry and Donaldson in 1862, he could not have captured Vicksburg in 1863. If he had not taken Vicksburg in 1863 he could not have taken Lee in 1865. If the Republicans cannot in November 1935 build up brigades in Lackawanna County, in Beaver County, in Philadelphia County, in Pennsylvania who are sworn to stop this illegal, unconstitutional usurpation of power, which is crushing the freedom of the American people, they cannot even find a general in 1936 to lead the scattered ranks.

Ladies and Gentlemen, if you do not cherish that liberty and freedom for which your forefathers gave their lives and which they attempted to preserve for you in adopting our Constitution, I am certain there is not one of you who does not cherish his home, his savings, his standard of living, his pocketbook. But do you realize that the reckless spending of the federal government—a million dollars per day to enforce the N.R.A. and tell you how many hours you could work and for what price, is about to wipe away the value of the few dollars you have still been able to hold for the "rainy day."

> Dickens' famous character, Micawber, gave young David Copperfield a piece of financial advice that is universal in its application. He said,
>   "Annual income 20 pounds,
>   Annual expenditure 19, 19 shillings sixpence
>   Result, Happiness
>   Annual income 20 pounds
>   Annual expenditure, 20 pounds ought
>   And six
>   Result, Misery"

Those who continually fail to live within their income, whether they be individual or nations, sooner or later come to grief. History is replete with testimony regarding the soundness of Micawber's advice. But those who now ignore it feel that unusual circumstances justify their action. Motive and circumstances, however noble or unusual, play no part in the matter. Yet we are told in this country by those in authority that the exigencies of the times—the social need—justify the accumulation of enormous deficits. This is the same old story; circumstances are always unusual. Motives are always of the highest. It is one thing to rationalize on a deficit. It is another thing to liquidate it.

In the fiscal year 1931, the Federal Government incurred a deficit of $902,000,000, in 1932 a further deficit of $3,148,000,000 was created, another $3,063,000 was added in 1933. In 1934 the Federal Government was $3,989,000,000 in the red. The 1935 deficit was $3,575,000,000 and present budget estimates place the 1936 deficit at $4,529,000,000. This indicates a cumulative deficit of about $19,206,000,000, in a period of six years.

Among all modern nations, the United States today has the largest deficit, both in total amount and in relation to income. The $11,000,000,000 deficit incurred in the four fiscal years from 1931 through 1934 was more than 100 percent of the government revenues for the same period. In the fiscal year 1935 it was almost 100 percent of the revenues collected. In other words, the government has been spending more than twice as much money as it has received.

A comparison of the position of other leading nations shows that from this standpoint Italy's record is next poorest. But Italy's accumulated deficit of $780,000,000 from 1931 through 1934 was only one-fourteenth as large as that of the United States and represented only one-fifth of her revenues for the period in which it was incurred.

Many other leading nations of the world have incurred deficits in recent years. But in nearly all cases they have been involuntary. The deficits that have resulted have been primarily by the failure of revenues to materialize in accordance with budget estimates. But the deficit of the United States has been planned and deliberate. It has budgeted its deficits in advance. The President's budget statement of September 29, 1935 estimated the deficit for 1936 at $3,281,982,860. Billions of dollars! There was a time when even a million dollars seemed a stupendous figure. But today a billion dollars appropriated to P.W.A. [Public Works Administration], F.E.R.A. [Federal Emergency Relief Administration], A.A.A. [Agricultural Adjustment Administration] has become as commonplace in daily news that we fail to appreciate the real significance of the word. Familiarity with it breeds contempt.

How much is a billion dollars? Upon reflection it staggers the imagination. A man with a $5,000 annual income would have to work 200,000 years to earn a billion dollars. Only a billion minutes elapsed between the birth of Christ and the year 1902 A.D. A billion dollars laid end to end would girdle the earth four times. A billion dollars should never be thought of as merely a sum of money. It should be thought of as representing many years of labor by many thousands of people. At our present average rate of individual income, a city of 100,000 people would have to work more than fifteen years to earn a billion dollars. Only when we consider such facts can the significance of our enormous national deficit be appreciated. Only then can we realize the extent to which we have mortgaged our future.

We all know the disaster that comes to the individual who spends more than he makes. He finally goes bankrupt and his creditors seize his property, leaving him penniless. But we do not realize that excessive spending by a government brings bankruptcy to all the people. Governments never go bankrupt in the sense that an individual does. Like individuals, governments have the power to appropriate and expend money. They also have further power that the individual does not have—the power to manufacture money. When its credit becomes impaired, a government does not file a petition in bankruptcy. Instead, it issues additional money. The United States suffered a number of times from deficits that compelled the manufacture [of] fiat money, such as Colonial paper money, the Continental currency, and the infamous greenbacks. Inflation and collapse have always followed. Today, instead of issuing paper money, the United States has sold bonds to banks, which in time issue the money with which to pay for such bonds. The difference is only one of method. The effect of the fiat credit is slow but insidious. The continued issuance of such money leads to steady reduction or dilution of the value of the currency. Ultimately the currency will become valueless. The cheapening of the value of money wipes out the accumulated savings of the people, until in the end an amount formerly regarded as a small fortune may no longer be sufficient to buy a loaf of bread. The great middle class, which is the backbone of any nation, is always the chief sufferer. Prices rise as the value of money is diluted. Wages cannot be adjusted upward, in such a period, rapidly enough to offset the tremendous increase in the cost of living. As a consequence, the standard of living declines rapidly and the entire population suffers. Moreover, the threat of currency depreciation has so impaired the confidence necessary to foster the investment of funds that there is no hope of industry opening and bringing about the reemployment of labor. Instead we have the employment of idle workers by the government in unproductive tasks. But despite this frantic effort of the government to create artificial employment, the total number of unemployed people has increased and the industrial production of the nation has decreased. The statistical reports of the League of Nations carry indices of industrial production for all the great nations. These indices show that from June of 1933 to the spring of 1935, the industrial production of Great Britain increased 20 percent, that of Germany 26 percent, that of Italy 31 percent, and that of Canada 17 percent, while industrial production of the United States during the same period decreased 8 percent.

Must the reckless spending continue, which brings neither employment nor increased industrial production but which does bring the loss of your savings, unemployment, low standards of living, suffering and poverty—a discredited nation? Grover Cleveland said on April 13, 1895, "This nation can promise safety and protection only as long as its solvency is unsuspected, the honor unsullied, and the soundness of its money unquestioned."

Ladies and Gentlemen the freedom, the security of the American people lies in your hands. Will you repudiate these unlawful intrusions upon your rights, will you protest against this insufferable, unsurmountable public deficit by voting on November 5th for home rule, constitutional government, sound finances under a Republican administration?

"Coming Events Cast Their Shadow/ Address in Detroit," 1939

When Richard Allen was pulled from his knees in St. George's M.E. Church in Philadelphia in 1816, he decided to establish a church where Negroes in America might enjoy that freedom of worship sought by the founders of this country, the seat of which had been the city of Philadelphia, yet where it was denied men not because of their faith but because of the color God had given them. About thirty years later, to be exact in 1844, the Methodist Episcopal Church split; the M.E. Church South seceding because it would not admit as members those descendants of Allen's race who still hoped to experience in the Methodist Episcopal Church the brotherhood which was a cornerstone of that faith as established by Charles Wesley. And so for another seventy or more years, Negro members of the Methodist Episcopal Church worshiped in separate buildings, attending joint church conferences, only to realize in 1936, more than one hundred fifty (150) years after Richard Allen had left the M.E. Church rather than submit to individual segregation, that they must submit to mass separation or accept Allen's decision. When the largest Protestant religious organization in America is willing publicly to declare such a position on its relation to the Negro members of its church; when it prefers union of its white members, North and South, to even a semblance of observance of the preachment that all men are the children of one God the Father, members of the same Mystical Body of Christ and temples of the same Holy Ghost, a black shadow hovers over the hopes of all Negro men and women in America.

We have but to trace the development of racism in Europe to realize the significance of such events as the attitude of the Methodist Episcopal Church in America. The cause of the plight of Jews in Central and Eastern Europe today goes far back in history. In the time of the Crusades and the Black Death, they were driven eastward to Poland, Lithuania, and Hungary, where they were admitted as middlemen, to a position between that of the nobles and the serfs. Between the fifteenth and seventeenth centuries, the Jews lived principally in Poland, where they were protected by the Polish kings and granted a large measure of autonomy, but restricted in their right to own land and indulge in commercial pursuits because they were excluded from the guilds which were the labor unions of their time. The partition of Poland between Russia and Lithuania resulted in the breaking up of any cultural or communal autonomy among the Jews, who found themselves under the domination of the Tsarist regime, rivaled until now only by Hitler in its oppression and complete exclusion of the Jews from the political, economic, and social life of the country. Excluded from the ownership of land, the Jews congregated in the towns and cities, engaged in petty trading, tailoring, and cabinet making. With the coming of the Great War to make the world safe for democracy, followed by peace treaties designed to protect minorities, for the first time in centuries, the Jews believed a new day had dawned. Poland was re-established in the Balkans, Jugoslavia and Albania were created, and Rumania's borders were enlarged. All of these newly created countries were bound by minority treaties to give the Jewish subjects political and economic equality and cultural rights.

But, as the events of the years following have so clearly established, international guarantees and treaties cannot create for a minority people the rights enjoyed by the dominant majority. The ink on these postwar treaties was scarcely dry when the Nazi platform was adopted in 1920. It provided that only Aryans constitute the racial state. They alone shall fill state jobs and be placed in position to make a livelihood. They alone must be editors of and contributors to the German press, and they alone shall enjoy equal rights and duties. A non-Aryan was described as one whose Jewish ancestors could be discovered to have lived after

January 1, 1800. All government and civil service employees were compelled to take an oath that they had no such Jewish ancestors and that they appreciated the consequences of their oath being false. With the rise of the National Socialist Party to power followed the series of decrees which are all too familiar to us. Non-Aryans were barred from holding any kind of office, the German Bar Association was dissolved and replaced by the National Socialist Lawyers' Society, which forbade Non-Aryans as members. Jewish students were first limited in number, next denied internships, and then excluded from the medical schools while the physicians eventually were forbidden to practice. Non-Aryans were denied membership in the Reich Chamber of Culture, which supervised literature, the press, radio, films, and music, and in which organization membership was made compulsory for everyone in those fields. They were barred as landowners or from land inheritance and permitted to take only one-fifth of their property if they emigrated, the remaining four-fifths being seized by the National Socialist Government.

What has happened to the minorities in Rumania is not so frequently spoken of but is equally significant to the American minorities. Rumania, forced at the conclusion of the Great War to sign on September 4, 1920, a Minorities' Treaty which specifically provided, "Rumania undertakes to recognize as Rumanian nationals ipso facto and without requirements of any formality, Jews inhabiting any Rumanian territory, who do not possess another nationality," on February 23, 1924, passed a nationality law which made the acquisition of citizenship subject to proof of ten years' continuous residence in the same place (known as Heimatsrecht) before December 1, 1918. Many Jews, owing to compulsory immigration and the misfortunes of war, were unable to show this qualification. The result was about twenty thousand Jews, in Rumania, who were "stateless." Even those Jews whose citizenship could not be attacked have been made to realize daily that theirs is but a second-class citizenship. They are not allowed to hold positions in the government or municipal services. They are equally barred from positions in the army, although they are compelled to discharge their military duties. They are largely represented in chambers of commerce and stock exchanges, but they are left out of the governing councils. They may provide the bulk or even the whole capital of a limited company, but they are required by law to reserve a number of administrative posts for persons of the Rumanian race. They cannot obtain credit from a Rumanian bank; and they have difficulty in obtaining the requisite facilities for importing goods and raw materials from abroad. Jewish landowners, like others, were expropriated through the Ayranian [sic] Reform of 1926, but the Jewish peasantry have been denied their proportionate share of the expropriated land.

The students have suffered as elsewhere in Central and Eastern Europe by the demand to restrict the admission of Jews to the universities to a small percentage. The Congress of Rumanian Lawyers adopted a resolution in May 1933 to exclude from membership all persons not of "pure Rumanian blood." Jews and members of other minorities were refused admission to the bar in Bucharest and other cities, while Jewish lawyers who went to the courts ran the risk of being attacked by so-called "lawyers' police," young barristers entrusted with the task of forcibly ejecting them. The Congress of the National Federation of Liberal Professions decided last June to exclude all Jews and members of other minorities from the vocations they represented; and the Association of Secondary School Masters passed a similar resolution.

Nor is this intensified racism by any means limited to Central and Eastern Europe. In Mexico the Committee for the Defense of Mexican Merchants is carrying on a campaign against Jewish traders, and a short while ago the so-called Bloc of Revolutionary Action for Small Commerce tried to pass a bill in Congress that would virtually drive Jews out of business in that country. In Costa Rica the establishment of a colony of Jewish refugees from Germany aroused anti-Semitic objections. Several Nazi leaders admitted the Germans in Costa Rica had instructions from Hitler not to trade with Jews.

In Brazil, Minister of Justice Campos and other advisers of Vargas drew up a new immigration bill that resulted in a thousand Jews who entered the country as tourists ordered out of the country.

In Ecuador, Dictator Enriquez [Alberto Enríquez Gallo] decreed the exclusion of all Jews except those engaged in farming or industrial pursuits "advantageous to the nation."

What is the significance of this portrayal of rampant racism in the list of present conditions in the United States? Only a few years ago we believed ourselves facing an unprecedented era of prosperity. Capital was being freely invested in new and old enterprises. There existed an unsupplied demand for goods and services. The requirements for the production of these required goods and services existed within our own borders in that we had ample raw materials, skilled and unskilled labor, and established manufacturing plants. There existed little, if any, serious concern about the survival of our democratic theories. We of the black minority believed, like the Jew in Europe, that the Great War had more firmly established these principles and broadened their application; that with education, improved economic opportunities afforded by the shortage of labor in the overworked factories, we, too, might actively share the benefits of a democracy. And then, almost in a flash, the stock market fell, steel production declined, freight car loading decreased, production generally slowed down, pay rolls were curtailed, unemployment mounted sky high.

Dissatisfaction and discontent with the economic condition of the country have given rise to the race-baiting speeches of such men as Father Coughlin and Major George Van Horn Moseley to the cry for an American party. Northwestern Pennsylvania, which has always been friendly in its attitude toward Negroes, carried the Republican ticket in the recent gubernatorial campaign to victory on the fact that every man on the ticket was an American protestant. It is a common expression to hear from the man on the street, "Hitler is right!" And when he says it to a Negro, rest assured he has no more respect for you than for the Jew on whom Hitler is placing the blame for a world economic condition put in motion when the German troops in 1914 goose-stepped into Belgium. Medical colleges in America that once freely admitted Negro students have either restricted the number now admitted to a percentage of the total enrollment or have entirely closed their doors to Negro students. In the entire state of Pennsylvania, we have not three Negro students in a law school, and none has been admitted to the bar in the past five years. Theoretically, Negroes can obtain mortgages from the Federal Housing Association, but the application is usually returned unaccepted. Private corporations do not hesitate to state their policy not to accept mortgages on properties owned by Negroes. In other words, the law permits us to purchase land but the mores of the community deny us the means.

Yes, the shadows that followed the Jew in Germany and Rumania to South America are overcasting the Negro in America. We who have for three hundred years lived in a democracy where the most rudimental principles of a democratic civilization were denied us are nevertheless aware that the fate which overtook Europe threatens to overtake minorities in the United States. However deeply traditional American democratic ideals may be rooted, the events of the past few years, such as the attitude of one of the strongest branches of Protestantism in the world, the restriction of opportunities for education, the refusal of men who have been declared liberals to make pronouncement against racism as indicated by their declining to serve on Jewish propaganda committees; the campaigning of a dominant political party on its freedom from affiliations with minorities; the refusal of the Daughters of the American Revolution to permit Marian Anderson to sing in Constitution Hall, are shadows that indicate that we in America may not be able to withstand the accumulating economic dissatisfaction and discontent that in Europe made men's minds fertile beds for racism.

I remember in 1932, on a visit to Germany, Mr. Alexander and I engaged a young student as a guide. He cursed every Jewish merchant whose shop we passed because they had a business while his father, a retired army officer, was impecunious. The young student, obsessed with the financial success of a few Jewish merchants, daily told us, "Someday a strong man will drive them all out and give us their wealth." He came that very year on an exchange fellowship to Dickinson College, Carlisle, Pennsylvania. How many young, plastic minds he affected will never be known. One thing we do know is that he found in 1932 many young men discontented because of lost family fortunes, ready to place the blame on anyone but themselves. President Roosevelt, well aware of this situation, in his fireside chat to the nation on April 14, 1938, sums it up as follows: "Democracy has disappeared in several other nations, not because the people of those nations disliked democracy, but because they had grown tired of unemployment and insecurity, of seeing their children hungry while they sat helpless in the face of government confusion, government weakness, through lack of leadership in government. Finally, in desperation, they chose to sacrifice liberty in the hope of getting something to eat."

It is no longer in America a matter of solving the farmer's problems, or those of organized labor, or those of the tenant farmer, or those of the industrialist. It is a matter of making the mechanism of democratic government work effectively in preventing all of these problems from plunging us into economic paralysis, when property values evaporate, the unemployed mount to such proportions that relief agencies cannot meet the burden—when men and women who have lost hope demand a dictator to take over the reins of government, feed the starving, restore the homeless, drive out the minorities, "and give us their wealth" as prophesied by my German guide.

It is therefore obvious that the maintenance of democratic institutions in America depends first upon the development of an economic system which, as stated by the National Policy Committee, will provide an adequate measure of economic security and justice; which will give the public some effective control over their economic as well as their political liberty; and which will find methods of controlling economic activity so as to

(a) insure liberty of occupation and consumption, and

(b) effectively stimulate the production of wealth.

In order to accomplish this purpose, the government will have to work out controls or regulatory devices which will diminish the fluctuations of business cycles under private enterprise and thereby mitigate severe business depressions. Such regulation contemplate[s] crop control so as to assure a market for produce as well as produce for a market; regulation of bank reserves, so as to make them available for the credit needs of the country; regulation of securities and the markets where they are sold, so as not to inflate the market with watered stocks; regulation of tariffs within limits, so as to supply the demand for domestic consumption, and more especially, so as to afford an even balance of trade; creation of equalization control so as to stabilize the ratio of exchange between the dollar, pound, and franc, and thereby protect payments to manufacturers who sell to foreign markets; [and] control of public utilities so as to protect millions of small investors as well as consumers. Such governmental control is absolutely essential to assure economic security, which is vital to the survival of democratic institutions in America.

In addition to economic controls to prevent severe business fluctuations, the government must alleviate suffering through relief measures extended both to capital and labor. All of us are familiar with the forms of direct and indirect relief created for the benefit of the individual under the nomenclature of W.P.A., P.W.A., N.Y.A., and C.C.C. Relief must, however, also be afforded the investor. Loans should be available for industry as well as for the workmen who labor in industry. Taxes must be adjusted so as not to drive private capital out of operation. To effect the latter result, one of the greatest present needs is uniform state laws governing corporation taxes, so that an investment which has become profitable will not suddenly be driven out of one state into another by increased capital taxes in the former state and empty promises of no capital taxes in the new location. This has in the past four years been the cause of at least one thousand industries leaving the state of Pennsylvania, where the capital tax increased from eight mills to 2 percent, and locating [in] southern states where there is at present no capital tax. The hazards of moving an industry are so great that private investors hesitate to place their funds in a business where there is no protection from severe losses. So that if private capital is to be put back to work, it will have to be offered relief and protection of the nature provided the individual worker.

While we are awaiting the results of these governmental efforts to provide economic security which is a foundation for democratic security, minorities must be alert that the pressure of discontented majorities does not destroy whatever benefits of democracy we now enjoy. What should be our program? First, it should include a plan for adult education in the principles of economic security that underlie democratic principles. If by health education we have been able to cut the tuberculosis rate two-thirds, to eliminate 90 percent of diphtheria, and almost abolish typhoid, then it cannot be considered too great a task to educate men's minds to the facts that will secure their freedom. We must realize that periods of depression arise when private capital is withdrawn from industry because overproduction reduces or brings no return to the investor; that this can be averted only by controlled production and by assuring an adequate return to capital. We must realize that private investors are entitled to as fair a return on their investments as we expect for our labor; that confiscation of private capital means the taking of the small and the big man's savings and ultimately the freedom of each—as has occurred in Russia. We must further realize that the presence in our midst of no minority group creates economic problems, but that they are [sic] the creatures of an uncontrolled economy. We must understand that the promises of no one man can bring prosperity, but that the working out of the principles of economy underlying the structure of any country are dependent upon the combined efforts of all people. If crop control is to be a success, the smallest farmer, as well as the plantation operator, must comply with the regulations. The cause of economic insecurity and how it can be overcome must be made clear to all classes of the public in language that each can understand in order that America may await the orderly solution of the problem and not in despair turn over its freedom in exchange for the vain promises of a self-proclaimed Messiah.

The National Urban League, a pioneer in interpreting economic conditions, is the best equipped organization by experience and proven success to present to the industrialist and the working man the basic economic facts underlying economic recovery. We are fortunate to have such an established organization already existing in the principal cities of America, respected for its sound judgement and leadership. If we realize the impending danger of democratic institutions in America being destroyed, we who would be most severely affected, must give complete financial and moral support to the Urban League, that it may further spread its program of economic recovery, the basis of democratic security.

The second step in our program should be education in tolerance for the younger generation. You in Detroit have done more along this line and set a higher standard than any other American city by the program conducted in Garfield High School by its principal, Charles A. Daly. Not until Mr. Daly's article on racial enrichment of the curriculum was published in the *National Educational Journal* did those in control of our public schools begin to think that not only were we not teaching the Negro anything about his own literature and history, but that the millions of children of other races in this country were utterly ignorant concerning the culture of a people who constitute more than one-tenth of their population. A survey of the textbooks used by the children of the state of Mississippi found no reference to the Negro in the civics or history textbooks, other than under the topic "Slavery." Another text on prominent Americans did not refer to a single Negro. If Mississippi has become aware of its deficiency in educating its white citizens concerning their Negro neighbors, is it not time that we Negroes in every city, town, and state awake to the necessity of Negro history being an integral part of the curricula of every secondary school?

The foundation of tolerance between people of varied races and religions is a mutual knowledge of the people and their religion. If we are all children of God, if He has breathed into each of us the breath of life, then there is enough of the Divine in each of us to be a person in whom another can find something to admire. How many times have you experienced a feeling of dislike for a man or woman whom you never intimately knew? Some chance, perhaps membership on a committee, association at work, or distress, brings you together and you find this person, whom you previously said you disliked, a very likeable chap. It is the person we do not know whom we dislike. In all of the people you know well, you can find some admirable qualities. The same situation exists concerning the relation between races of people. The white man who says he hates a Negro never intimately knew one and never read an intelligent book about one. Yet, we Negroes are doing little, even now, to educate ourselves in the face of the darkest shadows that have threatened our freedom since slavery. The Association for the Study of Negro Life and History, under the capable and farsighted leadership of Carter G. Woodson, has ready a wide and varied group of accredited publications on the Negro. These books should be introduced in the schools of America, to teach the youth who are his black neighbors, what they have done, what they can do for him and his country, and thereby to lay a foundation for tolerance in the minds of the youth of America.

There is considerable difference of opinion among leaders of Negro thought regarding the third point in a program to preserve our democratic institutions in this period of stress. There are those among us who think that at such a time we should lessen pressure for a fuller share of the rights legally ours for fear that by so doing we may arouse even greater racial hatred. Opposed to this line of thought, is the steady and relentless effort being made by the N.A.A.C.P. to open state-supported institutions of higher learning to Negro students or to provide for them an education equal to that provided white students. In my opinion, the N.A.A.C.P. is pursuing the only proper course. To begin with, we must be ever vigilant and watchful of our rights. Postponing action on a demand for fundamental rights will only result in the loss of greater rights. If we become inarticulate and inactive in pressing for the full benefits of a democratic government, it will be taken for granted that not only do no greater rights have to be given to us, but the meager benefits of a democracy that we now enjoy can be taken from us. There must be no compromise with reaction.

Furthermore, never was there a time when the conduct of America toward her minorities was subject to greater world criticism. Secretary Hull has been embarrassed repeatedly concerning his criticism of Nazism and Fascism by the latter's retorts concerning the position of the Negro in the United States. The present administration can consistently take but one position concerning any legal demands by minorities. The time to strike is here. And we on the side lines must back up with all of our means the efforts of that militant organization, the N.A.A.C.P., which is leading the way in showing America its duty toward its own minorities; a duty that becomes more patent with each blast of criticism of Germany and Italy from the State Department.

Democratic institutions can be preserved only if the people are willing to pay the price. Those of us who would suffer the most by their loss must be willing to pay the greatest price for their continuance. And, my friends, the time to pay has arrived. But we must pay in more than empty words and unfulfilled pledges. When I hear Negro men and women boast of their love of race, proclaim, "right or wrong, my race first," crowd out public meetings called in the interest of racial issues, but send up empty collection plates; when I see the budgets of our national organizations, such as the Advancement Association and the Urban League still subscribed in the main by white men and women, I tremble for the future.

I have a friend who has developed a hobby of raising roses into a successful business. In talking with her about the culture of her flowers, I remarked that "You must love your work." She replied, "Yes, I put a lot of love into my work, but I also put most of the money I make into it. I buy a highly developed fertilizer that is very expensive. I mix money with my love." We Negroes have got to mix unselfishly our money with our love of race if we hope to continue to live under a democratic government. Not only our future economic position but our position in America depends upon our willingness to support those organizations, men and women, who are striving to overcome the onslaught of racism in America. Democracy must be defended today, at any cost. Tomorrow, when the principles which we can defend today have been passed into the hands of a totalitarian state, will be too late. The ultimate solution, therefore, lies in our hands, in whether we are willing to pay in money, not in promises, for the security of democracy.

"The Place of a College Fraternity in the Life of a Student, in the Life of a University, in the Life of the Negro Race," 1939

Madame President, Sorors, and Friends of Delta Sigma Theta Sorority:

Gathered in your midst today are representatives of 107 chapters of a collegiate sorority, representing a membership of four thousand Negro women college graduates and undergraduates, located in various cities and towns extending from the Pacific to the Atlantic, from the Gulf of Mexico to the Great Lakes. Organized at Howard University in November 1912, we were the first Greek letter sorority established by Negro college women. From this humble but pretentious beginning almost twenty-six years ago, Delta Sigma Theta Sorority has spread its influence, ideals, and principles to all of the leading American colleges.

While sororities and fraternities are now commonly referred to by the college student and the public, few people understand the place of such an organization in the life of a student, or of a college or university, or in the life of a race of people. We notice the pins worn by members of various fraternities. Few of us are sufficiently learned in Greek to read the alphabet but have learned the letters appearing on the pins from seeing frequently the insignia worn by members. I doubt that the public realizes that the Greek letters are initial letters of secret mottoes forming a part of the basic ritual of the organization. A further doubt that is generally realized [is] that this ritual, which is usually a combination of Greek mythology, Biblical law, and idealistic thoughts, is the significant feature of a fraternity, that sets it apart as different from any other type of organization. The ritual defines the aims and objects of the sorority or fraternity, depicts its historical background, delineates its program of brotherly love and friendship, of scholastic excellence and quality of character and morals. The ritual is used in the initiation and is the background for the opening and closing ceremonies of the weekly chapter meetings. Beautifully written, full of high ideals and sentiments, the ritual serves to place the sorority or fraternity on a plane far above any other college organization or social club. No normal girl or boy could fail to derive benefit from constant exposure to such ideals. Each day, when the pin bearing the Greek letters representative of the fundamental principles of the sorority as set forth in the ritual, is placed by the member on her dress, she repledges herself to the ideals of her sorority.

Such an organization has a far-reaching and lasting effect upon the life of a student who in his sophomore year, pledges himself to the principles enunciated by his [or her] chosen fraternity. The scholastic standing of a student is of the foremost importance for admission to a college fraternity. No student can be initiated until the college or university has certified that his scholastic standing conforms with the requirements. Having been initiated, the scholastic record conforms with the requirements. Having been initiated, the scholastic record remains an important part of undergraduate fraternity life, because of campus inter-fraternal scholastic competition as well as competition from non-fraternity students. Records of the national Fraternity Conference and the results of a comparative study of the quality of academic work done by fraternity and non-fraternity students at Brown University show that during the last few years the scholarship average of fraternity men and women has been improving steadily and that their standing consistently equals or is a little better than that of the non-fraternity member.

In addition to inspiring and encouraging scholastic excellence, the sorority or fraternity teaches the young college student in a most practical manner his obligation to individuals and to Society. The average college student, in order to reach college, has been outstanding in his or her local high school and town career. She is frequently the pride of the family, the choicest flower of them all. Such a student comes to college with the purpose of furthering his or her own evolution from dependence to independence. In order, however, to make even the pledge club of a college fraternity, the student must demonstrate respect for the individual and collective rights of others; she must prove herself able to subvert self-interest to the benefit of the welfare of the group. Having proved herself capable of respecting the rights of the individual and sacrificing one's own desires and rights for the benefit of the group, she is qualified for admission to her chosen sorority. Once admitted, the process of developing social-mindedness continues at an even greater speed. The rating of a sorority or fraternity by the college or university authorities as well as in the minds of the public, depends upon the degree to which the sorority or fraternity is able to corral from its members complete obedience and united cooperation in the maintenance of scholastic, moral and societal standards. Government, whether by the State, the College, or by a group of sorors, is most successful when it prescribes the least; and government prescribes least when the individual embraces the spirit of its principles, instead of being forced to yield to the power of its command. The college fraternity or sorority attains this success in government not by vigilance committees, not by terror or threats, not by innumerable laws and regulations, but by instilling into its members a spirit of loyalty, of brotherly and sisterly affection, a flaming desire that the sorority or fraternity, not the individual, excel. Imbued with the spirit of the principles set forth in the ritual, the individual member learns that individual success is dependent upon group cooperation, that her sorority or his fraternity can attain no higher position than its weakest member; that while it is the inherent right, as well as the obligation of the individual, to further his or her evolution from dependence to independence, from self-interest to social-mindedness, in so doing she or he must respect the individual and collective rights of others.

The presence on a college or university campus of six or more such organizations, controlling by an intangible process, one those of us hardened to the world frequently deny any longer exists, controlling through the installation of ideals the conduct of their members, is of the greatest importance in the development of the educational process. Since man is to operate in life, with and in groups, the college or university must recognize, as an essential feature of its purposes, a properly organized and maintained student life, to which as large a degree of responsible control as possible should be delegated. Self-government and self-control are essentials to good citizenship, and therefore should be primary objectives of college training. The sorority and fraternity chapter, when they attain their full potentialities, present an unexcelled opportunity for discipline in group living, for the practice of self-government, for the development of leadership, for group cooperation through individual effort. The fact that as long as students who are members of a fraternity are nevertheless under the jurisdiction of the college, and the college has the ultimate responsibility for the student, means that when the college grants a sorority or fraternity the privilege of organizing and maintaining its own social life, such a grant constitutes only a delegation to the group of immediate responsibility for the social life of its members. The college or university has the right at any time to recall this delegation of responsibility. No instances of recall of authority delegated a Negro sorority or fraternity are known to me in the more than twenty years that I have actively been connected with the fraternity movement throughout the United States. This in itself clearly indicates the success with which Negro college boys and girls through their fraternities and sororities have governed themselves, provided for their own social life, adjusted their individual desires to the best welfare of the fraternity and the university, and integrated the group fraternity or sorority life with the college life, intellectually as well as socially, physically, and morally. Therefore, I say advisedly that through sorority and fraternity life on a college or university campus, the process of education is better achieved, because such life stimulates self-expression, fosters self-government, develops responsible leadership, encourages the attitudes and imparts the techniques needed for self-development, and strengthens zeal for service.

Each graduation presents to the various American cities a fresh group of young fraternity men and sorority women. Filled with the idealism of fraternity life, confident in their ability to succeed because of the degree of self-government attained by them in college, and equipped with scholastic achievements, they promptly affiliate with local graduate chapters, in the hope of finding there some remnant of college fraternity life to which to anchor their idealism and faith. In many of the smaller cities and towns these groups of graduate members of the various fraternities and sororities constitute the only source of cultural contact for the members and, through their efforts, for the entire community. They foster the presentation of artists, lectures, and other persons of talent and ability to an otherwise arid community. They are torch bearers of hope for thousands of young boys and girls, and struggling parents who see in them the fulfilment of their dreams. The contribution of such a graduate group of fraternity men and women can not be estimated in words or counted in dollars. Theirs is a human contribution beyond the realm of calculation.

In the larger cities the graduate fraternity and sorority frequently find themselves duplicating effort in an endeavor to function as a group in community life. Thus we find the "Go to High School, Go to College," and the "Guide Right" movements overlapping the work of national organizations equipped for vocational guidance. We find other groups undertaking health programs which are definitely the work of medical organizations, equipped by experience, training, and purpose best to administer to the public health. Other groups place their energies in emphasizing the importance in American life of Negro history, on work capably done by another national organization whose sole purpose is to study and disseminate facts concerning Negro history and achievement. As a result of this overlapping of effort by graduate chapters of the various fraternities and sororities, national organizations chartered for the purposes adopted by these fraternity and sorority groups, as well as the public, have criticized the college graduate for devotion to his fraternity rather than to the various organizations established to serve the varied social problems of the American Negro. Understandable as it is that college men and women, who in the most formative stages of their lives, have pledged devotion to the ideals of a fraternity, should continue in this devotion after graduation, it is nevertheless surprising that none of our college fraternities or sororities has defined the place of the graduate chapter in Negro life.

To begin with, the college graduate who has had the advantage of fraternity life integrated in the college or university life, should first of all recognize his responsibility to organized society. Whatever program he adopts should be subservient to that of good government and social progress, as was his college program required to be consistent with the program of the college or university that delegated authority to organize his own social life. Next, the nature of a program that the graduate fraternity member adopts must necessarily vary with the needs of the times. It must change with changing conditions and can not remain static in a dynamic world. Today, when the very existence of the American Negro, like that of other minority races, is being threatened, the program that we adopted ten years ago can not meet the requirements of a program looking forward to the world of tomorrow. Recently, when speaking to an audience, I chose a subject, "Coming Events Cast Their Shadows." I pointed out as the shadows that threatened the security of the American Negro: First, the segregation of the Negro members of the Methodist Episcopal Church. I say to you, as I stated to that audience, that when the largest protestant religious organization in America is willing publicly to declare such a position on its relation to the Negro members of its church; when it prefers union of its white members, North and South, to even a semblance of observance of the preachment that all men are the children of God the Father, members of the same mystical body of Christ and temples of the same Holy Ghost, a black shadow looms over the hopes of all Negro men and women in America. When the descendants of men and women who came to America because of religious persecution and who fought to preserve economic and religious freedom in their new found country, have so far forgotten why they call themselves Daughters of the American Revolution, as to close their walls to the world's greatest living voice because God placed it in a brown breast, I shudder as the shadows darken. When I realize that preparatory schools, colleges, universities, and especially professional schools that once freely admitted Negro students, have an impregnable waiting list when we apply; when I notice in my own State of Pennsylvania a dominant political party campaigning for votes on the platform that every candidate is white, native-born, and protestant; when I note men who have been declared liberals refusing to make pronouncements against racism, in spite of the darkness of these clouds, I read the handwriting on the wall.

Yes, the shadows that followed the Jew in Germany and Rumania to South America are overcasting the Negro in America. We who have for three hundred years lived in a democracy where the most rudimental principles of a democratic civilization were denied us are nevertheless aware that the future looms even darker than the past as the fate which overtook Europe threatens to overtake minorities in the United States. With such a situation imminent, can there be any doubt concerning the program that confronts college men and women in their fraternity and sorority life? The rampant spread of racism in American life must be stopped *now*. Achievement Weeks, Guide Right Programs, Go to College movements, preventative health measures, will be needless if we do not keep democracy alive in America by acting today. What should be our program to accomplish this? It should be a program of studied cooperation with national agencies equipped to combat racism.

Foremost in such an effort is adult education in the principles of economic security that underlie democratic principles. If by health education America has been able to cut the tuberculosis rate two-thirds, to eliminate 90 per cent of diphtheria, and almost abolish typhoid, then it can not be considered too great a task to educate men's minds to the facts that will secure their freedom. The public must be made to realize that periods of depression arise when private capital is withdrawn from industry because overproduction reduces or brings no return to the investor; that this can be averted only by controlled production and adequate return to capital; that the presence in our midst of no minority group creates economic problem[s], but that they are the creatures of an uncontrolled economy; that the promises of no one man can bring prosperity, but that the working out of the principles of economy underlying the structure of any country are dependent upon the combined efforts of all the people. The cause of economic insecurity and how it can be overcome must be made clear to all classes and all races, in language that each can understand, in order that America may await the orderly solution of the problem and not in despair turn over its freedom in exchange for the vain promises of a self-proclaimed Messiah.

The National Urban League, a pioneer in interpreting economic conditions, is the best equipped organization by experience and proven success to present to the industrialist and the working man the basic facts underlying economic recovery. We are fortunate to have such an established organization already in the principal cities of America, respected for its sound judgement and leadership. Fraternities and sororities, who have neither the accumulated experience nor training to direct adult education in the principles of economic security, should in my opinion confer with the officials of the National Urban League as to how the leadership of the fraternities can be used to effect the program of the League.

The second step in our program to combat racism in America should be education in tolerance. A recent article in the national *Educational Journal* reviewed a program established in the Garfield High school, of Detroit, Michigan, by its principal, Charles H. Daly, for the Racial Enrichment of the Curriculum. It was this article which brought forth general comment in American educational circles on our failure not only to teach the Negro facts concerning his own literature and history, but also the failure of our educational systems to enlighten the millions of children of other races in this country, concerning the culture of a people who constitute more than one-tenth of their population. A survey of the text books used by the children of the State of Mississippi found no reference to the Negro in the civics or history text books other than under the topic "Slavery." Another text used by the children of the State of Mississippi on prominent Americans, did not refer to a single Negro. If Mississippi has become aware of its deficiency in educating its white citizens concerning their Negro neighbors, is it not time that we Negroes in every city, town and state, awoke to the necessity of making Negro history an integral part of the curricula of every school?

The foundation for tolerance between people of varied races and religions is a mutual knowledge of the people and their religion. If we are all children of God, if He has breathed into each of us the breath of life, then there is enough of the Divine in each one of us to be a person in whom another can find something to admire. How many times have you not experienced a feeling of dislike for a man or woman whom you never intimately knew? Some chance, perhaps membership on a committee, association at work or common distress, brings you together and you find this person, whom you previously disliked, a very likeable chap. It is the person we do not know, whom we dislike. In all the people you know well, you can find admirable qualities. The same situation exists concerning the relation between races of people. The white man who says he hates a Negro never intimately knew one and never read an intelligent book about one. Yet we Negroes are doing little even now, in the face of the darkest shadows that have threatened our freedom since slavery, to educate Americans concerning our culture and contributions to American civilization. The Association for the study of Negro Life and History, under the capable and far-sighted leadership of Carter G. Woodson, has ready not only a wide and varied group of accredited publications on the Negro, but also has by reason of years of effort and study, accumulated experience in the best methods of disseminating these publications. No group of people is better equipped to assist the Association in its purposes than a college sorority or fraternity, the great mass of whose members are students, teachers, school directors, or parents of students. We are the source through which the work of the Association for the study of Negro Life and History can be most effectively realized. To sporadically, or annually, or daily attempt to duplicate the work of this established organization is no less than ridiculous. But to throw our resources back of its vital work in combating racial intolerance is our clear duty.

There is considerable difference of opinion among leaders of Negro thought regarding the third and my final point in a program to preserve our democratic institutions in this period of stress. There are those among us who think that at such a time we should lessen pressure for a fuller share of the rights [that are] legally ours for fear that by so doing we may arouse even greater racial hatred. Opposed to this line of thought is the steady and relentless effort being made by the N.A.A.C.P. to pen state-supported institutions of higher learning to Negro students or to provide for them an education equal to that provided white students. In my opinion, the N.A.A.C.P. is pursuing the only proper course. To begin with, we must be ever vigilant and watchful of our rights. Postponing action on a demand for fundamental rights will only result in the loss of greater rights. If we become inarticulate and inactive in pressing for the full benefits of a democratic government, it will be taken for granted that not only do no greater rights have to be given to us, but that the meagre benefits of a democracy that we now enjoy can be taken from us. There must be no compromise with reaction.

Furthermore, never was there a time when the conduct of America toward her minorities was subject to greater world criticism. Secretary Hull has been repeatedly embarrassed concerning his criticisms of Nazism and Fascism by the latter's retorts concerning the position of the Negro in the United States. The present administration can consistently take but one position concerning any legal demands by minorities. The time to strike is here. We, of the college fraternities and sororities, who represent the largest group of Negro intellectual power, reflect upon our own intelligence when we fail to give group support to the efforts of that militant organization, the N.A.A.C.P., which is leading the way in showing America its duty toward its own minorities.

Democratic institutions can be preserved only if the people are willing to pay the price. Those of us who would suffer the most by their loss must be willing to pay the greatest price for their continuance. Not only our future economic position but our existence in America depends upon our willingness to support those organizations, men and women, who through year[s] of accumulated experience and training are equipped to meet and overcome the onslaught of racism in America. Democracy must be defended today at any cost. Tomorrow, when the principles which we can defend today have passed into the hands of a totalitarian state, will be too late. Members of the Delta Sigma Theta Sorority, with your ninety-five chapters spread from border to border of the expanse of this great nation, with four thousand college trained women in their professions and businesses influencing the lives of thousands more, you can be the most potent force in overcoming the rampant spread of racism in America. Your years of experience on the college campus, having taught you that your program must be consistent with the welfare of the larger university group, you are therefore prepared to adjust your after college program to the welfare of your race. An opportunity for cooperation and integration of your program with that of national agencies equipped to meet the threat to democracy in America awaits you. I have no doubt that in your forthcoming deliberations you will devise means to meet this challenging opportunity.

"On the Status of the Philadelphia Negro," 1942

Mr. Poley, our distinguished guest, Roger Baldwin, members of the Committee on Race Relations of the Society of Friends, and my Friends:

I have been asked to talk with you tonight very briefly about the Status of the Philadelphia Negro, as a test of our faith in the Bill of Rights. Mr. Baldwin has forcefully and with rare insight portrayed the dangers we face in a misplaced patriotism threatening the security guaranteed us under the Bill of Rights. I wish, however, to call to your attention the fact that our appreciation of these rights, having been systematically weakened by years of unconcern as to whether they were enjoyed by all the people, has rendered the majority unfit to protect itself in a time of crisis, such as war, from the loss of these rights, so fundamental to free men.

For to understand the Bill of Rights is to understand what it means to be free. That there might be no uncertainty about the meaning of freedom, those men who in 1776 had fought for freedom, like those who in the thirteenth century produced the Magna Carta and in the eighteenth century the Bill of Rights, passed by the English Parliament, so the men of America who had won a glorious revolution wanted no uncertainty about what they had fought, one hungry, ragged, cold, and shed their blood. Determined that removal of the burdens imposed upon them by the British government should not be the only result of the hard, long war they had fought, but that the rights which they cherished and believed every man was by God endowed should be preserved not only for them but for all men in all times, the men of 1776 began a campaign against the adoption of the Constitution itself because it contained no guarantee of these rights. Fearful that this document might strip from them the ideals which made it possible for them to fight against over-whelming odds, concerned that the rights of free men might be lost in the interpretation of the Constitution, they demanded a charter in which to anchor their faith in men's right to freedom.

Their demand first successfully expressed itself in state action. Even before the Declaration of Independence in 1776, Virginia adopted a Dec-laration of Rights. Other states followed. The Pennsylvania Convention, with Benjamin Franklin at its head, adopted a Bill of Rights in July 1776. But the Founding Fathers, assembled in the Constitutional Convention of 1787, having lived through weak governments, were more concerned about a strong government to insure stability than about guarantees of freedom. On the other hand, the men who had borne the arms, whose families had suffered privation and want, demanded not only a consti-tution as a symbol of strength and unity, but also a Bill of Rights as a symbol of their freedom. The demand of the common men and women of America for more than order and authority, for a Bill of Rights defin-ing the privileges of free men, was realized when on December 15, 1791, Virginia ratified the first ten Amendments to the Constitution. These restrictions against encroachment on particular rights, and those safe-guards between the people and the government, although whipped into form by Madison, were not the product of any single mind or group of minds. They were the product of hundreds of years of man's struggle to create an appreciation of those rights with which God has endowed every man into whom he has breathed the breath of life, God-given rights, which no man can surrender and which no man who believes in God dare deny another.

To what extent have we in Philadelphia respected these inalienable rights guaranteed by natural law to black men as well as white men?

I am mindful of the fact that the Bill of Rights constitutes restric-tions on the power of government. These limitations, framed in the negative, express anxiety for freedom from the possible arbitrary powers of government. This freedom, which the framers of the Amendments individually believed in and accepted, they feared might be lost through the strength of the sovereignty, even if it be named a democracy. They failed, however, to anticipate that rights can be withheld as effectively by barriers established by a majority of the people, these customs having the strength of laws as effective as if the laws were passed by Congress or any other legislative body.

The first guarantee of the Bill of Rights respects Freedom of Religion. How free are Negroes in Philadelphia to select a religion according to the dictate of their own hearts? They may, with few exceptions, join only those churches that have established separate branches for christians [sic] of dark complexions. If the faith that appeals to them has not such a branch, in most cases, they may not become members, or even worshippers. Churches that send missionaries to the dark continent of Africa to the teeming heathens of the Orient, to the isles of the seas, social workers to feed the starving Europeans, will not share their spiritual fellowship with their dark neighbors. The Bill of Rights has not been infringed by Congress, nor by the Legislature, but it has been successfully stultified by the conduct of the christian majority. The common people of the eighteenth century, who conceived the dignity of man and gave effect to it by adopting the first ten Amendments to the Constitution, little dreamed that a century and a half later their own acts would be nullified as effectually by the common people for whom they fought and died to give them a free country, as by any tyrant.

What about the press? How free is it? The day of the pamphleteer has gone. We are dependent upon newspapers to create public opinion through the press. Recently the Philadelphia newspapers did a magnificent job in helping cause the United States Housing Authority to return the Richard Allen Homes to the low income people for whom they were built. We heartily commend the press for this unselfish service. Would that the press were always as concerned about the rights of the underprivileged masses of Philadelphia. If they had exposed the men responsible for the mass arrests in North Philadelphia and demanded an investigation of this unheard of abuse of the right to freedom, the liberty of all the people would be more secure. May their active interest in the Richard Allen Homes be the beginning of an honest crusade for freedom and justice for all the people.

The Second Amendment gives to the people the right to bear arms. Philadelphia is to be criticized, along with the rest of America, in not insisting that its Negro citizens be permitted to bear arms in every branch of the armed forces of the nation. By refusing to accept the services of Negro men in the United States Marine Corps in any capacity, and the Navy, other than as menials, we destroy national unity and make a mockery of an all-out effort to win a war to preserve democracy. Where are the Philadelphia press, the church, the society to preserve freedom and democracy, on this issue? Are their voices too weak to be heard or their faith too little to dare speak?

Passing on the Fourth Amendment, which guarantees security of the home from search and seizure, I am immediately reminded of Harry Carpenter, the Negro who was charged with treason. He said:

> You Negroes are—fools for going over there fighting those Japs. You go over, get all shot up and come back and get kicked in the pants just the same.

His arrest is typical of the manner in which Negro homes are subject to unwarranted search and seizure. Carpenter, a man never before arrested, regularly employed, living with his wife and family, was sitting in the home of a friend, where twelve persons, all employed, were assembled, enjoying a friendly game of cards. Suddenly, there entered, without warrant or other legal process, two white officers in plain clothes and a colored military police sergeant in uniform. It is now admitted that the wrong house was entered and that the soldiers being sought did not frequent this house. Had the process guaranteed by the Bill of Rights been pursued, these facts would have been ascertained and Carpenter would not have gotten in an argument which resulted in the first charge ever made in America of treason against a black man. Nevertheless, no action has been taken, no criticism raised concerning the unlawful and unwarranted entry of the house where Carpenter was visiting. Excitement over his alleged treasonable conduct, now reduced to sedition, has wiped away all concern over the protection guaranteed by this Fourth Amendment.

But war hysteria should not be attributed as the sole cause for loss of the right of Negroes to be free from unwarranted search in their homes. To those of us who talk with and live among the Negro masses, it is not unfamiliar to hear the expression, "The law came in." By this they mean that an officer clothed with the authority of the law knocked on their door, entered when it was opened, or knocked it down if it was not opened. I distinctly recall the case of Samuel Shelton, a respectable colored man who owned his own home at. . . . Stiles Street where he lived comfortably with his wife. One evening about three years ago officers without a warrant broke the beautiful plate glass of his front door, rushed into the house and began to search for an escaped criminal, whom they had heard was hiding in this house. Mr. Shelton was taking his bath. He had locked the door. When the officers knocked, he refused to open the door as he was in no condition to receive an invited or uninvited guest, and he was too excited to know what to do. Within a few seconds the bathroom door was broken down. The officers ordered him to put on his clothes, dragged him into their waiting car and put him under arrest. After being put to the expense of employing counsel, and the humiliation of an arrest, not to mention the mental and physical anguish and pain suffered by Mr. and Mrs. Shelton, Mr. Shelton was discharged. The officers who made the arrest without a warrant were not even reproved but only ordered to replace the plate glass in the front door and the bathroom door.

You ask, is not this an exceptional case? How often, if ever, has such happened or since? From my own experience of fourteen years at the bar, I can say it is a constant occurrence which our people in congested areas repeatedly experience. The right of the people to be secure in their persons, houses, papers, and effects against unreasonable search and seizure still remains on the statute books as the law of this commonwealth. But so callous have we in Philadelphia become to the constant infringement of this right, that not an individual or an organization has publicly protested against the unlawful entry of the home where Harry Carpenter was arrested. Protests have been loud against his being charged with treason or sedition. But we have not been heard to protest against this flagrant abuse of the right to be secure in one's home against unwarranted entry.

The Fifth Amendment provides among other things, as you know, that no person shall be compelled in any criminal case to be a witness against himself, or be deprived of life, liberty, or property without due process of law. To be compelled to be a witness against one's self is not the infrequent procedure of the prosecution in a criminal case, when a defendant's guilt is established by his own confession. Doubtless you recall that about three years ago there was a brutal hold up resulting in the murder of a druggist at 17th and Montgomery Avenue. It was alleged that two colored men committed the crime. For days various men were apprehended and examined as suspects. Finally, some time after the crime, a young colored boy was arrested, thoroughly grilled and examined, but he steadfastly denied that he had anything to do with this crime. The so-called tip that caused this boy's arrest was the statement from an alleged accomplice that this boy was a participant in the crime, but the latter insisted upon his innocence.

All of a sudden, weeks later, newspapers carried the story that this boy "broke" and had signed a confession. In fact, he did more. The detectives who "broke" this boy took photographs of his alleged re-enactment of the crime, photographing every step, stage, and detail of the crime, the place where it happened, the spot where the man was shot, how the boy entered the drug store and how he left. He was promptly indicted for first degree murder and in due course came up for trial to face [a] first degree murder jury.

The Commonwealth was prepared with the alleged confession, the photographs and statements taken by the detectives, when suddenly it was discovered and proven beyond a doubt that this boy was a confined prisoner in a penal institution, serving a sentence for another crime at the time of this brutal murder, and was in jail and could not have possibly committed the murder which he had always stoutly denied, although a confession had been wrung from him. The defendant, of course, was discharged. What happened to the detectives who had forced him to confess a crime against himself? *Nothing.* They are still "breaking" crimes by "voluntary" confessions. It was only last week that a colored defendant named William Young confessed to a murder. A few days later he was brought into court, showing visible signs of torturous beatings. The Honorable James Gay Gordon held that the confession had been extorted and forced by threats and cruel beating of the prisoner. His Honor, Judge Gordon, ruled the confession not worth the paper upon which it was written and held the detectives, McCormick and Murphy, for the Grand Jury. But rare, indeed, is the case where the defendant has the opportunity to obtain counsel before the physical evidence of beating has disappeared. Usually he is held incommunicado, "on ice," until he has recovered from the severe beating to which he has been subjected in order to obtain the confession which, when introduced in court, is always stated to be "a voluntary confession of the defendant, John Doe, made of his own free will and accord, after having been duly warned that whatever he says will be used against him at the time of his trial in court."

Equally reprehensible is our failure to protect the Negro masses from the deprivation of their liberty, without due process of law. Who in Philadelphia does not hang his head in shame when he recalls the mass arrests in 1941 in Northern Philadelphia of over two hundred Negroes without warrants or probable cause, who were held in jail for twenty-four to forty-eight hours? Every colored person in this neighborhood, on the streets, in a store, about to enter his home, was arrested on the basis that, because of frequent pocket-book snatching, attacks and assaults, it was necessary to round up every colored man or woman on these streets. Coincidentally, if not particularly significant, is the fact that a political campaign had just closed in which the people of this neighborhood had dared assert their political freedom.

The Fifth Amendment also secures the right to enjoy property ownership. The courts of our city have given Negro property owners all the protection which the law provides. But, as Negroes who want to buy or rent decent homes frequently say: "Who wants to buy a law suit?" That is what most of us buy when we purchase a home in what is designated as a white neighborhood. If the mortgagee does not call the mortgage or refuse to place it when the color of the purchaser is revealed, the hoodlums will break the windows, throw bottles filled with acid in the doors and make life so miserable that we cannot enjoy the newly purchased home. As you well know, recently in North Philadelphia the head of Girard College, two of the leaders of the white clergy in that neighborhood and others formed together to purchase every house that was offered for sale in the neighborhood, to prevent Negroes from entering. The right of colored people to purchase homes, to live peacefully in them, to enjoy the attributes of ownership, has been limited and defined in Philadelphia, not by restrictive covenants which may be held unconstitutional. No, we have taken no chance on the courts fairly and honestly ruling in favor of the Negro; we in Philadelphia have left the law on the statute books and put the Negro in restricted areas either by refusing to sell or finance for him property in certain areas or running him out if he bought it.

The test of our belief in the Bill of Rights is the extent to which these rights are enjoyed by the minority. The object of these restrictions on the government was to assure the common man the enjoyment of certain God-given rights, outlined in the first ten amendments to the Constitution. If their object is to protect the average man, then the acid test as to whether or not he is protected is found, not in the rights enjoyed by the majority, which are incidental, but in the rights enjoyed by the minority, which are essential. When the minority of our people can choose their religion, but may not, with few exceptions, exercise their choice except in churches set apart for the spiritual fellowship of black men only, when their homes and persons are not safe from unwarranted entry and seizure, when they are frequently compelled to be witnesses against themselves, and when they are deprived of their liberty without due process of law, and are denied by organized effort enjoyment of property rights, the majority have lost faith in the belief that all men are endowed by their Creator with certain inalienable rights, and having lost this faith, put in jeopardy the right to be free men themselves.

Fragment, "Concerning the Loyalty Pledge Statement of Security Principles and the House Un-American Activities," 1947–1948

. . . daily living in every state of these United States.

There is no evidence in our history that our faith and freedom of thought and expression is not well founded. In fifty years the most violent dissidence of political expression has been permitted. It is not apparent why today the American people should be so wanting in courage, so fearful of our foundations as to fall victims to the frightened men inside and outside of government as evidenced by the Loyalty Pledge Statement of Security Principles and the House Un-American Activities Committee. Persecution for opinions may soon reach a point in America never before attained. Today it threatens the fundamental right of every American to freedom of conscience and expression.

The American Negroes are not beggars for privileges but rather we are leaven in the bread of [the] American way of life, prickers of the conscience of the people, sentinels of justice—Yes we are God's chosen children, imported to this land and permitted to multiply in the midst of disease, ignorance, undernourishment, unemployment—in ghettos on the other side of the railroad tracks called South Street in my town,

Jefferson Avenue in your City and Lenox Avenue in New York. When the American people recognize us and all others whom they have denied, as God's children endowed by our Creator with the same rights as all people who inhabit the earth, then and then only will she prove herself capable of leading the people of the world to eternal peace and security.

"To Secure These Rights," 1948

This title was borrowed from the well-known section of the Declaration of Independence which reads, "Man is endowed by his Creator with certain inalienable rights. Among these are life, liberty and the pursuit of happiness. *To secure these rights*, governments are instituted among men." Twenty-five thousand copies of this report were printed and distributed by the United States Government Printing Office. Significant as are the findings and recommendations of the report, they cannot overshadow the significance of the President of the United States appointing a committee of private citizens to determine to what extent existing laws are inadequate to protect the civil rights of the American people; and the forthright report of this committee which exposes our shortcomings and recommends ways to correct them; and the approval with which the public received the report as indicated by the fact that the twenty-six thousand copies printed by the United States Government were exhausted within two days after their release. *Only in America* would the head of the government, by executive order, charge private citizens with critically examining the civil rights of the people of the country; *only in America* would a committee of private citizens dare render such a critical report of government itself and *only in America* would such a report be received with great approval by private citizens and government. The action of President Truman in appointing the committee, the nature of the report rendered by the committee, and the general acceptance of the recommendations by the American people are clearly indicative of the fact that we are still a *free people in America*. Only in a free government may people continue to appraise the adequacies of their institutions.

President Truman, upon receiving the report, said, "I am going to read and study this report with great care and I recommend to all my countrymen that they do the same." Every American should follow the advice of our President and read this report. It points out that twice before in American history the nation has found it necessary to review the state of its civil rights. The first time was between 1776 and 1791 when we were drafting the Declaration of Independence on down to the time of the writing of the Constitution and the Bill of Rights. The second time was when the Union was temporarily torn asunder over the question of whether it could exist half slave and half free. We have today come to a time for a third re-examination of the situation and a sustained drive ahead.

Our reason for this statement is based first on moral grounds. The gap between what we state we believe to be our American heritage and how we act in daily practice toward one another in America is so great that it is creating a kind of moral dry rot which eats away our democratic beliefs. There are times when the difference between what we preach about civil rights and what we practice becomes absolutely shocking. The fact that many white people and many black people have not been allowed to vote in some states has made a mockery of our laws guaranteeing universal suffrage. As a result of this denial of the right to vote to a majority of population in the poll tax states where 10 percent of the potential vote in 1944 voted, many men in public and private life do not believe that these people are capable of voting. The fact that here in Philadelphia, the birthplace of our Constitution, the City Fathers attempted to prevent people from assembling in Independence Square, to protest against universal military training, because the views of the protestors are not shared by the legal guardians of this sacred cradle of liberty, is a threat to that freedom of assembly and of speech guaranteed by the Constitution itself. Moreover, the fact that many people share the opinion that any person opposed to universal military training is opposed to our system of government and should not be permitted to voice his opinion in Independence Square, is proof that our beliefs in one of the most fundamental guarantees of the Constitution has been weakened by repeated denials until many of us justify such a refusal without realizing that in so doing we threaten the foundation of our own liberty. Such situations destroy our democratic processes and beliefs.

Second, now is the time to read this report and re-examine the state of our civil rights for our own economic protection. The withholding of jobs and business opportunities from some people does not make more jobs and business opportunities for others but rather drags down the whole economic level. You cannot sell an electric refrigerator to a family that cannot pay an electric bill. Economic progress demands that the whole nation move forward at the same time. Job boycott and discrimination is a cancer, malignant growth in the economic body of the nation. We cannot feed the people of Europe and Asia and supply our own citizens with full market baskets unless we make full use of all our resources. The report of the President's Committee on Civil Rights indicates clearly with specific illustrations that the withholding of jobs and business opportunities from some people because of their race, national origin, or religion has cost this country in money, production, inventive genius, and leadership a price beyond estimate. The United States can no longer afford this heavy drain upon its human health and upon its national accomplishments.

Third, the protection of our civil rights is vital to the mental health of our citizens. Experiences which result in frustration, insecurity, fear, and hate undermine the mental health of individuals and create an unhealthy relationship between persons and groups. Such persons and groups create subjects for investigation and witch hunts, which lead eventually to purges and concentration camps. At no time has it been more important to insure the mental health of the American people [with] the social conditions necessary for which the psychiatrists tell us are the four basic rights stressed in the report of the President's Committee viz.,

The Right to safety and security and security [*sic*] of the person;

The Right to citizenship and its privileges;

The Right to freedom of conscience and expression;

The Right to equality of opportunity.

Because these rights affect mental health, we should strongly urge the responsible government authority promptly to take action to secure them to our citizens. A mentally healthy people could not have produced a Hitler nor have permitted Nazism to flourish. A mentally healthy people in the United States won't let it happen here!!!

"The Responsibility of
Minorities," 1948

The Great American experiment in Civil Liberties has been forged by peoples from many lands and continents, from innumerable nations and races. Our population has come by immigration from four continents. We are essentially a nation of minorities who only become a majority when groups of minorities are combined. Beginning with colonial days we had two great streams of immigrants; the first was from Northern or Western Europe and the second, beginning with the Civil War and continuing to the end of World War I, was from Southern and Eastern Europe. The majority of the early population was Protestant, although some were Catholics and a small number Jews. In the second group came a larger number of Catholics and Jews. Southern European immigrant groups are today a minority group in relation to older, English-speaking immigrants. But they are part of the white majority in relation to the Negro community. Catholics and Jews are a part of the white majority in relation to the Negro community but a part of a minority when considered beside the dominant majority of Caucasian English-speaking Protestants in the United States. Yet this majority of white Protestants is but a combination of minorities when we consider the cleavage in many communities between Baptist and Methodist, Fundamentalists and Reformist, Jehovah's Witnesses and followers of innumerable cults and Divines.

Statistics are always dull and uninteresting but it may not bore you, but help me to present a clear picture of the diversity of our population and its many minorities to state that *one* out of every *four* Americans is today either a foreign-born white or the child of foreign-born white parents; that one out of every *five* white Americans speaks a language other than English in his home; that one in every ten Americans is a Negro; that over a million and a quarter Mexicans or persons of Mexican descent live in the United States, mostly in Texas and California; that 400,000 American Indians live mostly on reservations in the West and that almost 300,000 Chinese and Japanese live in the United States, mostly on the West Coast until after the evacuation incident of World War II.

By reason of this great variance in our population, different relations have arisen among the groups and individuals, not always reflecting our pronounced American belief in equality. Basic to this belief is a more fundamental belief that all men are created by one God, therefore in His sight they are brothers and entitled to equality of opportunity by man and groups of men in society. In order to insure the rights of the various minorities of which our country consisted from its infancy, James Madison, in 1789, introduced seventeen constitutional amendments protecting civil liberty. The Congress approved twelve which were then submitted to the states for ratification. Ten of the twelve were *ratified* and became our federal Bill of Rights.

I do not need here to enumerate what are the rights protected by ten amendments. You are well acquainted with the fact that these amendments are prohibitions against the federal government violating such fundamental rights as freedom of religion, speech, press, assembly, petition, unreasonable search and seizure, right to trial by jury. I desire rather to call to your attention the fact that the framers of the Bill of Rights knew that its brief list of civil liberties was not complete. The Bill of Rights of many states contained much more detailed and a longer declaration of civil liberties than those appearing in these amendments. Therefore, the founding fathers included in the Bill of Rights a provision known as the Ninth Amendment, which provides: "The enumeration in the Constitution, of certain rights, shall not be construed to deny nor disparage others retained by the people."

What are these rights retained by the people? I should classify them as follows:

1) The right to safety and security of the person. Certainly every man and woman has a right to life, the day and the hour of the end of life is in God's hands. Yet in our country so insecure has been the life of certain of our people that in the decade from 1936 to 1946 thirty-six individuals were lynched. The fear and insecurity which arouse in the breasts of the minority who were primarily the subjects of the hideous crime of lynching spread its curse upon other minorities by weakening their sense of responsibility to protect every man in his right to life and security. It made possible the evacuation from their homes of 100,000 Japanese at a time when our civil courts were functioning and our country was not under marshall [martial] law. The denial of the fundamental rights of trial by jury to those minorities can happen to other minorities tomorrow. It is the responsibility of all citizens and particularly to those groups who by reason of differences in national origin, race, or religion have been treated as a people apart—a minority—to create and preserve a public opinion which insists upon the generous and whole-hearted support of the spirit as well as the letter of the Bill of Rights, by which our civil liberties are protected.

2) The second right retained by the people is the right to freedom of conscience and expression. I am not unaware that in a world becoming increasingly divided, that our government must take all rational precautions against acts which threaten or seem to threaten our national security and existence. We need not, however, create a police state to escape a police state. It can make little difference to the citizen who loses his liberty and dignity as a human being whether his loss came from an enemy or from a native oppressor who subverts *democratic* government in the guise of protecting it.

There is in our history no evidences that our faith in freedom of thought and speech is not well founded. Jefferson, in his inaugural address, laid down a foundation for this freedom when he said "If there be any among us, those who wish to dissolve the Union, or to change its Republican form let them stand undisturbed as monuments of the safety with which error of opinion may be tolerated when reason is left free to combat it." Following this doctrine for one hundred and fifty years, the most violent dissidence of political expression has been allowed, not only as a monument to "the safety with which error of opinion may be tolerated when reason is left free to combat it" but in the firm belief that "the ultimate good desired is better reached by free trade in ideas."

It is now apparent that the American people have become so wanting in courage and skeptical of our foundations of government as to fall victims to the fears of frightened men inside and outside of government. The Group for Advancement of Psychiatry states that this fear is due to failure to protect the civil rights of our citizens. Experiences that result in frustration, insecurity, fear, and hate undermine the mental health of individuals and create unhealthy relationships between persons and groups. A mentally healthy people could not have produced a Hitler, nor a Mussolini, nor a Thomas Committee. Insecurity of the person, of the job, of life, produces fear, which in turn, results in investigations, witch hunts, public hearings, purges, gestapos, and concentration camps. There are alarming signs that persecution for opinion, if not soon curbed, may reach a point never before attained in American history. The more alarming aspects of the situation today include the Loyalty Order of last spring, the more recent, "Statement of Security Principles" by the department of State and the performance of the Un-American Activities Committee. It is the right and heritage of every American freely to form political opinions and to express them; when accused of an offense, to be presented with the charges against him, to be confronted by his accusers and given an opportunity to defend himself before a jury of his own peers, cloaked with the presumption of innocence and not the presumption of guilt. But the procedure followed by the Un-American Committee and that prescribed by the Loyalty Order and of the "Statement of Security Principles" are such as to subject the citizen to intimidation and abuse without redress and to expose another great minority, two million federal workers, to loss of reputation and livelihood, without the opportunity to defend their honor or their jobs.

3) The third right, which I shall discuss, retained by the people, is the right to equality of opportunity.

(a) The right to work is a prerequisite to the right to life. How can a man provide food for himself and his family if, because of God given differences in color, nationality, or his own religious convictions, he cannot find work. Prejudice produces no wealth. Discrimination is a fool's economic paradise.

(b) The right to rent or buy a house to protect one from the elements of nature is an equally fundamental right which is denied large segments in our society by restrictive covenants or the blatant refusal of banks and other financial institutions to afford credit to Mexicans, Japanese, Indians, Jews, Negroes, and other of the numerous minorities that constitute America.

(c) The right to an education is basic to man's need and desire to improve his cultural, religious, and economic status. Yet millions of Americans cannot attend the schools best fitted to prepare them for citizenship because of the badge of minority status.

I might continue to enumerate the denials of equality of opportunities not characteristic of any section of the United States but experienced throughout the nation by citizens of this country because of their race, religion, or national origin. I can never come to New York City to spend a night in a hotel without fear of refusal. Even though I carry a written confirmation of my reservation, I may encounter hours of waiting and disagreeable argument before the room assigned is given to me. To obtain a bed in a hospital is even more difficult in the North or South, in the East or West. Recently a distinguished diplomat of dark complexion, the Haitian Ambassador to the United States, was ordered from the airport in Nashville, Tennessee, because he took a seat. So varied is our population, so diverse the relationships between the groups, that one cannot describe even in so monumental a work as the *American Dilemma*, what may be the inequalities experienced by a member of one of the numerous minorities that constitute our heterogeneous population.

I am, however, a firm believer in a divine purpose for all the problems that face man in his daily concerns and irritating duties. The division of the American population into diverse minorities has its purpose. We are leaven in the bread of the American way of life; the central theme of which is the importance of the individual person. Stemming from this principle is the obligation to build social institutions that will guarantee equality of opportunity to all men, and the basis of which is a fundamental belief that man was created by God in his image. We, in America, have conquered nature—we have harnessed the waters, spanned the seas by air and boat, tunneled the mountains and extracted the wealth of the earth, smashed the atom and in a ball the size of my palm developed a bomb that can destroy man and his discoveries, but we have never been able to breathe into a test tube the breath of human life. We are forced to acknowledge God as the sole creator of man. Thus our American heritage places prime importance on the dignity and integrity of man, the son of God, who is the father of all mankind. Yes, we are all the children of God, each possessing some divine characteristic, that resembles his image. It is the duty and responsibility of those millions who compose the various minorities in America continuously to prick the conscience of the majority by our daily actions [to] secure that all men enjoy those "rights which shall not be construed to be denied nor disparaged others." Yes, we minorities are God's chosen people, transported to this land and permitted to multiply in the midst, frequently, of disease, ignorance, undernourishment, unemployment, in ghettos on the wrong side of the railroad track or of Park Avenue.

When we minorities unite our strength to protect, safeguard, and secure the rights endowed all the people, then and only then will America prove herself capable of leading the people of the world to eternal peace and security.

"Progress Made in Civil Rights in the United States Since the Publication of *To Secure These Rights*," ca. 1958

The change in the climate of public opinion in the United States regarding civil rights is, in my opinion, the most outstanding feature of the ten years since the publication of *To Secure These Rights*. The fact that the Governors of twelve states, each of whom has heavy responsibilities consuming all of his energy and time, have, nevertheless, taken the time to meet together to discuss further progress in securing civil rights is in itself evidence of the support their purpose has at the grass roots. Nor could the legislatures of these states have passed laws against discrimination had not they known that their constituents, in the main, supported their so doing. The decisions of the United States Supreme Court outlawing segregation in travel, various restrictions on the free exercise of the right of franchise, and the doctrine of separate but equal are not to be attributed to the election returns, but rather to a changed climate of opinion in this country.

What has produced this change? The farsightedness of President Harry S. Truman in appointing fifteen private citizens to examine the status of civil rights in the United States, and charged with the responsibility of making a report of its studies and in particular recommendations of more adequate means and procedures for the protection of the civil rights of the people of the United States laid the ground work and initiated the forces that are largely responsible for the change in public opinion. The Report, while extremely critical of [the] government, Mr. Truman caused [it] to be published at government expense, it being thereafter widely reprinted. For the first time in the history of this country there appeared, under the aegis of the President of the United States, a factual, indisputable record of the great discrepancy between what we in the United States say we believe and how we act. The complacency of our free society was shocked into action and thousands of voluntary committees, groups, and organizations began studying the Report, and developing plans and programs to make practices in their respective communities and the nation conform to our democratic pronouncements. As a result sufficient support was given to City Councils in more than thirty cities and the legislatures of twelve states to pass laws against discrimination. The incorporation of fair play, which most Americans deeply respect, in public policy through ordinances, statutes, or clearly stated policy in these cities and states has given strength to the courageous and support to the timid citizens of good will throughout the United States. We have, therefore, seen that a vast majority of Americans, having respect for law and a sense of fair play, have welcomed the enactment of a law against discrimination, which gives them the opportunity to do what they know to be just and right, but which they did not have the courage to do in the face of anticipated community or neighborhood criticism.

The precipitation of the United States into world leadership has had a profound effect upon civil rights. The man on the street, as well as the experts in the State department, realize that we cannot hope to influence the thinking of the people of the world to choose the democratic way of life, as opposed to totalitarianism, unless we prove by our daily conduct that democracy works at home. Thus for the first time since the ignominious Hayes Compromise of 1877, federal troops were sent to Little Rock in 1957 to protect the civil rights of Negroes, as defined by the United States Supreme Court in its epic making decision of May 17, 1954 (*Brown et al. v. Board of Education*, 347 U.S. 483). The mobs at Little Rock and the rise of the White Citizens Councils were no new phenomena in the life of the Negro. New, however, to the Negro and their detractors was the climate of opinion in the nation, which realizing that world respect for our democracy depends upon the extent to which we make freedom the right of every man, demanded that the President act, even by sending federal troops to protect the rights of eight Negro children.

The McCarthy episode has also had its effect upon the thinking of the American people regarding civil rights. When the Senator had over played the communist scare and shown his real self before the millions of television viewers, he was finished. The people began to realize the damage McCarthy had done in breaking down the sanctions and safeguards guaranteeing the rights of the individual by due process. The intellectual, whom McCarthy identified as the trouble maker, the fellow traveler, as well as the uneducated, who were bewildered and confused, not knowing why they were before a Congressional Committee, now knew that the prejudice which identified them with an unpopular cause is only a short step from the Hitler method of identifying in similar method any group, in order to gain control of the machinery of government. The American people, belatedly and slowly, have awakened to the realization that the denial of the fundamental rights guaranteed by the constitution to any one group is but a stepping stone to the denial of them to another group, be they of different religious, national, or racial backgrounds. The urgent task that confronts the nation is to bring speedily to the understanding of the people in every section of this country, before too many "little rocks" have destroyed our world reputation and freedom to act, the knowledge that "To Secure These Rights" to all of the heterogeneous elements of our population, we cannot possibly have a broader base than that which includes all the people, with all their rights and with equal power to maintain their rights.

"Founders Day Address," 1963

Dr. Manley, Members of the Board of Trustees, Members of the Faculty, Students and Friends of Spelman College: I consider it a privilege and honor to have been invited to deliver the Founders Day Address at your renowned institution. The high academic standing of Spelman is recognized not only by your membership in the Southern Association of Colleges and Schools, and the appearance of your College on the approved list of the Association of American Universities, as well as the American Association of University Women, but more important by the distinction attained in the life of our country by too many of your graduates for time to permit me to enumerate.

When Spelman College was established on April 11, 1881, only sixteen years after the Civil War, both Negroes and concerned whites, such as your founders, *Sophia B. Packard* and *Harriet E. Giles,* realized that the Emancipation had only freed the Negro from physical shackles and that if the mind of the Negro was to be freed so that he could develop the ability and will to secure for himself and posterity the rights guaranteed under that Constitution of the Bill of Rights, emphasis must be placed upon education. At the beginning, as evidenced by the training provided the eleven students of the first class of your college, who were "eager to learn to read the Bible and write well enough to send letters to their children," the courses of study involved only the most rudimentary elements such as learning to read, write, and count. From this meager start developed classes in sewing, cooking, millinery, nurse training, but as public education began to fulfill these needs, Spelman, along with similar Negro institutions, began to train for leadership.

From your College and other Negro colleges and universities came most of our professional men and women who have assumed leadership at the local and national level[s]. There is indeed little racial strategy today which was not to some degree developed by them, including the pickets and sit-ins. In 1913 [*sic*] my uncle, Doctor Nathan F. Mossell, a graduate of Lincoln University, class of 1879 and of University of Pennsylvania Medical School, class of 1882, from which latter institution he was the first Negro to receive a degree from any department, having protested in vain to the Mayor of Philadelphia against the showing of *The Birth of a Nation* led more than a thousand Negroes in a march from the heart of the Negro population to the center of the city, where the theatre was located. This tumultuous demonstration broke up the show. Moreover, the relatively small number of colored men and women who were *trained* at the eastern and western colleges and universities made notable contributions. Among these were Doctor W.E.B. Dubois, the first historian to study sympathetically and scientifically Negro communities and institutions; Carter G. Woodson, who dedicated his life to recording and preserving Negro History; Abram Harris in Economics; E. Franklin Frazier in Sociology; Ralph Bunche in Political Science; Charles Houston, who brought the first successful civil rights actions, taught and gave inspiration, which produced Thurgood Marshall and his volunteer staff of consultants.

It is my studied opinion that had it not been for the continuous, never ending efforts and demands of the Negroes in America to secure the rights guaranteed by the fundamental law of this nation, the United States might never have even approached the goals set for this country in the Constitution and Bill of Rights. Let me remind you that when the founding fathers wrote:

> We hold these truths to be self-evident, that all men are created equal, that they are endowed by their Creator with cer-

tain inalienable Rights, that among these are Life, Liberty and the Pursuit of Happiness. That to secure these rights governments are instituted among Men, deriving their just powers from the consent of the governed.

only a limited number of white, protestant, rich men enjoyed these rights and this privileged class governed without the consent of the rest of the population.

Nowhere was voting and office holding open to all men.

In New Hampshire voters had to be Protestant tax payers.

In Massachusetts voters had to own freehold estates yielding an income of three pounds a year or have a personal estate worth sixty pounds.

Virginia limited the right of franchise to a male who owned twenty-five acres of land, properly planted, with a house thereon at least twelve feet square on a foundation, or who possessed fifty acres of wild land, or a freehold or estate interest in a lot in some town established by law.

Georgia limited the right to vote to any white male inhabitant owning ten pounds of property and paying a tax, but such a person was required to vote or be subject to a fine of five pounds for failure thereof.

It should further be noted that the right to vote did not carry the right to hold office. To qualify for the lower House of Legislature,

In New Hampshire a voter was eligible only if he was Protestant and owned an estate of one hundred pounds.

In Massachusetts a voter was eligible if he owned real estate with a value of one hundred pounds or personal estate of two hundred pounds. In addition, he was required to swear that he believed in the Old and New Testaments and in divine inspiration.

In South Carolina a representative had to own five hundred acres of land and ten (10) Negro slaves or real estate worth 150 pounds sterling clear of debt.

In Georgia he was required to own 250 acres of land or property worth 250 pounds and believe in the Protestant religion.

The man of little means might vote, but only well-to-do Protestants could legislate and in many states none but a rich Protestant could govern. No Hebrew, Atheist, or Roman Catholic could be governor of New Hampshire, New Jersey, [or] South Carolina, and none but a Christian could be a governor of Massachusetts, Pennsylvania, Delaware, Maryland, and South Carolina. Furthermore, representation in the lower House of Legislature was in no state based upon population but on a series of variables, such as the number of taxable voters, or the amount of taxable property, or an arbitrary assignment of votes to each county.

Not until 1962 were the white people as well as the Negroes of the great State of Georgia freed from the unit system of counting votes, a hangover from colonial days. And how were the people of Georgia freed? By a decision of the United States Supreme Court, yes. But the forces which produced the climate in which the Attorney General of the United States argued his first case before that august body and its historical decision, which threatens to destroy the electoral college, were the long, steady process of enlightenment of the American people and the demands of Negroes as well as liberal whites for the right to vote and the right to have each vote given equal weight in representation.

I repeat, it is my confirmed opinion that had it not been for the continuous, never ending efforts and demands of the American Negro to "Secure These Rights" guaranteed by the fundamental laws of this nation, the United States might have forgotten and lost its claim to being a democracy. Not until the Hitler holocaust did the Jews in America join our fight for equality. Not until the Japanese-Americans were placed in concentration camps did they even form an organization of their own people. The Negro ministers, whose church doors have always been open to us; the pioneer political and social workers of the stature of Walter White, Eugene Kinckle Jones; educators such as Mary McLeod Bethune and John Hope; Negro lawyers, such as Charles Houston, Austin Walden, [and] Raymond Pace Alexander have carried on a relentless battle to keep alive and give meaning to the rights guaranteed American citizens.

On the other hand, we must never overlook the fact that the founding fathers drafted a social and political structure capable of peaceful change. Throughout history men have sought to bring order among themselves by erecting social and political structures that reflected in institutional form only the power, mores, and morality of a particular period. These institutional forms proved generally incapable of change. When they could no longer withstand the shifting forces of community and national power, they were destroyed by violence or war.

The United States, founded on revolution, adopted a constitution and Bill of Rights based upon a declaration of human rights. A second revolution, known as the Civil War, made clear to all who could read— even if some refuse to read—that this is one nation, indivisible in which the federal government is supreme in protecting rights guaranteed [to] its citizens. From these two revolutions have come and still are emerging a system of law and respect for law, unique in the world for peaceful social and political change. I do not mean to indicate or suggest that we have attained Utopia in any part of the United States but only that changes have taken place in social, economic, and political life of the United States within my lifetime that once were so controversial and are so fundamental that they could have come about in most countries only by violence, if not war.

Take but one example, the District of Columbia, the nation's capital. On December 5, 1946, when President Truman met with his Committee on Civil Rights and handed them his charge, outlining their powers and duties, we were served lunch in the White House. I stated that I was honored to have been requested by the President to serve on this committee, the work of which was of great concern to me and my people, and that I felt deeply privileged to be a luncheon guest in the White House, but that I would not agree to continue eating meals in the White House nor would I ask friends to give me a place to sleep while attending meetings of the President's Committee on Civil Rights unless my government could provide me with accommodations equal to those enjoyed by other members of the Committee. I was supported in this expression not only by James B. Carey, then Secretary of CIO, but equally by one of Atlanta's most distinguished citizens, Mrs. M. E. Tilley. As a result, the White House secured accommodations for us at the Statler Hotel, which hotel made a condition that all the members of the Commission stop at the Statler. This was the first time that the Statler had accepted Negro guests. Today the presence of Negroes in not only the Statler but all Washington hotels is a common occurrence. The hotels in Washington, D.C., actually seek conventions of Negro organizations.

Again in the National Airport, built on federally owned land, I was refused in 1947 a glass of milk at a counter and told by the manager of the eating facilities that I could carry it in the toilet to drink. My plane had been called and I had to make it in order to keep a speaking engagement in Richmond. I took up this matter directly with President Truman. Within a few months thereafter colored people were not only drinking milk at the counter in the National Airport but eating full meals in the restaurants.

In the Roosevelt administration we had our first appointments of Negroes in any number to responsible positions, but they were all special assistants or advisors. Today they hold policy-making positions in government which no Negro even hoped to attain fifteen years ago. Negro Congressmen hold important committee chairmanships. Negro Judges sit on the United States Circuit Court of Appeals, one step removed from the United States Supreme Court.

These changes in the social structure of our nation's capital have come with so little excitement and so gradually that many Americans are unaware of them. For those of us who have lived through them they afford our great hope in the capability of the United States to secure through peaceful means the social, economic, and political changes which are so absolutely necessary if America is to remain the leader of the democratic world.

In the Far East, Asia, Western Europe, Central and South America, college students have over the years taken the lead in effecting social change. Two years ago I witnessed in Japan the demonstrations of students against rearmament. I also saw students in Chile marching in protest against an increase in bus fares. I have seen unnumbered hordes of students in India stopping all traffic as they filled the streets of New Delhi protesting the delay of the United States to ship wheat. Where there has been hunger, imperialism, dictatorship, exploitation, college students have in many countries often demonstrated against what they believe to be unjust. In the United States and England the usual protestation has been, until recently, by debate rather than by positive action. It was the southern Negro student who first in this country undertook sustained direct action. First he started the "sit-ins" and later was joined by "Freedom Riders." These activities reflect a growing sense of security of an increasing middle class and the effect of a world pressure on the United States to root out and destroy discrimination. The rise of twenty-one independent African states has had tremendous influence on Negroes in the United States and caused them to be determined to secure freedom for the oppressed peoples of their native country.

You students of Spelman College, and your counterpart in other colleges and universities of the United States, will live after your graduation in communities of a nation where there is constant agitation and action for the eradication of the situations which cause us to be called Negroes rather than Americans. Your problem will be one of strategy and techniques. You must realize the calculated risk inherent in any leadership efforts and be prepared to face criticism if your approach proves not to be generally acceptable to the community or if you refuse to join a movement which, after careful consideration, you do not believe is sound morally and technically. What is the best approach?

I am by no means wise enough, nor foolish enough, to offer you the answer. If you knew the division of opinion on action now taking place in my own city of Philadelphia because a white man has been chosen to head a multi-million dollar Ford Foundation pilot project seeking to find the causes of social ills in a predominantly Negro depressed area almost as large as the City of Atlanta, in which matter along with other citizens I have contended that the objection to the Director based upon race is fallacious and should not be an issue, but rather competency regardless of race, you would very rightfully tell me to go home and settle the problems in my own backyard. Therefore, I shall certainly not attempt to tell you how you should settle racial problems in your various communities, nor in Atlanta, where your progress has been phenomenal. However, based upon long years of experience in the vineyard, I should like to suggest some guiding principles and point out a few of the problems you and I will face in the next decade:

1. There is an expression used by some colored people when referring to others of their racial background, viz., "She is colored just like I am." The mentally enslaved Negro who makes such a remark well knows that you college students, your professors, your president, and other leaders are subject to the same disrespect and indignities by the ignorant, poor, socially unaccepted white man, as is he. Only by achieving equality of opportunity for the lowest man on the totem pole do we secure the rights of all of our people—white and colored alike.

Recently the *Philadelphia Evening Bulletin* carried a lengthy letter from a colored man who said that he was a college graduate, had a good paying job, worked eight hours daily in a large industry, owned a home in a white neighborhood where he and his family were well accepted, and he had no patience with Negroes who were always talking about and participating in actions against discrimination. In other words, his personal problems he believed had been solved and he was not concerned about those men and women at the bottom of the totem pole. But the day he loses his job and soon thereafter his home, he will be concerned. Not until we make equality of opportunity and respect for human dignity a living fact for all men, regardless of their color, religion, or national background, will any individual make it secure for himself. I was born in Philadelphia, have lived there practically all my life, and been active in my profession as well as community life. As a consequence my face is well known. When I drive up to the International Airport in Philadelphia, I can park my car in space reserved for officials, because of my official position. The porters run to my car. The airline clerks give me V.I.P. treatment. When, however, the plane lands in another city, be it Atlanta, Chicago, New York, or Birmingham, I am just another colored woman passenger, subject to the whims, prejudices, or reactions based upon the experience of the people I encounter. If the only people of color they have ever met or heard of are in criminal statistics, I will receive the kind of reception and treatment it is their experience to give such unfortunate people. Only by achieving equality of opportunity for the lowest man on the totem pole can you and I protect and strengthen the rights of all people, including ourselves.

2. Only by making democracy work in the United States, not tinkling cymbal and sounding brass, do we make secure our way of life. The people of the world have the choice between democracy and communism or possibly annihilation. There is no question that all of us, regardless of the inequities, privation, and suffering we have so long endured in the United States, would choose first to live and next to live in the democratic way of life. You and I are free to criticize our leaders and our government. We have no fear that because you, here assembled, have listened to me criticize government because it has not secured equality of rights to all citizens, for which according to the constitution our government was constituted, that you will be routed from your beds and arrested tonight. I am certain that you agree with me "that it is a good government of which the people can say that which is bad" and that our responsibility, for which the colored people of the United States have long assumed the burden, is to make democracy work. Every great civilization of the past, regardless of its glory, has perished. It is not written that our civilization will not join those of ages past, regardless of whether it will be buried by communism or die by its own folly. We are not pessimistic when we recognize the potential discrimination creates for decay. In our struggle to secure equality of opportunity, personal security, respect for individual dignity, and rights of full citizenship we are making a heroic struggle not only for ourselves but of greater importance a struggle for the survival of the United States. America cannot hope that the uncommitted nations of the world, nor those controlled by dictatorships, will choose the democratic way, if our failures to put into practice our pronounced belief in freedom continue to be heralded around the world. By destroying every vestige of discrimination at home, we make democracy secure at home and in so doing the hope of the people of the world. Yes, the freedom riders and the sit-ins work not only to free themselves but to make America free.

3. The capacity of peaceful, orderly change in America has kept this nation vigorous and alive. It is the hope for change which must motivate

the masses of American Negroes. But despite all that has been accomplished, we are still suffering from racial and religious discrimination. It exists in education, employment, housing and public accommodations; North, South, East and West. Here and there individuals have been able to break through the barriers in the communities in which they reside. But, as you and I know, they are exceptions to the rule. If you will pardon a personal reference, my elder daughter told me when she was in college: "I knew from the day I was born that I had to go to college." She started life with a set of values. Everybody she knew or of whom she heard in her family for generations had gone to college. The parents of her friends were college graduates. My children, like many of you students, started life with values and goals. But the great mass of colored people in the United States have had no such advantage. As a result we have been slow in developing even a small middle class. According to the census of 1960, only 13,056 non-whites in Philadelphia and 1,644 in Atlanta made over $6,000 in 1959.

The great mass of our people, discouraged by years of closed doors, have not accepted middle class goals and values. For the past ten years I have been a member of the Philadelphia Commission on Human Rights [sic]. We have a staff of twenty-nine persons, including eleven highly trained professionals and a budget of close to $300,000. We do not receive in one year thirty complaints in discrimination in employment. Filing a complaint is meaningless to a man who has worn thin the soles of his shoes filing applications for work and watched later, less skilled, white applicants being employed. Our Commission has to send inspectors into the industries to count the number of colored employees, skilled and unskilled, and examine employment applications in order to ferret out the discrimination. We must subpoena the records when the employer is uncooperative and hold expensive, prolonged public hearings to throw the light of public opinion on the employment problem.

The great mass of people ask themselves either consciously but more frequently, unconsciously:

What's the need of complaining? Nobody has ever done anything for me.

Why save money for a home, when all I can buy is some old house in a neighborhood just as bad as where I live? I'll get me a nice, new car and throw dust in those white folks' faces!

And in cities where the schools are integrated, why work my head off, when the scholarships will all go to the white kids?

Or in communities where college trained men and women are unemployed, why go to college and be too good to work in a ditch, when you can't work in an office?

Why volunteer to ring doorbells for the Red Cross or the Community Chest or any other community effort when re-gardless of your ability they seldom, if ever, consider you for membership on policy making boards?

Why develop a taste for fine music, good plays, art when all I can do is listen to my television, radio or read those books I can buy or borrow?

When the masses of Negroes upon whom lack of opportunity has imposed low horizons, limited aspirations, and motivation reflect con-sciously or unconsciously on these matters they conclude it is not worth-while trying to emerge into the middle class. The chance of succeeding is too slim to be worth the terrific effort. This attitude will not change by the masses seeing, reading, or hearing about the limited number of Negroes who have emerged into the [main]stream of American life. It will change only as the unceasing number of educated youths dedicate their lives not exclusively to making money but to convincing the Ne-gro masses that the rewards of the American way of life are available to all who are willing to make sacrifices and to arousing the people in the communities in which they live to the acceptance of the Negro, the Puerto Rican, the Mexican, all the people of this heterogeneous nation into the main stream of American life, into the churches, industries, places of public accommodation, amusement, and culture.

4. The opportunities for unskilled labor, filled by mass migration in World War I and the employment of a million Negro workers in World

War II in civilian jobs within four years, gave us an opportunity to prove ability to perform basic factory operations in a variety of businesses, in semi-skilled and skilled capacities. Today, however, the demand is no longer for unskilled nor semi-skilled workers, but in the present industrial expansion in electronics, television, air conditioning, spacecraft, and plastics, a worker is required to be highly skilled. Thus the man or woman without skills today is either destined to excessive or continuous periods of unemployment. Are you college students and alumnae prepared with the high degree of skill that employment requires today? In my profession we call the secretaries "the prima donnas." A competent, legal secretary demands and receives better pay than the average public school teacher. The shortage is so great that white law offices are seeking capable colored secretaries who know how to spell, can comprehend what they read and the meaning of the material dictated to them.

There is without question a shortage of trained Negroes to fill the new opportunities for skilled and technical positions. Advertisements by the public employment services, career forums, [and] recruitment of Negro College graduates produce only a small number of qualified Negroes for the highly technical jobs of modern industry.

There is, of course, a reason for the paucity of talent. Among Negro labor it is generally due to refusal to admit them to apprenticeship training and on-the-job training, resulting in denial of admission to many unions. Inadequate and inferior schools are an important cause especially in rural and large urban areas, where there is de facto segregation. A fundamental cause which affects the young colored boy or girl from the privileged and underprivileged family is his reaction to long established discrimination which causes him to believe there will never be an opportunity for him in the new industrial fields. How well I recall the students of the University of Pennsylvania criticizing my husband more than thirty years ago when he entered the Wharton School of Business and Finance. They would satirically ask: "What are you going to do when you graduate? Who ever heard of a Negro studying Finance?" He later used all he had learned, not only in his private practice representing corporations, but as a Councilman of the City of Philadelphia, where he served as Chairman of the Committee on Public Property and a member of the Appropriations Committee, responsible for the raising and spending annually of about $200 million dollars. Finally, a primary cause is lack of excellency in one's studies. It is not enough to secure a diploma. This piece of paper may admit you to an examination, but what you learned and how well you learned will determine whether you place high enough in an examination to qualify for a position. Whether you will be privileged to enjoy the opportunities created by student sit-ins will depend upon your individual qualifications and not the number of hours you as a student spent away from class sitting in.

The Freedom Riders, Sit-Ins, [and] Boycotts are performing a service which history alone can fully evaluate. These activities have proven their effectiveness by the results you have seen in Georgia, where the legislature adopted a local option law which permits localities to determine whether or not schools are to be desegregated; where by edict of the United States Supreme Court, the unit voting system has been broken and as a result the first time in ninety-two years a Negro Senator has been elected to the Georgia State Legislature. Certainly much remains to be done in Georgia as well as all over the United States. But the momentum that has opened the dike, and the hole, pouring out the forces of opposing desegregation, is constantly widening.

My concern is that you and I be prepared to live in the highly competitive world in which we will find ourselves as the walls of segregation come tumbling down. Will the few who secure the first top jobs remember the many who are still at the bottom of the ladder and continue to bring them to the top? Will we remember that our apparent security is dependent upon the degree of security employed by all citizens of this country and the world, and thus concern ourselves with Foreign Affairs, World Disarmament, the plight of the deprived at home, in South America, Asia, and the world? Will we be determined to prepare ourselves with such excellence in skills needed in this atomic age that our talents will be sought after with more zeal than we who seek the opportunity to use them? To what degree we answer these questions will depend not only the freedom of Negroes in the United States but also the securing of freedom to all the people of this nation and the world.

"Education and Social Change: The Citizen's Role in Achieving Civil Rights," ca. 1966

It is a tragic reflection upon America's claim to world leadership that racial riots from coast to coast had to awaken the nation to the realization that instead of a great society, we have produced ghettos, slums, [and] shocking inequities in public school education in the North and the South, as well as in the East and on the West coast.

In the eleven deep Southern States in 1965 there were only approximately sixty-four thousand Negro students attending public schools with white children. This figure represents slightly more than 2 per cent of the Negro enrollment. This year there are by various estimates, according to the United States Office of Education, about 180,000 Negro students attending schools with white students in the same eleven State area. This, however, represents only a very small percentage of the Negro students in these States. Title VI of the Civil Rights Act of 1964 provides that Federal funds must *not* be used to support programs and activities in which there is discrimination based on race, color, or national origin. The 1966 Guidelines for School Desegregation issued by the Office of Education are pointed at measures to eliminate a dual school system, composed of white students taught by white teachers, administered by white supervisors, and composed of Negro students, taught by Negro teachers, administered in part or in whole, by Negro supervisors.

These guidelines proposed to eliminate racial segregation of children where there is a dual school system primarily by "Free Choice Plans." The "Free Choice Plans" require students or their parents to choose their own school, regardless of where they live. These plans are not acceptable to the Segregationists nor the civil rights leaders. Governor Wallace was recently reported as stating at a meeting with Alabama County and City School Superintendents that the State will not comply with the desegregation guidelines because, "These new regulations attempt to take over every aspect in education." Other political and educational leaders in the South have charged that the guidelines go beyond the law and the latest Federal Court decisions on school integration. Fewer than three hundred of the two thousand school districts asked to submit declarations of intent to comply had done so on April 12, 1966, although April 15th was the deadline (*NY Times*, 4/12/66). On the other hand, civil rights leaders point out the impossibility of exercising free choice in those states maintaining a dual system of public education. To begin with, the parent or child who dares exercise "free choice" knows from bitter experience that the parent faces loss of job, eviction, or possibly destruction of his home, if not loss of life. The Federal Government I venture to say would have to send inspectors into the rural towns and most of the urban areas to secure and distribute the Choice Forms and deliver them to the office of the Superintendent. Based upon experience in registering voters in these states, hours would be fixed when the Superintendent's office was open to secure Free Choice Forms resulting in a limited number of forms being issued and those Negroes who returned the form would later learn it had never been received. Therefore, the civil rights leaders rightfully state that the "Free Choice Plans" are inviting trouble, because the Negroes intend to desegregate the public schools, if it means sit-ins, marches, boycotts, and every other peaceful means of integrating the public school which peaceful means we know from experience result in anything but peace.

What then is the answer? The Guidelines state that "The School System, not the State or Federal Government is responsible for making

the plan work." If this be so, I suggest the Guidelines require the school
system to follow the other suggested plans of desegregation, viz.,

1. Close small, inadequate school buildings now used for
    Negro students and assign these students to desegregated
    schools;

2. Where there are adequate school buildings now used for
    Negro students only, make these buildings a part of the
    whole school system, by re-organizing the grade struc-
    ture, such as the K4-4-4 so that these schools contain
    fewer grades but are desegregated.

3. Federal government must provide irresistible incentives
    to states and localities to advance breakthroughs in de
    facto segregation by making substantial sources of money
    available for school construction and transportation to
    stimulate and encourage local school systems to meet the
    problem of integrating our public schools.

Admittedly, as stated in the Revised Statement of Policies by H.E.W.
[Department of Health, Education, and Welfare], no single type of plan
is appropriate for all schools. Equally true is the fact that Free Choice
Plans are not an appropriate or reasonable means of securing desegregation. "Free Choice" places an insurmountable burden on the Negro
parent and child rather than on the school board; it forces civil rights organizations to use the weapon of peaceful protest, which too frequently
results in anything but peace and the plan promotes non-compliance.
All a school board has to do is to adopt the "freedom of choice plan," get
a few Negro children to sign up for a white school, [then] let the community pressure cause them to withdraw their applications or reject the
Negro children because of overcrowding, improper registration, or any
other excuse the school board might want to give.

The above mentioned minimal enrollment of Negro students in
white schools has resulted in 452 Negro teachers in the South losing
their jobs or being demoted to jobs beneath their qualifications. Respect
for the dignity of the individual requires that citizens support the free-

dom of the right of a qualified teacher to work at her profession be it teaching children who are black or white, regardless of their race or national origin.

A school manned by all white or all colored teachers is as destructive of democracy, and incapable of building a fully rounded individual, as one attended by children of one race or color or national origin. The white child, who has never personally known a Negro other than as a servant or the child of a servant, is robbed of an important and valuable experience in establishing and maintaining respect for every individual. Similarly, the Negro child, who has never known that a white teacher is as humane, concerned, and devoted as his colored teacher, has in fact grown up and spent his most formative years in a "No Man's Land." He knows no man of another race or nationality, unless it be the corner store keeper with whom his relations are not always cordial. Smoldering resentment and deep frustration arise and deepen as he compares his life with the T.V. picture of American life and too often these emotions erupt into open rebellion against social evils, commonly referred to as race riots.

By reason of fortuitous occurrence, I arrived in Los Angeles in the midst of the Watts riots. Through the courtesy of City and State Officials I was permitted to drive through the area and talk with some of the residents. Almost every person I interviewed conveyed the same thinking, viz., "We Won!" It took deep prodding to ascertain what these people thought they had won. Finally, I realized they meant that despite their continuous protests, for the first time they had won the attention of the City, the State, the Federal Government, and the nation to the shocking inequities in education, employment, recreation, and housing to which they had so long been subjected. It is indeed ironic that in fact the Negro revolution had to focus national attention on the inadequacies of public education in Metropolitan areas not only for Negro children but also white children. Boston, New York City, Rochester, Syracuse, Philadelphia, Wilmington, Delaware, Washington D.C., Cleveland, Ohio, Chicago, St. Louis, Los Angeles are but a few of the cities outside of the border and Southern States that have only in recent years undertaken massive programs to provide quality education for all students and supplemental programs for socially deprived children.

The 1965 Task Force of the National Education Association has proposed, as a means of achieving integration of faculties in the deep south, massive programs of intergroup and compensatory education for large numbers of southern teachers, both colored and white. Such a program is needed in the North as well as the South . . . indeed all over the United States. There are white teachers in every section of our country, who have never had a colored classmate, or a colored student or a colored friend and have never read a book on Negro history. But the most informed and understanding teachers of intergroup relations can not solve the problem of race relations without communal support. The total society is involved in education and every segment must be reached if we are, in the foreseeable future, to build an integrated public school system, truly representative of a democracy.

As previously stated, the Guidelines for School Desegregation and the Revised Statement of Policies for School Desegregation Plans Under Title VI of the Civil Rights Act of 1964, as promulgated respectively in 1965 and 1966 by the Office of Education, apply to public elementary and secondary school systems undergoing desegregation to eliminate a dual school structure. They have absolutely no effect upon racial segregation in urban areas, where by law, a dual system is forbidden. With an ever increasing shift of Negro population to urban areas grave problems of segregation have arisen. In 1910 only 29 percent of American Negroes lived in urban areas. The great migration which accompanied World War I continued through World War II, the Korea Conflict, and with less intensity continued thereafter, until in 1960, 65 percent of the American Negroes lived in urban areas and of the Negroes who lived in these urban areas, 80 percent were concentrated in the center of the inner cities.

As a result of this concentration, de facto segregation has become a fait accompli in almost every metropolitan city. In Chicago, 90 per cent of the Negro elementary students and 63 per cent of the Negro high school students attend schools which are 90 per cent Negro. In Philadelphia, 73 per cent of Negro elementary students and 54 per cent of Negro high school students attend schools with a population of more than 90 per cent Negro. In New York City less than one-fourth of the Negro elementary schools have fully licensed teachers, while over two-thirds of the white schools have teachers fully licensed. A similar situation exists in other urban areas.

What can we as citizens, concerned that children who live in large urban areas or in the suburbs receive a rounded education, and realizing that either because of poor facilities, inadequately trained teachers, or lack of contact with and knowledge of children of different colors, races, or national origins—I repeat, what can we do, to eradicate de facto segregation?

We can:

1. Support reorganization of the school structure by adopting such plans as K-4-4-4 or the campus school, where children of all ages attend classes and where opportunities for specialized training, not otherwise available, are provided.

2. Agree not to move because one Negro family buys a home in our block but determine to maintain our neighborhood, the highest standards for our neighborhood schools, our church, our home and welcome the new neighbor.

3. Encourage the Board of Education to solicit the publication and use of textbooks which fairly and adequately portray the Negro and his contribution to America.

4. Demand quality education for the entire school system, so that regardless of where a child lives he receives equal teaching skills, physical facilities, and educational opportunities.

5. Support Bond issues for public education so that the [city's] public school becomes so superior it will attract back to the city the families who fled to the suburbs.

6. Insist upon the breaking down of the ghetto by rehabilitation of boarded up and vacant land so as to make the inner city so attractive that home owners of every race,

color, or national origin will seek to live in the attractive, convenient inner city.

I know from personal experience that these purposes can be accomplished by dedicated citizens. I live in an area of Philadelphia known as Mt. Airy. It is contiguous to Germantown. When colored people bought the first houses in this part of the City, some realtors began a siege on the owners to sell their houses, with the old bugaboo cliche "your values will decrease." The Quakers organized. They put signs in their windows: "My house is not for sale." They refused to move. They refused to desert old neighbors [and] familiar sights, and abandon their homes located in a most desirable environment. The flight of children from the public schools started. The enrollment in the Henry School, located in my immediate neighborhood, dropped from approximately 90 percent white to about 20 percent. A strong principal decided to meet the challenge. She and her faculty decided that first and foremost Henry School must maintain the highest standards. Second, parents must be made partners in their efforts. Leaders of the community agreed to make Henry School Home and School Association an instrument for encouraging parents not to move but help improve the standards of Henry School. An organ was purchased for the school through contributions by parents and neighbors of the school. The first colored teacher was transferred to Henry School to set a pattern for respect for Negroes. Today the faculty is 32 per cent Negro and the student body is almost equally white and colored.

The problem of desegregating our public schools is not a Negro problem, it should not solely be a civil rights problem, although the civil rights organizations can and must be a catalytic force in arousing public attention, support, and providing solutions. The desegregation of our public schools is an American problem—how to upgrade to a level of excellence the quality of education for children, not only in the inner city, but throughout this country, so as to make the most effective use of our human resources. To accomplish this purpose requires billions of tax dollars, the development of diverse curricula to prepare children for work in a highly scientific age, well prepared teachers not only academically but in intergroup relations, buildings equipped to train children to meet the requirements of reaching other planets and living on them as well as living in peace and harmony with a Negro neighbor on this planet. The total society must be involved in this tremendous task. The power of Government, Labor, Industry, as well as that of politicians, civil rights and civil liberties organizations, educational and social welfare leaders must be combined to demand and secure a complete reorganization of the public school system beginning with nursery school. As stated in 1926 by Alfred North Whitehead:

> If mankind can rise to the occasion, their lies in front a golden age of beneficent creativeness. . . . The problem is not how to produce men, but how to produce great societies. The great societies will put up the great men for the occasion.

We can not produce a great society with our citizens in practically every town and hamlet divided by the railroad track, whether the name of the track be The Seaboard Air Line, State Street, South Street, Sixteenth Street, or Park Avenue and a different quality of education provided for those on each side of the track. What we have accomplished today in adopting the Civil Rights Act of 1964 and the Guidelines of 1965 and as revised in March 1966 is, as Winston Churchill said, ". . . not the end, it is not even the beginning of the end. But it is, perhaps, the end of the beginning."

"The Catalytic Role of Commissions in Helping Alienated Communities," 1967

Mr. Chairman and fellow delegates, I want to express the extreme gratitude of my Commission for the privilege to address such a distinguished
Conference. This annual meeting, which brings together representatives
of those local and state governmental agencies having responsibility in
the field of human rights, is without parallel. Therefore, this is a signal
honor and opportunity.

I should like to start my remarks with a discussion of the meaning of the central area of our concern this morning: the problem of
alienation.

The term "alienate" is variously understood to mean: to make indifferent or adverse; to make inimical; to turn away; to estrange; to dis-
unite; to disaffect; to separate; to make unfriendly; to set against or to
divide. If one considers such well publicized ghettos as Watts, Harlem,
Hough, Southside Chicago, or North Philadelphia, it is easy to accept
at least one, if not most, of the above definitions as descriptive of the
atmosphere and attitude of many communities across the continent of
North America.

I will not attempt in this paper to describe in detail and analyze
the forces which have contributed to the alienation of these communities other than those causes which our commissions may review such
as needing its careful evaluation. All the causes for alienation could in

itself occupy all the time we have in this conference. Furthermore, I do not think it necessary for an audience of this kind. But let me offer a few descriptive reminders of the circumstances contributing to the alienation—the disaffection which manifests itself in rioting, vandalism, protest demonstrations, etc.

These are communities where job-seekers have been rebuffed at employment offices or frustrated in their ambition to move up the ladder through internal training and promotion procedures. They have been turned aside at union hiring halls or denied the opportunity to enter apprentice programs and secure the skills which would lead to gainful and satisfying work careers.

These are communities where fathers and mothers cannot [provide], and see no possibility of providing, the wholesome living environment they would like their children to have. They cannot avoid overcrowding—cannot offer home conditions conducive to study, reading, or wholesome entertainment. We can imagine how these frustrations debase the self-respect of fathers and mothers experiencing such helplessness and futility in their roles.

These are communities where law enforcement is too often a mockery. Where police brutality, disrespect, and discourtesy are often experienced and suffered at the hands of the most visible representative of a suspect governmental power structure.

In these communities the process of education is not an exciting adventure nor does it seem to point the way to broader opportunity. Classrooms too often are a mere extension of the drab and desolate environment of the home.

Civic and political life seem not to be realistic channels leading toward enjoyment of the fruits of our affluent society. Voluntary citizen efforts too often grind to dismal and ineffective inaction by its leadership or those who might offer encouragement and produce effective changes.

Social esteem is quite naturally low in these communities. There is so little to nourish it.

I have viewed my assignment, therefore, not as one of discussing the complex ramifications of the problems which exist in these communities. I prefer, rather, to discuss with you the philosophy, the functions, and the effectiveness of our human rights agencies as we try to offer succor to the kinds of communities which we label as "alienated."

But before I go further with the matters which I want to discuss in more detail, let me add a warning. We must avoid stereotypical and myopic thinking about these communities. We must not assume that all the men lounging on the street corners prefer their idleness. The fathers and mothers do not prefer the shabby and rundown tenements they cluster in. They do not want to be insulted and brutalized by agents of our law enforcement bodies. The people of the alienated communities are human beings who share a common humanity with all human beings—individuals who want to share and enjoy all the fruits of an abundant society.

With these mental pictures as a guide, let us now turn our attention to the phenomenon of public human rights agencies. I think it is essential that we examine what seems clear as regards the perceptible purpose and intent underlying the establishment of most, if not indeed all, of our agencies. We need to look beyond the rhetoric of enabling legislation. Obviously, the language content of our mandates is important and deserving of interest and respect. However, it must be viewed in combination with other factors.

The necessity for such an approach is readily discernible. Let us compare the import of language which is embodied in the declaration of the policy provisions in most of our enabling legislation with the companion language which defines powers and duties.

Except for its reference to the Universal Declaration of Human Rights proclaimed by the United Nations, the policy provisions of the Ontario Human Rights Code [are] quite similar to that found in many of our laws. The Ontario language is as follows:

"Whereas, recognition of the inherent dignity and the inalienable rights of all members of the human family is the foundation of freedom, justice and peace in the world—

"And whereas, it is public policy in Ontario that every person is free and equal in dignity and rights without regard to race, creed, color, nationality, ancestry or place of origin—"

The Des Moines, Iowa, Ordinances on Human Rights further support this contention. Some of its language is as follows:

"Whereas, the State of Iowa—, proclaims that all persons are by nature free and equal; and

"Whereas it is necessary and proper to provide for the safety, preserve the health, promote the prosperity, improve the morals, order, comfort and convenience of the City of Des Moines and the inhabitants of said city; and

"Whereas, there exists a need in the city—for the establishment of a body—to the end that an effort be made to eliminate prejudice, intolerance, bigotry, and discrimination—, now, therefore"

Let us make no mistake as we examine these sweeping declarations of policy. The words are noble and compelling testimonies to our intent. One might conclude that our governing bodies had arrived at a determination to enact laws that completely prohibit and eliminate every vestige of discrimination. Listen again to the phrases:

. . . recognition of the inherent dignity and the inalienable rights of all members of the human family is the foundation of freedom, justice and peace in the world . . .

. . . every person is free and equal in dignity and rights without regard to race, etc. . . .

. . . proclaims that all persons are by nature free and equal . . .

. . . a need . . . for the establishment of a body . . . to the end that an effort be made to eliminate prejudice, intolerance, bigotry, and discrimination . . .

But were our law-makers determined to enact the laws which we need? Unfortunately the evidence does not support a conclusion that such determination existed; if so, it was rare.

Instead, we generally find that our agencies are required and empowered to conduct educational programs to promote the equal rights and opportunities of all persons.

In addition to that, most of us are *empowered to administer certain types* of legislation which prohibits *various kinds* of discriminatory acts.

Permit me to use, as an example, the legislation presently in force in Philadelphia to illustrate the limitation on us as we try to prohibit discrimination in housing.

As we publicize the provisions of our housing legislation in Philadelphia, we boldly proclaim it is against the law to discriminate in the sale or rental of housing. In doing so we more often than not ignore the small print which actually, and legally, exempts 65 percent of the housing in Philadelphia from the provisions of the law. We cannot apply any legal sanctions against the owner of a one or two family dwelling if the owner lives in one of the units and wants to discriminate in the sale or rental of his property.

Many of us are also entrusted with the authority to advise other governmental departments and, in many instances, private agencies and organizations as well.

Perhaps I will leave it to each of you to review your own experiences with other governmental bodies when you attempted, or even contemplated, advising or consulting with them regarding their policies and practices relating to equal employment, for example. Or think of what the response has been when your agency expressed itself regarding policies of a board of education, or a housing authority. I assume we have been somewhat more successful in our dealings with private agencies and organizations but I suspect we have encountered problems in these areas as well.

Regrettably, the enforcement powers which we all feel are indispensable tools, are rather primitive instruments for the tasks before us. They are the first proof that our governing bodies manifestly determined that our human rights agencies were not meant to achieve the condition which they so eloquently declared to be public policy.

They almost universally contain exemptions or limitations of one order or another that limit our ability to completely and aggressively perform our tasks.

These exemptions or limitations frequently start with the religious institutions that are the guardians of our moral fiber and extend to certain classes and sizes of profit-making businesses. However, even more debilitating are the gaps in essential legislative coverage that make it absolutely patent that announced public policy is not expected to come to fruition.

Coupled with the aforementioned disabilities one finds that every existing Commission lacks adequate budget and staff to effectively develop and implement the variety of programs necessary to deliver the *summum bonum* inherent in our policy pronouncements. These glaring deficiencies, however, must largely be laid at the doorstep of those of us who have accepted mantles of responsibility in the civil rights field.

We have failed miserably to perform as competent administrators.

We have not, as public civil rights commissioners, deemed it our responsibility to adopt an attitude which assumes that oaths of office impose upon us the obligation to make policy a living reality. Instead, most of us appear to have embraced the position that it is our role to construe our legislative mandates as narrowly as possible. Many of us, in fact, behave as if it is our job to stand as a buffer between our professional staffs and their innovative efforts to subject our enabling powers to the broadest possible interpretation.

I wish to suggest that the oath of office that we have taken gives us the direct responsibility to take the initiative. We should not have to be persuaded, educated, or motivated by our staffs to seek new vistas. Indeed, it is we who should be demanding of our staffs [sic] to seek new vistas. Indeed, it is we who should be demanding of our staffs new concepts, improved programs, and innovations.

In any event, since our topic concerns dealing with alienated communities, what can we as public agencies hope to do to remove at least some of the causes that create and perpetuate alienation[?] Quite obviously, we can try to work to eliminate overt acts of discrimination. However, we must realize that the elimination of discrimination, if accomplished, will not alone remove the plethora of concerns affecting our ghetto communities. It will not yield a solution to distressing conditions in housing, education, employment, welfare services, transportation, etc.

Nonetheless, we must all recognize that the underlying purpose behind the creation of our agencies has been the desire of our governments to minimize unrest and to prevent alienation. We, therefore, must all face up to this reality and create policies and programs that go far beyond the mere matter of discrimination. It is not enough to provide prompt solutions to complaints, to conduct effective contract compliance programs, or to develop and implement sound intergroup educational programs.

If we as public agencies are to deal effectively with alienated communities, if we are to implement the language of our sweeping documents, we must devise ways and means to eradicate the problems which impinge so distressingly upon our ghetto populations. Where adequate legislation is lacking, we must spearhead efforts to correct the situation.

However, of equal, if indeed not of greater importance, is the need for Commission members to demand the stature, the cooperation, the budget, and the staffing that will make it possible for our agencies to have a significant impact upon urban renewal and housing programs, upon manpower training and job development programs, upon our police departments and upon our educational systems.

We must demand that our agencies be brought into the policy making councils where decisions are made that affect ghetto residents.

We must seriously examine our past staffing practices and begin to see that we have available and responsible to us personnel with special professional competence in urban planning, in economic development, in the field of education, etc. We have not in the past, nor will we in the future, be very useful to the ghetto dweller or to our mayors and governors if we continue to limit our agencies by having professional competence only in the human relations field. Such persons should continue to form the backbone of our staffs but they must be augmented by other disciplines.

We must, however, realize that appropriate agency policy and effective staffing can be only optimally productive if they serve a catalytic role both in the ghetto and in the halls of government. It is for that reason that I have referred to the need for additional areas of professional expertise within agency staffs. I am thoroughly convinced that in order to exercise the influence we wish to exert within our administrations and be an aggressive catalyst there, we must have the ability to talk the language and provide technical competence that is respected and acknowledged. We must be able to review and offer professional critiques to the wide range of proposals and programs that directly or indirectly affect ghetto residents. Reaction to the efforts of other governmental departments or of private groups, however, is not enough. With new professional expertise, we must join with those who feel alienated to develop new or counter proposals, or programs that are specifically designed to be of maximum benefit to the poor and disadvantaged.

It is the reagent of professional competence that can beckon as the substance which can enable human rights agencies to create a sense of hope and a sense of positive involvement for the presently alienated, thereby helping them to effectively interact with government and the community at large to make progress. It will be our capacity to provide advocacy planning talent that will enable us to have true and meaningful relevance to our alienated communities. It is only through professionalism that we can hope successfully to challenge the status quo. In fact, I firmly believe that until our agencies can produce valid facts and figures, until we develop the ability to offer comprehensive and sound program packages in the area of housing, job development, and training, we will continue to be able to meet only one portion of the tremendous need that is such an overwhelming reality in our ghettos.

The same is equally true in our relationship to our administrations. We must be able to provide them with more than expressions of concern regarding negative citizen reaction to the implementation of various programs or the absence or alleged inadequacy of other programs. I strongly question the wisdom or the right of our agencies to hurl challenges unless we are able to produce professionally developed alternatives.

Let us now turn our attention to some of the implications of my proposal. How can we justify what to many may appear to be a duplication of skills that presently exist in other departments? I think it can be done and I am positive that it needs to be done. I think we can start to present a justification by pointing to the fact that ours are the only governmental agencies having direct responsibility to eliminate the barriers which restrict minority groups from full participation in our American society.

As I have indicated earlier, this cannot be accomplished solely by programs dealing with the eradication of overt acts of discrimination. It requires an improvement in the problem areas frequently mentioned above. It has been demonstrated that planning which is not specifically designed with the alienated as a prime consideration may not positively affect or improve the lot of the alienated. The agencies confronted with the responsibility should, and must have, the capacity to supply advocacy planning.

I think we can categorically assert that only through such a capacity can public human rights agencies be relevant to that segment of our society that is most likely to explode. I think, further, that we can assure our governors and mayors that the existence of planning capability within our agencies will cause the traditional agencies with planning or program responsibilities to increase their awareness of the deprived and significantly reduce the number of situations which create tension, conflict, and unrest.

However, even if all of our agencies are able to win over our administrations, we may still have trouble obtaining adequate budgets. Unfortunately, some legislatures and some city councils fail to appreciate the wisdom of some executive proposals. Confronted with this possibility, it might be wise to seek planning capacity in only the most pressing problem area until we are able to demonstrate the value of such an investment. Failing that, or as a supplement, we might seek to develop an arrangement with a university which is willing to undertake such an approach on a cooperative basis. Another approach might be found through cooperation of a chapter of a professional society. In any event, the point we seek to make here is that there are many possible avenues to the development of professional expertise.

On the other hand, there are many ways in which we can use our new skills and new knowledge to improve conditions in alienated communities. In almost all such communities there are organizations or private agencies that need and are willing to use professional assistance. In some situations, existing organizations or institutions, such as churches, can be persuaded to create special committees which can make use of our new talent. As an example, my own Commission has been able to organize human relations councils in a large number of churches and public housing projects. Each of the councils carry on projects in such areas as housing or employment.

In some special situations it might be desirable to seek to work through the leadership structure of an ethnic community. In Philadelphia we have frequently found this to be true in working with our Puerto Rican population. I would suspect that the same might well be true for those Commissions having to do with American Indian, Mexican American, Asiatics, or other similar communities.

No matter what leadership or organizational entity is used, an agency should be able to find crucial areas within which to exercise its professional competence. Most frequently, it will probably be in a situation in which community leaders are seeking solutions to a problem their community wants to solve. In other instances, a Commission might go to a community to seek its ideas, involvement, and support as it participates in the development of its city's Community Renewal Program Report, new anti-poverty programs, or its Model Cities Program. If in doing so it can supply competent planning personnel, the Commission can readily be perceived as a vital tool for community use.

Fellow Commissioners, what I have proposed to you today may appear to some to be impractical, or at best too costly in terms of traditional commission staffing. It may also strike some of us as far beyond the scope of normal commission operational philosophy. Nonetheless, I say to you that nothing short of a radical and agonizing reappraisal of our old methods and techniques will make it possible for public Commissions to deal with and offer aid to either the alienated or the general community.

As I said early in my talk, let us face up, openly and persuasively, to the fact that our agencies have been and still are being created to eliminate the potential for explosion and revolt. We are institutions to which reference is made when political leaders or the general community find it necessary to defend their interest or intent concerning minority group citizens. We, as members of Commissions, have allowed this situation to prevail by standing mute or actively supporting contentions that our agencies realistically represent meaningful effort to deal with ethnically isolated citizens. I suppose we have justified our position by making ourselves accept the belief that we have discharged our responsibility when we adjust or eliminate acts of discrimination that are prohibited by our legislative provisions. In so doing, we are turning our backs on the fact that past and presently existing programs have not made enough of a contribution to keep our minority populations from experiencing a declining position relative to society generally. We are, in matter of fact, failing in the very task that led to our creation: the prevention of tension, unrest, and civil outbreak.

I think it is our job to speak out forcefully, telling our states and our towns that traditional planning and programming are not succeeding. We should say these efforts are failing to a large degree because the Negro, the Puerto Rican, the Indian, and the Spanish-speaking American have not had on their side and at their disposal professionally qualified planning advocates. They have lacked representation at the decision making table; and because of that lack of representation they come off poorly. If our agencies are expected to be effective governmental agencies, with an interest and a responsibility for opportunities for minority citizens, we must be given the capacity to identify programs, measure their effectiveness, and to pin-point deficiencies and offer proposals for additional programs in housing, employment, education, etc.

We can all agree that there are an increasing number of programs, at all levels of government, that are designed to improve the plight of the ghetto dweller. We can also agree that minority groups have had countless pieces of legislation enacted on their behalf. However, what has been the sum effect of these numerous programs and this mountain of legislation[?] Has the gap between economic status of the Negro, the Indian, the Puerto Rican and other minority groups and the general population of America been closing? To the contrary; the national figures show continuing and, in some instances, growing disparities between the general population and minorities in housing conditions, incomes, unemployment, infant mortality, school drop-out rates, etc.

Discontent and unrest are festering in our ghettos; they are like armed nuclear bombs. We are not adequately equipped to defuse this explosive situation. It is my considered judgement that if this 1967 meeting of our Commissions accomplishes nothing else, it will have made an outstanding contribution if it adopts a resolution calling attention to this critical situation. It should ask all existing Commissions, members and non-members alike, to initiate prompt appropriate action to seek such additional professional competence as they require to realistically offer assistance to the alienated in their communities.

Notes

Throughout the notes, the Sadie Tanner Mossell Alexander Records, located at the University of Pennsylvania Archives in Philadelphia, are cited as STMA.

Preface

1. Julianne Malveaux, "Missed Opportunity: Sadie Tanner Mossell Alexander and the Economics Profession," *American Economic Review* 81, no. 2 (May 1991): 307–310. Malveaux compared Alexander's scholarly output to that of renowned scholars Abram Harris, Oliver Cox, W. E. B. Du Bois, and D. Parke Gibson. She speculates that if Alexander had been allowed to work as an economist, she might have chosen to research similar topics as these scholars in the areas of Black businesses, social classes, and Black consumption, or she may have continued to focus on other aspects of her dissertation research on Black families and migration patterns from a macroeconomic perspective, using case study analysis.

2. For an outstanding analysis of the intellectual thought of the other early African American economist, Abram Harris Jr., see William Darity Jr., *Race, Radicalism, and Reform: Selected Papers, Abram L. Harris* (New Brunswick, N.J.: Transaction, 1989).

3. Sadie T. M. Alexander to Mrs. Jeanetta Welch Brown, Executive Secretary of the National Council of Negro Women, August 21, 1944, STMA, box 59, ff9.

4. Sadie T. M. Alexander from Mrs. Goldie E. Watson, Executive Secretary of the Bi-Partisan Committee for a Pennsylvania F.E.P.C., March 19, 1945, STMA, box 60, ff3; and Sadie T. M. Alexander to Beth Anderson, August 13, 1958, STMA, box 3, ff20; *Daily Courier* (Connellsville, Pa.), July 16, 1958, 1.

5. Rae Alexander-Minter, "The Tanner Family: A Grandniece's Chronicle," in Dewey F. Mosby, Henry Ossawa Tanner, Darrel Sewell, Rae Alexander-Minter, and Philadelphia Museum of Art, *Henry Ossawa Tanner*, 1st trade ed. (Philadelphia: Philadelphia Museum of Art, 1991), 26.

6. Ibid., 27.

7. Lia B. Epperson, "Knocking Down Doors: The Trailblazing Life of Sadie Tanner Mossell Alexander, Pennsylvania's First Black Woman Lawyer," Women's Legal History Biography Project, Stanford University Law School, 1998, 8.

8. Ibid., 9.

9. Alexander discussed her mother's insistence that she attend the University of Pennsylvania in Alexander, "Address Before Delta Sigma Theta."

10. Sadie T. M. Alexander, "A Clean Sweep: Reflections on the Rocky Road to Winning a 'Boom Award' in 1918," *Pennsylvania Gazette*, 1972, STMA, box 72, ff10.

11. Alexander, "Response of Sadie T. M. Alexander, Esquire, at a Luncheon in Her Honor."

12. Sadie T. M. Alexander, "The Best of Times and the Worst of Times," *University of Pennsylvania Law Alumni Journal* (1977), STMA, box 72, ff15.

13. Sadie T. M. Alexander to Eugene Kinckle Jones, May 1, 1951, STMA, box 61, ff25.

14. Consumers League of Eastern Pennsylvania, *Colored Women as Industrial Workers in Philadelphia: A Study Made by the Consumers' League of Eastern Pennsylvania*, 1920, available at https://babel.hathitrust.org/cgi/pt?id=yale.39002004336278&view=1up&seq=7 (accessed October 24, 2020).

15. Sadie Mossell, "The Standard of Living Among One Hundred Negro Migrant Families in Philadelphia," Ph.D. diss., University of Pennsylvania, 1921, 5.

16. Ibid., 10.

17. Mossell wrote to Raymond Alexander on May 16, 1921, and mentioned press coverage of her graduation (STMA, box 3, ff1).

18. Sadie Mossell took two graduate courses with Professor Bye: History of Economic Thought, and Recent Developments of Economic Theory. Professor Bye's mother made the hood that Mossell wore. STMA, box 76, ff15.

19. Sadie T. M. Alexander to Mr. Frances R. Smith, Chairman, Democratic County Executive Committee, December 14, 1964, STMA, box 71; "Sadie Tanner Mossell Alexander," interview by Walter Massey Phillips, October 12, 1977, transcription, Walter Massey Phillips Oral Histories, SCRC 128, Special Collections Research Center, Temple University Libraries, Philadelphia; Francille Rusan Wilson, "'All of the Glory . . . Faded . . . Quickly': Sadie T. M. Alexander and Black Professional Women, 1920–1950," in *Sister Circle: Black Women and Work*, ed. Sharon Harley (New Brunswick, N.J.: Rutgers University Press, 2002), 164–183.

20. Alexander, "The Best of Times and the Worst of Times," 20.

21. Susan Carter, "Academic Women Revisited: An Empirical Study of Changing Patterns in Women's Employment as College and University Faculty, 1890–1963," *Journal of Social History* 14 (Summer 1981): 615–697.

22. R. D. Green and A. Thompson, "Streams of Racial Progress: The Discipline of Economics at Howard University at Its Sesquicentennial," *Negro Educational Review* 68, nos. 1–4 (2017): 31–55, 157; Malveaux, "Missed Opportunity," 2.

23. Sadie Tanner Mossell, *A Study of the Negro Tuberculosis Problem in Philadelphia* (Philadelphia: Henry Phipps Institute, 1923).

24. Alexander, "Role of Negro Women in the Economic Life of the Post-War South."

25. Alexander, "The Best of Times and the Worst of Times," 20.

26. Alexander, "Response of Sadie T. M. Alexander, at a Luncheon in Her Honor," 2.

27. Alexander, "The Best of Times and the Worst of Times," 20.

28. Sadie T. M. Alexander, "Forty-Five Years a Woman Lawyer," 1975, STMA, box 72, ff13.

29. See the scholarship of Kenneth Mack for further discussion of the role that the Alexanders played in the National Bar Association: Kenneth Walter Mack, "A Social History of Everyday Practice: Sadie T. M. Alexander and the Incorporation of Black Women into the American Legal Profession, 1925–1960," *Cornell Law Review* 87, no. 6 (September 2002): 1405–1474.

30. Epperson, "Knocking Down Doors," 19.

31. Alexander, "Response of Sadie T. M. Alexander, Esquire, at a Luncheon in Her Honor." According to Epperson in her "Knocking Down Doors," under Sadie Alexander's leadership the John Mercer Langston Law Club—a professional organization of Black lawyers in Philadelphia—established a legal aid bureau to assist and represent those Blacks in civil and criminal court who could not afford lawyers.

32. Mack, "A Social History of Everyday Practice," 1406.

33. Ibid.

34. Judge A. Leon Higginbotham, memorial service for Sadie Tanner Mossell Alexander, 1989.

Introduction to Part I

1. Henry S. Robinson, "The M Street High School, 1891–1916." *Records of the Columbia Historical Society, Washington D.C.: Historical Society of D.C.* 51 (1984): 119–143.

2. Sadie T. M. Alexander, "A Clean Sweep: Reflections on the Rocky Road to Winning a 'Boom Award' in 1918," 1972, STMA, box 72, ff10.

3. Rayford W. Logan, "Carter G. Woodson: Mirror and Molder of His Time, 1875–1950," *Journal of Negro History* 58, no. 1 (1973): 1–17; Robinson, "M Street High School."

4. National Urban League, *Negro Heroes: True Stories Told in Full Color*, no. 2 (Summer 1948).

5. Alexander, "Coming Events Cast Their Shadow/Address in Detroit," 166.

6. Alexander, "Clean Sweep."

7. Sadie T. M. Alexander, "Fragment of 'The Contribution of the Negro to American Life,'" speech, ca. 1920s, STMA, box 71, ff24.

8. Ibid., 2.

9. William Darity Jr., "Many Roads to Extinction: Early AEA Economists and the Black Disappearance Hypothesis," *History of Economics Review* 21 (Winter 1994): 47–64.

10. Ibid., 48.

11. Annie L. Cot, "'Breed out the Unfit and Breed in the Fit': Irving Fisher, Economics, and the Science of Heredity," *American Journal of Economics and Sociology* 64, no. 3 (July 2005).

12. Abram Harris Jr., "The New Negro Worker in Pittsburgh," master's thesis, University of Pittsburgh, 1924, 35.

13. James N. Gregory, *The Southern Diaspora: How the Great Migration of Black and White Southerners Transformed America* (Chapel Hill: University of North Carolina Press, 2005), 14.

14. Harper Barnes, *Never Been a Time: The 1917 Race Riot That Sparked the Civil Rights Movement* (New York: Walker & Company, 2008); Elliott M. Ruckwick, *Race Riot at East St. Louis, July 2, 1917* (Carbondale: University of Illinois Press, 1982); Charles L. Lumpkins, *American Pogrom: The East St. Louis Race Riot and Black Politics* (Athens: Ohio University Press, 2008).

15. See historian Karen Sieber's website Visualizing the Red Summer, at http://visualizingtheredsummer.com (accessed October 24, 2020); also DeNeen Brown, "Tulsa's Ugly Racial History: From Trail of Tears to Deadly 1921 Race Massacre," *Washington Post*, June 20, 2020; Leonard Green, "Tulsa Race Riot of 1921, the Most Destructive Act of Racial Violence in the U.S., Was Whitewashed from History," *New York Daily News*, January 19, 2020.

16. B. R. Boxill, *Blacks and Social Justice* (Totowa, N.J.: Rowman & Allanheld, 1984).

17. For a discussion of Du Bois's analysis of cooperative endeavors to strengthen Black communities, see Derrick P. Alridge, *The Educational Thought of W.E.B. Du Bois: An Intellectual History* (New York: Teachers College Press, 2008).

Introduction to Part II

1. For a discussion of the interaction between notions of civilization, race, and gender, see Gail Bederman, "'Civilization,' the Decline of Middle Class Manliness, and Ida B. Wells' Antilynching Campaign (1892–92)," *Radical History Review* 52 (Winter 1992): 4–30.

2. Ibid.

3. Robert W. Dimand, "The Neglect of Women's Contributions to Economics," in *Women of Value: Feminist Essays on the History of Women in Economics,* ed. Mary Ann Dimand, Robert W. Dimand, and Evelyn L. Forget (Aldershot, UK: Edward Elgar, 1995), 1–24.

4. Susan Carter, "Academic Women Revisited: An Empirical Study of Changing Patterns in Women's Employment as College and University Faculty, 1890–1963," *Journal of Social History* 14 (Summer 1981): 615–697.

5. Evelyn L. Forget, "American Women Economists, 1900–1940: Doctoral Dissertations and Research Specialization," in *Women of Value: Feminist Essays on the History of Women in Economics*, ed. Mary Ann Dimand, Robert Dimand, and Evelyn L. Forget (Aldershot, UK: Edward Elgar, 1995), 25–38.

6. See arguments in Alice Dunbar-Nelson, "The Negro Woman and the Ballot," 1926, in *Words of Fire: An Anthology of African-American Feminist Thought*, ed. Beverly Guy-Sheftall (New York: New Press, 1995), 86–88.

7. Evelyn Brooks Higginbotham, "In Politics to Stay: Black Women Leaders and Party Politics During the 1920s," in *Women, Politics, and Change*, ed. Louise Tilly and Patricia Gurin (New York: Russell Sage, 1990); Glenda Gilmore, *Gender and Jim Crow: Women and the Politics of White Supremacy in North Carolina, 1896–1920* (Chapel Hill: University of North Carolina Press, 1996); and Joyce A. Hanson, *Mary McLeod Bethune and Black Women's Political Activism* (Columbia: University of Missouri Press, 2003).

8. Elise Johnson McDougald, "The Double Task: The Struggle of Negro Women for Sex and Race Emancipation," *Survey Graphic* 53 (March 1, 1925): 689–691.

9. See, for example, negative assumptions that social scientists made about Black mothers' employment during the early Great Migration era, which are detailed in Louise V. Kennedy, *The Negro Peasant Turns Cityward: Effects of Recent Migrations to Northern Centers* (New York: Columbia University Press, 1930).

10. Rosalyn Terborg-Penn, "Discontented Black Feminists: Prelude and Postscript to the Passage of the Nineteenth Amendment," in *"We Specialize in the Wholly Impossible": A Reader in Black Women's History*, ed. Darlene Clark Hine, Wilma King, and Linda Reed (Brooklyn, N.Y.: Carlson Publishing, 1995), 487–503.

11. Paula Giddings, *When and Where I Enter: The Impact of Black Women on Race and Sex in America* (New York: Quill, 1984).

12. See the historical description of the Gamma chapter of Delta Sigma Theta Sorority at the sorority's website: https://www.dstgamma.com/new-page (accessed October 30, 2020).

Introduction to Part III

1. Ira Katznelson, *When Affirmative Action Was White: An Untold History of Racial Inequality in Twentieth-Century America* (New York: W. W. Norton, 2005).

2. Juan F. Perea, "The Echoes of Slavery: Recognizing the Racist Origins of the Agricultural and Domestic Worker Exclusion from the National Labor Relations Act," *Ohio State Law Journal* 72, no. 1 (2011): 95–138.

3. Darlene Clark Hine and Stanley Harrold, *The African-American Odyssey* (Upper Saddle River, N.J.: Prentice Hall, 2000).

4. Franklin D. Roosevelt, State of the Union Message to Congress, January 11, 1944, available in full at http://www.fdrlibrary.marist.edu/archives/stateoftheunion .html (accessed November 22, 2020).

5. Alexander, "Role of the Negro Women in the Economic Life of the Post-War South."

6. Alexander's files have two letters indicating that she had requested information on the "employment of Negro women in Southern industries." A letter from Warren M. Banner, Director of Research and Community Projects, National Urban League, was dated February 26, 1945, and provided information on employment in various places.

Alexander also received a letter from Julius A. Thomas, director of the Department of Industrial Relations, regarding the employment of Negro women in southern industries, dated March 1, 1945. Research Assistant Soni Madnani made the connection to Alexander's upcoming Florida A&M talk and surmised that the information would have come very late in order for Alexander to write a speech based on the data. UPT 50 A374, STMA OS-O4.

7. Nina Banks, "The Black Woman Economist Who Pioneered a Federal Jobs Guarantee," Institute for New Economic Thinking, New York, February 22, 2019.

8. Jerome De Henau et al., "Investing in the Care Economy: A Gender Analysis of Employment Stimulus in Seven OECD Countries," *Report by the UK Women's Budget Group Commissioned by the International Trade Union Confederation* (Brussels: International Trade Union Confederation, March 2016); John Schmitt, "Investing in Social Infrastructure as an Anti-Recession Tool," Washington Center for Equitable Growth, Washington, D.C., April 11, 2016.

Introduction to Part IV

1. William E. Juhnke, "President Truman's Committee on Civil Rights: The Interaction of Politics, Protest, and Presidential Advisory Commission," *Presidential Studies Quarterly* 19, no. 3 (1989): 593–610. Truman was outraged by lynchings and vicious attacks on Black World War II veterans, including the attack on U.S. Army Sergeant Isaac Woodard, who was beaten and blinded by police officers in South Carolina. See Audra D. S. Burch, "Why a Town Is Finally Honoring a Black Veteran Attacked by Its White Police Chief," *New York Times*, February 8, 2019.

2. Sadie T. M. Alexander, "Address to Americans for Democratic Action," Washington, D.C., 1947, STMA, box 71, ff84.

Bibliography of Speeches
in the Volume

Alexander, Sadie T. M. "Acceptance Speech of the Award of the Pennsylvania Society for Promoting the Abolition of Slavery." 1975. Sadie Tanner Mossell Alexander Records, University of Pennsylvania Archives, box 72, ff14.

———. "Address Before Delta Sigma Theta Sorority." 1939. Sadie Tanner Mossell Alexander Records, University of Pennsylvania Archives, box 71, ff62.

———. "Address on Negro Achievement." Speech given at the Tindley Temple during Negro Achievement Week, 1936. Sadie Tanner Mossell Alexander Records, University of Pennsylvania Archives, box 71, ff51.

———. "Address on the Economic and Occupational Status of Negroes." Speech delivered at the Elks' Educational and Economic Conference, Washington, D.C. (August 1935) and Business and Professional Women's Club, Philadelphia Commission on Human Relations (July 1936). Sadie Tanner Mossell Alexander Records, University of Pennsylvania Archives, box 71, ff50.

———. "Address on the Theme 'War Must Cease.'" Speech delivered at Bethel A.M.E. Church, Baltimore, October 13, 1935. Sadie Tanner Mossell Alexander Records, University of Pennsylvania Archives, box 71, ff49.

———. "The Catalytic Role of Commissions in Helping Alienated Communities." Address at the 19th Annual Conference of Commissions for Human Rights, Toronto, July 5, 1967. Sadie Tanner Mossell Alexander Records, University of Pennsylvania Archives, box 72, ff5.

———. "Coming Events Cast Their Shadow/Address in Detroit." Speech, 1939. Sadie Tanner Mossell Alexander Records, University of Pennsylvania Archives, box 71, ff59.

———. "Constitutional Guarantees of Civil Rights to American Negroes." Speech before the National YWCA Conference, May 9, 1934. Sadie Tanner Mossell Alexander Records, University of Pennsylvania Archives, box 71, ff42.

———. "The Contributions of the Negro to American Life." Speech, ca. 1920s. Sadie Tanner Mossell Alexander Records, University of Pennsylvania Archives, box 71, ff25.

———. "A Demand for Women as Executive Officers of the Church." Speech delivered on Women's Day at Union A.M.E. Church, Philadelphia, 1928. Sadie Tanner Mossell Alexander Records, University of Pennsylvania Archives, box 71, ff28.

———. "The Economic Status of Negro Women, an Index to the Negro's Economic Status." Speech, ca. 1930s. Sadie Tanner Mossell Alexander Records, University of Pennsylvania Archives, box 71, ff31.

———. "Education and Social Change: The Citizen's Role in Achieving Civil Rights." ca. 1966. Sadie Tanner Mossell Alexander Records, University of Pennsylvania Archives, box 72, ff2.

———. "The Emancipated Woman." Speech, ca. 1930s. Sadie Tanner Mossell Alexander Records, University of Pennsylvania Archives, box 71, ff30.

———. "For the Republican Party in the Lackawanna County Elections." Speech given November 1, 1935. Sadie Tanner Mossell Alexander Records, University of Pennsylvania Archives, box 71, ff47.

———. "Founders Day Address." Speech delivered at Spelman College, April 11, 1963. Sadie Tanner Mossell Alexander Records, University of Pennsylvania Archives, box 71, ff106.

———. Fragment. Speech, ca. 1920s. Sadie Tanner Mossell Alexander Records, University of Pennsylvania Archives, box 71, ff22.

———. Fragment, "Concerning the Loyalty Pledge Statement of Security Principles and the House Un-American Activities." Speech, 1947–1948. Sadie Tanner Mossell Alexander Records, University of Pennsylvania Archives, box 71, ff86.

———. Fragment, "Contributions [We Can] Make." Speech, ca. 1920s. Sadie Tanner Mossell Alexander Records, University of Pennsylvania Archives, box 71, ff23.

———. "Negro Women in Our Economic Life." *Opportunity: Journal of Negro Life* (July 1930): 201–203.

———. "New Tempos—New Concepts." Address of Sadie T. M. Alexander, Chairman, Philadelphia Commission on Human Relations, Before the Annual Conference of Commission on Human Rights in Pittsburgh, 1963. Sadie Tanner Mossell Alexander Records, University of Pennsylvania Archives, box 107, ff71.

———. "On the Status of the Philadelphia Negro." Address before the Whittier Committee on Race Relations of the Society of Friends, 1942. Sadie Tanner Mossell Alexander Records, University of Pennsylvania Archives, box 71, ff70.

———. "Outstanding Achievements of Negro Women." Speech, ca. 1930s. Sadie Tanner Mossell Alexander Records, University of Pennsylvania Archives, box 71, ff33.

———. "The Place of a College Fraternity in the Life of a Student, in the Life of a University, in the Life of the Negro Race." Address at Delta Sigma Theta Conference, 1939. Sadie Tanner Mossell Alexander Records, University of Pennsylvania Archives, box 71, ff61.

————. "Progress Made in Civil Rights in the United States Since the Publication of *To Secure These Rights.*" Speech, ca. 1958. Sadie Tanner Mossell Alexander Records, University of Pennsylvania Archives, box 71, ff100.

————. "Response of Sadie T. M. Alexander, Esquire, at Luncheon in Her Honor." Speech given to the Commission on Human Relations, January 31, 1968. Sadie Tanner Mossell Alexander Records, University of Pennsylvania Archives, box 72, ff6.

————. "The Responsibility of Minorities." Address at Central Synagogue, Rockville, Long Island, April 9, 1948. Sadie Tanner Mossell Alexander Records, University of Pennsylvania Archives, OS 4 Scrapbook 1946–47. An earlier version of this speech is located in box 71, ff91b.

————. "The Role of the Negro Women in the Economic Life of the Post-War South." Speech given at Florida Agricultural and Mechanical College in Honor of Mary McLeod Bethune, March 1, 1945. Sadie Tanner Mossell Alexander Records, University of Pennsylvania Archives, box 71, ff80.

————. "Segregation in Public Schools." Speech given at the Dunbar Theatre in Philadelphia, 1925. Sadie Tanner Mossell Alexander Records, University of Pennsylvania Archives, box 71, ff27.

————. "Speech Before the Eastern Federation of Negro Republicans." Speech delivered at Wesley Church, Philadelphia, September 6, 1935. Sadie Tanner Mossell Alexander Records, University of Pennsylvania Archives, box 71, ff48.

————. "Statement of Mrs. Sadie T. M. Alexander at the White House Regional Conference on Equal Employment Opportunity." June 10, 1964. Sadie Tanner Mossell Alexander Records, University of Pennsylvania Archives, box 71, ff109.

————. "To Secure These Rights." Address at a Luncheon Meeting Speech of Americans for Democratic Action, January 10, 1948. Sadie Tanner Mossell Alexander Records, University of Pennsylvania Archives, box 71, ff90.

————. "Women as Practitioners of Law in the United States." Address before the National Bar Association, 1941. Sadie Tanner Mossell Alexander Records, University of Pennsylvania Archives, box 71, ff68.

Acknowledgments

My recovery of the economic life and thought of Sadie T. M. Alexander has been a very long journey and a labor of love. I have many people to thank, most of all my phenomenal research assistant Lily Shorney. Of the many faculty projects that an incoming first-year Presidential Fellow could choose, Lily chose to work with me on my Sadie T. M. Alexander book projects (biography and edited volume of speeches) because of her interest in women's studies and African American women in particular. For two academic years, Lily worked with me on all phases of the volume of speeches, including organizing my extensive print files, researching and compiling information from primary and secondary sources, and sending me vital materials that I needed during my semester spent in Ghana. Lily spent a good deal of time doing the seemingly impossible—deciphering Alexander's handwritten speeches and piecing them together into typed documents. There were many, many times when I went into our shared Google file—even during spring break—and found that Lily was already there diligently trying to figure out words that remained a mystery. In my final months of writing the introductions to each section, Lily not only proofed the speeches for typos (which was all that I asked), but also carefully read each sentence for clarity. She looked up historical information to verify that speeches with missing information were accurate, and she managed to figure out the logic of some of the changes that Alexander had included in her scribbled notes inserted between sentences and along the margins. Lily's research assistance was indispensable and I would not have been able to complete this volume without her superb work. I offer her my heartfelt gratitude in bringing to fruition a book to which she made a substantial contribution.

The Alexander family provided an invaluable gift to the nation when they donated their family papers to the University of Pennsylvania. This extraordinary collection contains critical historical information about African American institutions, cultural life, and leadership. I am so grateful to each member of the Alexander family for graciously sharing with me their memories of Sadie T. M. Alexander and for their enthusiasm for my book projects. I list them in the order in which I met them: Rae Alexander-Minter, Jeffrey Hayes, Tom Minter Jr., Mary Cannaday, Raymond Brown, and Virginia Brown. My deepest appreciation to each of them.

I am thrilled to acknowledge the staff of the University of Pennsylvania Archives for their skilled work in organizing the Sadie T. M. Alexander (STMA) collection and making it available to researchers. At every stage of my research, the archival staff provided me with resources, guidance, and assistance that enabled me to undertake the work needed to recover Alexander's life as an economist. In particular, I thank Mark Frazier Lloyd, university archivist emeritus, for granting me permission to publish Alexander's speeches and advising me on when to stop reading and start writing. In 2020, during the coronavirus shutdown, Jim Duffin promptly provided me with resources that I needed and gave me a wonderful gift by directing me to digitized home videos that allowed me to see Sadie Alexander in action. Tim Horning enabled me to do my research in a welcoming setting and patiently answered my many questions as well as obtained files and photos that I requested, sometimes with little advance notice. I am especially grateful to former staff member Nancy Miller for the many times that she pointed me in the direction of resources. Nancy brought to my attention the information on the fieldwork that young Sadie Mossell and Virginia Alexander performed for the Consumer's League of Pennsylvania.

On behalf of myself and Yale University Press, I would like to thank the following institutions and archives for so generously giving permission to publish the following copyrighted materials: the University of Pennsylvania Archives, Sadie Tanner Mossell Alexander Record Group (UPT 50 A374S), for select speeches, writings, and photos in the Sadie Tanner Mossell Alexander Records; Spelman College, for "Founders Day Address" by Dr. Sadie T. M. Alexander, April 11, 1963, which originally appeared in the *Spelman Messenger* in May 1963; and the National Urban League, for "Negro Women in Our Economic Life," which was first published in *Opportunity* 8 (January 1930): 201–203.

My heartfelt appreciation goes out to the staff at Yale University Press. I would still be reading archival materials had they not reached out to me about my plans for a book on Sadie Alexander. I thank Taiba Batool and Seth Ditchik for recognizing Alexander's importance to the economics profession and their unfailing support for the edited volume of speeches and the biography. I thank Seth for enthusiastically taking over the project and ensuring the timely publication of the edited volume to commemorate the hundredth anniversary of Alexander's doctorate. Karen Olson provided much needed editorial assistance and direction while shepherding my manuscript through the production process. I am very grateful to her. It was a pleasure working with Julie Carlson, whose meticulous and thoughtful copyediting greatly enhanced the quality of my book. And many thanks to Jeff Schier for his skillful handling of the volume through the final stages of production.

I am profoundly thankful to Bucknell University for funding my research. Were it not for Bucknell, I would not have been able to complete my in-depth study of Alexander's extraordinary life. The Bucknell Institute for Public Policy, under the leadership of Professors Amy Wolaver and Janet Knoedler, provided me with generous research funding at a critical time. Jan's unfailing support also took the form of writing many letters of recommendation for external and internal grants. One of those letters resulted in the Office of the Dean of Arts and Sciences awarding me a three-year Dean's Fellowship grant that enabled me to spend weeks each summer working at the archives. Race scholar Linden Lewis was an associate dean at the time and I suspect that he played a key role in the award decision.

Bucknell students provided very helpful research assistance as well as the enthusiasm that comes along with seeing things through fresh, youthful eyes. Darby Hamilton, my first research assistant, set up my filing system and helped catalog my voluminous materials based on his reading of key themes he found in them. Mark Small offered astute comments on a talk I had prepared about Sadie Alexander that enabled me to see my own life from a different perspective. Several students worked hard to decipher Alexander's handwriting and I thank them for their efforts: Jordan Bonner, Ty Chung, Sam Cowans, Michaella Irvine, and Joe Stephenson. Megan Ganning provided cheerful assistance with my Alexander speaking engagements and social media announcements. Soni Madnani conducted archival research with me during summer 2019 and set up an amazing digital filing system. Her keen insights are incorporated into this edited volume. Jingyi Zhou secured permissions and conducted research on events and people within Sadie Alexander's orbit. The stellar research assistance of these undergraduate students enabled me to pull together this volume.

In spring 2015, I spent a wonderful full day in the company of another group of bright, inquisitive undergraduate students in the economics department at Oberlin College. They were part of the Rethinking Economics movement and invited me to talk about my research because they wanted "education in economics grounded in theory and reality; not divorced from social justice but driven by it." This amazing group of young people included Claire Ciraolo, Sky Davis, Andrew Follmann, Julia Murphy, Miliaku Nwabueze, Ema Sagner, Mimi Stern, and Anais Stewart. They shaped my thinking on Sadie Alexander and economics as well as the many ways in which miseducation sometimes serves as a catalyst for critical thought and action as it did for Alexander.

Feminist economists' important research to recover the work of early women economists inspired my own efforts. I am thankful and indebted to my dear former colleague Jean Shackelford. Jean was there in the very beginning, encouraging me, giving me ideas, and setting up panels at Allied Social Science Associations (ASSA) conferences that featured my research findings. Jean introduced me to Cecilia Conrad and I thank Cecilia for the many ways that she supported my Alexander research through conference panels, journal editorial assistance, and answering the naïve questions of someone in the early stages of research.

I am grateful to Randy Albelda for providing very helpful comments on my Alexander papers.

I thank my colleagues in the Department of Economics at Bucknell University for their support. In particular, my former chair, Thomas Kinnaman, always came through for my research requests and showed genuine happiness for my successes. Nancy White enriched my thinking about urban migration through her own love of the topic. Christine Ngo provided much enthusiasm and very helpful information on the book publishing process. Winston "Jami" Griffith has been an inspiration and source of unwavering loyalty. Lindsey Hahn thoughtfully displayed my research on Alexander on social media and other department sites. My manuscript benefited from Marcellus Andrews's brilliance and deep knowledge of both economics and the African American experience.

A huge thanks to the many people who disseminated or helped me to disseminate information about Sadie Alexander's economic thinking through media outlets. They include Lori L. Tharps of the *Philadelphia Magazine*; Alex Eisenbarth, Matthew Kulvicki, and Aaron Freedman of the Institute for New Economic Thinking (INET); Mike Ferlazzo, Bucknell's Director of Media Relations; Jeff Canning of RW Jones Agency; Aimee Keane of the *Financial Times*; and especially Cardiff Garcia (NPR, formerly of the *Financial Times' Alphaville* podcast) for his determination to help right the historic wrong done to Alexander, the economist.

Sadie T. M. Alexander scholars whose research informed my thinking and paved a way for my economic analysis include Lia B. Epperson, Kenneth Mack, and Francille Rusan Wilson. Julianne Malveaux—the economist who has carried on the legacy of Sadie Alexander as a brilliant public intellectual—introduced Alexander to the economics profession through her incisive article "Missed Opportunity: Sadie Tanner Mossell Alexander and the Economics Profession." It motivated me to go to the University of Pennsylvania Archives in search of information that might indicate that Alexander had continued her interest in economics beyond her dissertation.

Early on, members of the National Economic Association (NEA) recognized the importance of my recovery of Sadie Alexander's economics and made sure that others were aware of it. They include Bernard

Anderson, Sandy Darity, Willene Johnson, Trevon Logan, Margaret Simms, Omari Swinton, Linwood Tauheed, Romie Tribble, Angelino Viceisza, and Valerie Wilson. NEA Board member Dania Francis helped to promote my research to media outlets. NEA participants in the Freedom and Justice conferences have been helpful in offering feedback. They include Geert Dhondt, Darrick Hamilton, Michelle Holder, Sam Myers Jr., and Bill Spriggs. I thank Gary Hoover and Ebonya Washington of Committee on the Status of Minority Groups in the Economics Profession (CSMGEP) for their role in helping to disseminate my Alexander research to a wider audience of economists. Above all, I thank Rhonda Sharpe for the wise counsel that she provided on many occasions, for being an ardent champion of my research, and for being a constant source of laughter and friendship.

I thank members of the Modern Monetary Theory (MMT) community and people connected to them for their embrace of Sadie Alexander's contribution to the discussion of full employment job guarantees: Raúl Carrillo, Rev. Dr. Delman Coates, Mathew Forstater, Poti Giannakouros, Rohan Grey, Joseph Polito, and Nathan Tankus.

In the final week of editing, I reached out to three Adam Smith scholars that my research assistant Lily had located and asked them if they could figure out two words attributed to Adam Smith that had baffled us for over a year. Within little time, all three scholars had solved our puzzle with Smith's original sentence and full bibliographic reference. My immense gratitude to Jack Russell Weinstein, Craig Smith, and Sam Fleischacker for their thoughtfulness.

Friends provided inspiration, wisdom, laughter, and validation that this historical research mattered. They include Gina Beavers, Janice Butler, Tameka Cage Conley, Monique Frazier, Jerry Harvard, Caroline Hossein, Karen Jows, Angèle Kingué, Jim Kunder, Sue Reed, Frank Sader, Khalil Saucier, Martha Shaunessy, Atiya Stokes-Brown, Paul Susman, Jennifer Thomson, and Hoda Zaki. Norlisha Crawford provided wonderful companionship, assistance with note-taking, and edifying conversations on trips to the archives during the early days of my research. There are no words to convey my deep appreciation to my closest friends Shantih Clemans and Leslie Patrick for their unswerving support and scholarly advice.

The women of the Sadie Collective have done much to generate enthusiasm for Sadie Alexander among young people. I thank Anna Gifty Opoku-Agyeman, Kayla Jones, Fanta Traore, and other members of the collective for promoting my research on Sadie Alexander.

My family has been my bedrock of love and encouragement: my parents, Timothy and Bobbie Banks; siblings Virginia Listach, Tim Banks Jr., and Bobbie Jean Hunter; and cousins Sherry Brown and Liliana Rodriguez. Finally, and especially, I thank my sons, Emiliano and Julián Torija, for being such good sports and wonderful companions during our summers spent in the great city of Philadelphia.

Index

AAA. *See* Agricultural Adjustment Act of 1933

Abbotts Dairies, 71

access to education: Blacks' educational attainment and, 7, 23, 30–31, 190; Black women's educational attainment and, 23–24; discrimination in, 234; importance of, 14, 18, 151; integrated schools in southern states, 151, 238–245; maladministration of law denying to Blacks, 157; quota systems of institutions of higher education, 184; racial equality and, 5, 155, 157; right to education, 220; separate but equal schools, 155, 222

achievements. *See* Black achievements

Adler, Felix, 34

adult education, 198

affirmative action, 97–98, 121, 124

AFL unions, 108

African Americans. *See headings starting with "Black"*

African discovery of America, 11

Agricultural Adjustment Act of 1933 (AAA), 29, 101, 163

Agricultural Adjustment Administration, 177

agriculture: Black farmers, 30; Black women working in, 43, 66–67; cotton-picking and sorting jobs, 101, 163; crop control, 188; foreclosure of farms in Great Depression, 170; Social Security Act exemption of workers, 102, 164; tenant farmers, 101, 163–164, 186; unemployment of Black workers in, 101

airlines, fair employment practices in hiring stewardesses, 120

Alabama, school desegregation in, 238

Alexander, Mary Elizabeth (daughter), xix

Alexander, Rae Pace (daughter), xix

Alexander, Raymond Pace (husband), xiv, xviii–xix, 98, 131–135, 185, 229, 236, 260n17

Alexander, Sadie Tanner Mossell acknowledgment of accomplishments of, xxii, 23
birth of, xiii
children of, xix, 234
doctorate in economics, xii, xiv–xvii, 23, 259n1
early years and education of, xiii, 3

"Response of Sadie T. M. Alexander, Esquire, at Luncheon in Her Honor" (1968), 98, 131–141

"The Responsibility of Minorities" (1948), 149, 216–221

"The Role of the Negro Women in the Economic Life of the Post-War South" (1945), 96, 104–116

"Segregation in Public Schools" (1925), 42, 45–47

"Speech Before the Eastern Federation of Negro Republicans" (1935), 147–148, 159–165

"Statement of Mrs. Sadie T. M. Alexander at the White House Regional Conference on Equal Employment Opportunity" (1964), 98, 127–130

"Women as Practitioners of Law in the United States" (1941), 44, 80–89

Alexander, Sadie T. M., writings by
"Negro Women in Our Economic Life" (1930), 42, 52–57
Opportunity Magazine article (1930), xx
"The Standard of Living Among One Hundred Negro Migrant Families in Philadelphia" (dissertation), xv–xvi
A Study of the Negro Tuberculosis Problem in Philadelphia (1923), xx
Who's Who Among Negro Lawyers (booklet, 1945), xx

Alexander, Virginia (sister-in-law), xv

alienation of communities, 151, 246–257; attitudes of public civil rights commissioners toward, 251; avoiding stereotypical thinking about, 248; budgetary shortcomings to remedy, 251, 254; church councils, role of, 254–255; circumstances contributing to, 247–248; community involvement, importance of, 255; declarations of government policies and, 248–249; enforcement powers of agencies, lack of, 250; failure of public civil rights commissions to

achieve their missions, 256; human rights agencies' role, 248, 249–250; meaning of alienation, 246; recommendations for improving, 251–257; working through leadership structure of ethnic community, 255

AME Church: "Address on the Theme 'War Must Cease'" (Baltimore AME Church 1935), 148, 166–172; "A Demand for Women as Executive Officers of the Church" (Philadelphia's Union AME Church 1928), 42, 48–51; General Conference (1924), 48; General Conference (1928), 48

American Association of University Women, 225

American Civil Liberties Union, xix

American Economic Association, 4

American Economic Review, xii

American Indians, 217, 255

American Jewish Committee, 123

Americans for Democratic Action meeting, Alexander speech to (1948), xix, 149

Anderson, Marian, 24, 44, 185

Anderson, Violette N., 86

anti-poverty programs, 255

anti-Semitism, 148, 181–183, 198

anti-war sentiments, 148, 166–172

apartment houses, fair employment practices in hiring, 120

apprenticeship programs, 122, 124, 129, 236, 247

Arkansas, admission of women to practice law in, 84–85

Armenians, 62

arms, right to bear, 205

arts and literature: Black artists, 36; Blacks' role in, 31; Black women artists, 24; Black women authors, 24–25; Harlem Renaissance, 15. *See also* music

Asian Americans, 217, 255

assembly, freedom of, 213, 217